THE TEXAS

The Tale of the River Card (Round II)

MIRACLE

JOHN MARSHALL

iUniverse

THE TEXAS MIRACLE
THE TALE OF THE RIVER CARD (ROUND II)

iUniverse books may be ordered through booksellers or by contacting:

iUniverse
1663 Liberty Drive
Bloomington, IN 47403
www.iuniverse.com
1-800-Authors (1-800-288-4677)

ISBN: 978-1-4917-9260-5 (sc)
ISBN: 978-1-4917-9259-9 (e)

Library of Congress Control Number: 2016907041

Print information available on the last page.

iUniverse rev. date: 07/20/2016

Contents

Introduction

*"If you can keep your head when all about you are losing
theirs ..."*

Rudyard Kipling penned those words in 1895 and went on to advocate
trust, truth, virtue, and betting it all on the "River Card."[1]

While Rudyard's words were thoughtful, they were not necessarily
actionable as he neglected to specify when to go all-in. This is especially
true if you define action as separating a man from his money or from his
real estate.

In January of 2009, it seemed that everyone was losing their heads
and then some. Those who regulate, marshal, and otherwise steer the
American economic system were collectively convinced that we were all
staring into the abyss. The S&P 500 had just lost ten years' worth of value
and the Great Recession was in full swing. Names like Bear Stearns and
Lehman Brothers had been reduced to entries in the history books and the
US Treasury Department was rebranding itself on a daily basis. Annual
bonuses for bankers and brokers were in question, and there was even talk
that freshly-minted Harvard MBAs might not find jobs upon graduation.
Fortune 500 CEOs were flying commercial for the sake of public relations

---

[1] Well, more or less.

and their CFOs were stockpiling cash to prepare for the worst. The US financial markets were paralyzed.

Since the executives on Wall Street are the only ones who actually know what an abyss looks like, the rest of us were required to look through their lens and gasp on cue. Expecting an abyss to be the beginning of the end, ninety percent of us were eventually relieved to learn that an abyss is simply a basket of pink slips that get handed out to the other ten percent of the workforce. For the remaining ninety percent of us who kept our jobs, an abyss turned out to be something that simply created lower prices for things like cars, gasoline, stocks, lake houses and, most important, the ground beneath those lake houses.

In Washington, D.C., January of 2009 ushered in an era of change. Who knows whether the American voters had looked into the abyss and recoiled, or simply considered the next option being offered by the Republican Party to be abysmal? For the first time in twenty years, a man who did not hail from Texas or Arkansas was about to be installed as the President of the United States. Moreover, the president-elect appeared to be the fulfillment of Martin Luther King's dream and he captured the attention of every vein of the media. As a result, no one gave a possum's ass about local issues such as the sale of surplus real estate in Palo Pinto County, Texas.

In Austin, Texas, January of 2009 was noteworthy for decidedly different reasons.

Four years earlier, US Senator Kay Bailey Hutchison had mounted and then abandoned a challenge against incumbent Texas governor Rick Perry. On January 14, 2009, Todd J. Gillman of the *Dallas Morning News* reported that Senator Hutchison would be mounting a second challenge in 2010.[2] Rick Perry and Kay Bailey Hutchison were both tenured leaders in the Texas Republican Party and the party faithful would be forced to choose sides.

At the outset, Kay Bailey Hutchinson enjoyed a twenty-five point lead in the polls with major newspapers across the state endorsing her candidacy. Rick Perry had never lost an election at any level—and losing to Hutchinson would surely doom his 2012 presidential bid before it even

[2] Todd J. Gillman, "Hutchinson Mounts Challenge," *Dallas Morning News*, January 14, 2009.

got started. In the face of this challenge, Perry could not have enough friends with money or influence. Now was the time for Perry to put his reputation as a governor who "transparently rewards friends and punishes enemies" to good use.[3]

Simultaneously, one of the largest battles in the history of the Texas legislature was reaching its climax. The Speaker of the House, a man by the name of Tom Craddick from Midland, had managed to alienate the entire Texas House of Representatives. The power struggle that followed in both parties became known as the "Anyone but Craddick" sweepstakes and the number of ambitious representatives seeking the Speaker's gavel was approaching double digits. So too, were the horse-trading opportunities that arose from the process. A new Speaker of the House would mean new committee chairs and new committee members. It would also mean new alliances.

During this period of unprecedented turbulence, a gentleman by the name of Michael Harold Patterson offered to pay $50 million to buy roughly 1200 acres of surplus real estate from the state of Texas. An analysis of the numbers strongly suggests that this property was worth closer to a billion.

As the story goes, the ensuing transaction represented a case study in collaborative commerce where a cabal of strategic partners worked in unison to achieve a mutually beneficial outcome. The outcome was so beneficial to Michael Harold Patterson that he claimed to have made $30 million in only 366 days.

Welcome to the great state of Texas, where we are "Wide Open for Business."[4]

---

[3] "Rick Perry is 2010 Texan of the Year," Editorial, *Dallas Morning News*, December 26, 2010.

[4] Texas Wide Open for Business® is the official brand for the Texas Economic Development Division within the Office of the Governor. Staff, "Texas Wide Open for Business," *Office of the Governor*, February 16, 2007, accessed November 1, 2015. https://web.archive.org/web/20150906110855/https://texaswideopenforbusiness.com/.

Acknowledgments:

This book is intended to provide a modicum of insight into the tangled web of Lone Star State politics and the requisite horse-trading that goes with that. If you find yourself half way through a chapter, and then find yourself having to go back to the beginning of that chapter to make sure that you caught something right—then you are paying attention and reading well.

For those parts that you find readable on the first pass, all of the credit goes to my editor.

Her name is Krista Hill.

For those parts that you had to read twice, the same credit and appreciation accrues. Were it not for Krista's work, you would have had to read those parts three times.

Thank you, Krista.

Dedication:

This work is dedicated to my wife of thirty years and to our two kids.

I had previously always found the standard dedication acknowledging the wife's and the kids' patience and understanding during the writing process to be somewhat pathetic and obligatory.

After having spent the last five years on this project...I now get it.

To my wife who gave me that fireworks-blowing-up-in-the-sky moment on our first date that very few men ever get the chance to experience – I love you more than you will ever know. The fireworks still go off every time I see you pull into the driveway. Thank you for putting up with this and everything else over the past thirty years.

To my daughter, who will always be my "Little Bear," but is now a young woman on her path—I love you more than you will ever know. It was not until you were born that I realized what I was supposed to do with my life.

Thank you for making me a father and for trying to teach me how to be a good one.

And, to my son who is the man who I hope to grow up and be someday—you are nothing short of amazing. It comforts me greatly to know that you will be taking over the family when the time comes. I love you.

Dad

Chapter 1

POWER CORRUPTS

"Power tends to corrupt, and absolute power corrupts absolutely."—Lord Acton, 1887

The words above are hard to argue with—so I won't.

I grew up in a small town in Texas where lofty thoughts related to the relationship between power and eventual corruption were a fool's luxury. Where I came from, everyone had to work for a living. There was simply no time in the day to be bothered by the privilege of others. Nor was there any time to worry about whether politicians in Texas were enriching themselves at the expense of the rest of us. We all assumed that they were and that was just a part of life.

From the end of Reconstruction, and through the first half of the twentieth century, the Democratic Party enjoyed total domination of the political landscape in Texas. During the 1950's, substantially more people voted in the Democratic primary election than in the following general election. If you could win your race in the Democratic primary in the spring, you were assured of your election in the fall. For better or worse, this one-party system produced the likes of President Lyndon Baines Johnson and House Speaker Jim Wright.

The Democratic Party's domination in the state of Texas began to erode during the 1960's. This erosion can be traced back to 1944 when the

U.S. Supreme Court ruled that "whites-only" primaries were illegal. That ruling, arguably, was the first modern-day example of the overreaching federal government attempting to infringe on the state rights of Texas. This ruling was also one of the factors that began to split the old Democratic Party of Texas in half.

On one side, you had the enlightened folks who were in favor of civil rights, voting rights, and things of that nature. On the other side, you had people who felt threatened by the pace of social change. These people remained in favor of the status quo.

The beginning of the end for the Democratic Party in Texas occurred in 1961 when John Tower was elected to the United States Senate as a Republican. This was the first objective evidence that a Texan with an "R" next to his name could win a statewide election. Things would soon get worse for the Democrats—if you allow the word "soon" to mean seventeen years.

In 1978, William P. "Bill" Clements ran for governor in Texas as a Republican. Clements won that race against John Luke Hill by a rounding error: 49.96% to 49.24%. As a result, Bill Clements became the first Republican governor since 1869. It appeared that the tide might finally be turning.

Four years later, in 1982, Bill Clements ran for reelection. Disappointingly, Clements lost that election to Mark White, who had been serving as the state's attorney general. To make matters worse, every other Republican candidate who ran for statewide office in 1982 was defeated by their Democratic opponent. This included George Strake, Jr. who was on the ballot as the Republican nominee for lieutenant governor. Strake had served as Bill Clements' secretary of state.

The Republican revolution in Texas had not yet found its footing, or its organizational footprint. To address this lack of traction, George Strake replaced Chet Upham of Mineral Wells as the chairman of the Republican Party of Texas.[5]

All the same, the success of John Tower and Bill Clements was a catalyst that spurred a great many Democrats toward a religious conversion of sorts. These born-again politicians rebranded themselves as Republicans.

---

[5] It is often stated that you could fit the entire Republican Party of Texas into a phone booth during Chet Upham's tenure.

One of the most notable of these converts was a fellow by the name of Phil Gramm. Gramm served as a Democratic congressman from 1979 until 1983. He then denounced his allegiance to the Democratic Party and ran as a Republican for reelection to the U.S. House of Representatives. Phil Gramm won the race handily.

In 1984, Gramm ran for the U.S. Senate to fill the seat that had opened up as a result of John Tower's retirement. Gramm defeated several opponents in the GOP primary, including a U.S. congressman by the name of Dr. Ron Paul. Gramm then went on to poll 58.5% of the vote in the general election. As a consequence, Phil Gramm became the poster boy for switching political parties in the state of Texas.

Phil Gramm's success as a Republican candidate also served to convince defeated governor Bill Clements that all was not lost. In 1986, Bill Clements ran for governor once again and won by a margin of 7.6%. The celebration of his political resurrection proved to be short-lived.

During this same period of time, Governor Clements served as the chairman of the Board of Governors of Southern Methodist University. Two months after he was sworn into office for his second term as governor, Bill Clements publicly confessed to his role in a scheme to pay salaries to thirteen of SMU's star football players.

Governor Clements explained that the board of SMU had agreed to phase out the "salaries" at the end of the 1986 season rather than halt the payments immediately. He further explained that the board felt duty-bound to honor its prior commitments to those thirteen players. His official quote on the matter was true to Texas heritage: "We had a payroll to meet."

Governor Clements' revelation was devastating for SMU as the university was already under NCAA probation. Once it was revealed, the decision to continue paying those players obliged the NCAA to shut down SMU's football program in 1987. This ruling has become known as the "Death Penalty" and the related scandal resulted in one of the best *30-for-30* episodes that ESPN has produced to date. A viewing of the segment, entitled *Pony Excess*, will reveal with utter transparency the culture of Texas politics during the era.

Recognizing that he was unelectable, Bill Clements chose not to run for reelection in 1990. In his stead, the Republican Party nominated a multi-millionaire by the name of Clayton Williams. Williams was a stereotypical Texan with a legendary gift for telling tales. Everyone referred to him simply as "Claytie" and everyone knew that he was a political wildcard. His Democratic opponent that year was a woman by the name of Ann Richards, who was equally salty. These two colorful characters produced an endless series of newsworthy anecdotes. Fortunately for both of them, there was no such thing as Twitter, or even the internet, at that point in time.

The race between Ann Richards and Clayton Williams should not have been close. Texas had already shifted hard right and Clayton Williams was enjoying an eleven-point lead in the polls, with only two months remaining before the general election. Claytie then got careless. While telling tales on his ranch in the presence of a few reporters, Clayton Williams uttered one of the most remarkable statements in the history of Texas politics: "If it is inevitable, just relax and enjoy it."

Clayton Williams was comparing a bad weather forecast to rape. To say the least, this highly publicized remark motivated more than a few females in Texas to get out and vote. When Clayton Williams refused to shake Ann Richards' hand during a public debate, the negative sentiments of the lady folk grew even stronger. Ann Richards wound up winning the race for governor in 1990 by two percentage points.

Despite the Bill Clements scandal and the Clayton Williams debacle, Texas was nonetheless shifting from blue to red during this period of time. This trend in political persuasions prompted another Democrat to repent and become the next born-again Republican on September 29, 1989.

The sins of this particular convert, who had served three terms in the Texas House with a "D" next to his name, were not insignificant. In 1987, he voted for a $5.7 billion tax increase. In 1988, he went so far as to endorse Al Gore in the presidential primary over George H. W. Bush. Moreover, he was often referred to as Al Gore's campaign manager within the state of Texas and this is a characterization that he has never refuted.[6]

That young sinner's name was James Perry.

---

[6] Abby Livingston, "8 Things to Know About Rick Perry," *The Texas Tribune*, June 4, 2015, accessed November 27, 2015. https://www.texastribune.org/2015/06/04/8-things-know-about-rick-perry/.

Having converted to the Republican Party, James ran for Agriculture Commissioner in 1990. He barely won that race. Four years later, in 1994, James Perry ran for reelection and brought home a decisive victory with 62% of the vote. This was the same year that George "W" Bush first ran for governor and soundly defeated incumbent Ann Richards.

One of the most important powers of the governor of Texas is the constitutional authority to make appointments. One of the earliest appointments that Governor George W. Bush made when he was governor occurred in 1995. This was when he appointed a young lawyer by the name of Greg Abbott to the Supreme Court of Texas. This appointment put Greg Abbott's political career on a gilded trajectory.

By the mid 1990's, Texas had officially become a "red" state and James Perry was widely recognized as an established winner. In 1998, James ran for lieutenant governor and won with 50.04% of the vote, making him the first Republican lieutenant governor since Reconstruction. Simultaneously, George W. Bush was reelected as governor with a record tally of 69% of the vote. George Bush's coattails were long and broad and the Republican Party of Texas won each of the statewide races that year. The Texas GOP has done so ever since.

Texas was now blood-red. If you could win the Republican primary in the spring, you were basically assured of your victory in the fall. The best example of this was a fellow by the name of David Dewhurst. In that same year, 1998, David Dewhurst ran for Texas land commissioner—even though he had never held a single elected office in his life. Nonetheless, Dewhurst won the general election with 57% of the vote.

Two years later, Governor George W. Bush was elected President of the United States. Per the Texas Constitution, the lieutenant governor ascended to what would eventually become a throne. By virtue of the presidential election in the year 2000, James Richard "Rick" Perry became governor of Texas. Following that, Rick Perry became the longest serving governor in the state's history.

Not one single Democrat has won a statewide election in Texas since 1994. For the past twenty years, Texas has existed as a single-party state yet again. As a result of this domination, established Republicans have continuously moved up the hierarchy. In 2002, David Dewhurst ran for lieutenant governor and won with 52% of the vote. In that same year, Greg Abbott ran for attorney general and captured 57% of the vote.

For the next twelve years, the top three elected offices in Texas were occupied by the same three politicians. In effect, Rick Perry, David Dewhurst, and Greg Abbott became the "Texas Trinity." And, they were not without deity-like powers. In fact, some claimed that they were capable of miracles. During the majority of their tenure, the United States was enduring the Great Recession while the state of Texas was enjoying substantial job growth and economic expansion. This envious outcome is now hailed by the office holders of that era as "The Texas Miracle."

The established leadership of the Republican Party of Texas takes full credit for sowing the seeds that produced "The Texas Miracle." Personally, I give the Good Lord most of the credit as He was the one who invented things like crude oil, natural gas, and fracking. On the other hand, I have never seen an "R" after the Good Lord's name, so it is uncertain as to whether or not He could ever win a general election in the state of Texas.

As noted earlier, absolute power tends to corrupt absolutely. On August 14, 2014, Governor Rick Perry was indicted on two counts of public corruption. The charges in this case are abuse of official capacity, a first-degree felony, and coercion of a public servant, a third-degree felony.[7]

The ill effects of absolute power are not limited to the highest elected offices. In fact, such power is most effectively wielded in the legislative chambers. The Republican Party of Texas now holds so much control over the House and the Senate that it is possible to pass virtually any piece of legislation desired by major contributors. The story that you are about to read will demonstrate this point, and it is but one example of what a genuine "Texas Miracle" actually looks like.

Again, welcome to the great state of Texas where we are "Wide Open for Business." If you are a business that can afford the services of a good lobbying firm, then you have come to the right place. If you are simply a Texan trying to raise a family and make an honest living, I wish you the best of luck.

---

[7] Jay Root, "Five Things to Know about the Perry Indictment," *The Texas Tribune*, August 16, 2014, accessed July 4, 2015.
http://www.texastribune.org/2014/08/16/five-things-know-about-perry-indictment.

Chapter 2

ICYMI – PLAYING POSSUM

In 1929, the Texas Legislature created the Brazos River Conservation and Reclamation District. This agency was renamed the Brazos River Authority in 1953 and is known as the BRA. The BRA was the first state agency in the United States specifically created for the purpose of developing and managing the water resources of an entire river basin. This particular river basin spans over 850 miles across the great state of Texas.

Although the BRA is a state agency, it does not levy or collect taxes. With the exception of a small number of government grants, the BRA is entirely self-supporting. It maintains and operates reservoirs and water treatment systems through revenues received from the customers to whom it sells water. Two of the largest such customers are the city of Round Rock, near Austin, and Dow Chemical Company.

The BRA's board of directors consists of twenty-one members who are appointed by the governor of Texas. These appointments are made subject to the advice, consent, and confirmation of the Texas Senate. Each director serves a six-year term; one-third of them are replaced or reappointed every other year. This structure is consistent with almost all of the other state agencies in Texas, and the purpose is to ensure that no single governor leaves an indelible mark on the political landscape of the state.

The Brazos River Authority functions under the direction of a general manager who serves as the CEO. During the *Tale of the River Card*, and as of this writing, that gentleman's name is Phil Ford. In his capacity as the

CEO of the BRA, Mr. Ford earns the modest sum of approximately $300K per year. Such compensation suggests that the BRA is a fairly important agency. If you have ever lived through a lengthy Texas drought, then you would probably understand why.

There are more than 42,000 square miles that make up the Brazos River basin. This sizable land mass is divided into four geographic regions and each of these regions enjoys a distinctive climate and topography. To illustrate this point, when Texas joined the United States of America, we demanded and received the right to divide ourselves into five states in the future— if we so desired.

The Brazos River Authority manages twelve reservoirs that can store more than 800 billion gallons of water. The BRA sells water from these reservoirs to municipal, industrial, and agricultural customers. These customers range from far northwest Texas down to the Gulf of Mexico.

In 1936, the first headquarters of the BRA was established in the Kyle Hotel in Temple, Texas. In 1940, the offices of the BRA were moved to two small rooms in the Baker Hotel in Mineral Wells. This relocation enabled the BRA to concentrate on its first major project: the construction of the Morris Sheppard Dam that created Possum Kingdom Lake.

The relocation of the BRA to the Mineral Wells area gave the local politicians in Palo Pinto County a monopoly position over the Brazos River Authority. It also helped transform the newly formed lake into a local resort that was subsidized by the taxpayers of Texas.

Possum Kingdom Lake is basically a dammed-up canyon. It is breathtakingly beautiful when the lake is full—and it can be rather ugly when the water level drops fifteen feet during a prolonged Texas drought. The original land acquired to create the lake came mostly from the cattle barons who were located in Palo Pinto County, and the majority of their land was originally acquired by those ranchers during the early Texas land grants. Most of these ranchers did not want to relinquish a half, or even a fourth, to say nothing of three-fourths of their ranches to the government. Instead, they took an all or nothing approach: "Buy my entire ranch or buy nothing at all."

As a result, the Brazos River Authority wound up owning approximately 14,000 acres of land surrounding Possum Kingdom Lake. Out of this total, eighty-five hundred acres was controlled by what would eventually become the Federal Energy Regulatory Commission, more commonly known as FERC. The FERC property consisted primarily of the shoreline and the islands that were created when the canyon was flooded.

Over the course of a few years, 310 miles of pristine shoreline had been created in one of the most visually appealing parts of Texas. And then, the shoreline simply sat there. It was truly a local paradise and it was being enjoyed by no one. As you might imagine, a waste of this magnitude could not—and would not—survive for long in a state that is "Wide Open for Business."

As the original incarnation of the Brazos River Authority was dominated by folks from Palo Pinto County, it is not surprising that the BRA soon decided that it would be a good idea to lease some of that shoreline to the local folks for their own personal amusement. And so they did.

In the words of Texas State Senator Craig Estes, here is a synopsis of the inevitable evolution:

> For more than sixty-five years, the Brazos River Authority has leased the shoreline property surrounding Possum Kingdom Lake to lessees for residential purposes.
>
> What began as rustic fishing cabins and camper trailers has evolved into a community of primary and secondary residences—some of them quite, uh, expansive—built on sites leased from the BRA.
>
> Over the years, and for a variety of reasons, the landlord-lessee relationship has steadily deteriorated between BRA and the residents of Possum Kingdom Lake.[8]

Senator Estes' assessment that this relationship had "deteriorated" was putting it mildly. For decades, the BRA had been leasing out parcels of its shoreline for virtually nothing. It did not take long before the word traveled from Palo Pinto County into the Dallas and Fort Worth areas. There was

---

[8] Sen. Craig Estes, "Senate Natural Resources Committee," *Texas Senate Video Archives*, April 17, 2007, accessed May 3, 2013.
http://tlcsenate.granicus.com/MediaPlayer.php?view_id=16&clip_id=2908.

cheap resort land to be had, for pennies on the dollar, and that lakefront property was only an hour's drive to the west.

The end result was predictable. By the early 2000's, the vast majority of the shoreline was occupied by weekenders who were paying seventy-six dollars per month, on average, to rent three-quarters of an acre of lakefront property. On top of these properties, the weekenders had built some really nice homes. And by "really nice," I mean dream homes.[9]

Because Possum Kingdom Lake was out there in the country, few people outside of Palo Pinto County and the Dallas/Fort Worth area knew much, or cared much, about it. You will never find another deal that was sweeter than this. Unfortunately, for the folks who were making Possum Kingdom their weekend hideaway, there was a handful of Texans who wanted to make the pot right. It would seem that every time some rich folks in Texas find themselves enjoying a sweetheart deal, a batch of bureaucrats comes along and tries to make things right. Damn it.

In the early 2000's, the board and the staff of the Brazos River Authority began to study the rental situation at Possum Kingdom Lake. To this end, the BRA had two different organizations perform a comprehensive analysis of the BRA's rental practices. The first was the Tennessee Valley Authority and the second was the Staubach Company. Both of these organizations recommended drastic changes.

The Staubach Company issued what became known as the *Staubach Report* in 2006. Among other things, the Staubach Company recommended that the Brazos River Authority begin charging the weekenders a fair market price to rent their lake lots. This recommendation set "The Texas Miracle" in motion, and the 84% of the homeowners who used Possum Kingdom Lake as their second home on the weekends went to work to protect their investments.

When wealthy Texans see a threat to their own personal largesse, their natural response is to contact the politicians whom they have been underwriting. Not surprisingly, the first response by the weekenders to the financial threat of the *Staubach Report* was to do exactly that. The call went out to State Senator Craig Estes and State Representative James "Jim" Keffer. Fortunately for the weekenders, both were accustomed to the process.

---

[9] See Pondera Properties at http://www.ponderapk.com.

Senator Estes obligingly authored Senate Bill 1326 in 2007. This bill was designed to force the Brazos River Authority to sell the leased property to the weekenders. There were no co-authors for his bill and there were there no sponsors. Simultaneously, Representative Jim Keffer authored House Bill 2923. Keffer's companion bill carried an identical caption to the one that was offered by Senator Estes:

> Relating to the sale by the Brazos River Authority of certain residential and commercial lots in the immediate vicinity of Possum Kingdom Lake to leaseholders of those lots.

To make a long story short, Senate Bill 1326 was shot down in a ball of flames in 2007 by Republicans and Democrats alike. This course of events was chronicled in detail in *Playing Possum—The Tale of the River Card, Round I*.

In addition to the members of the legislature, Senate Bill 1326 was also opposed by the board members of the Brazos River Authority, who had been appointed by the governor. Moreover, the bill was vigorously opposed by the state employees of the Brazos River Authority, who were responsible for acting in the best interests of the citizens of Texas.

By contrast, the effort in 2007 to force the Brazos River Authority to sell the shoreline property to the weekenders was supported by Governor Rick Perry, Lt. Governor David Dewhurst, and Attorney General Greg Abbott. The fact that this did not occur was an unusual challenge to their authority and their legislative will.

Mark Twain once observed: "Truth is stranger than fiction, but it is because Fiction is obliged to stick to possibilities—Truth isn't."

The following pages present the sad but true story of how the taxpayers of Texas were swindled out of hundreds of millions of dollars of prime Texas real estate. As you will see, the truth goes far beyond what anyone would think possible.

During the failed attempt to force the BRA to sell its shoreline in 2007, a good old boy by the name of Michael Harold Patterson was sitting on the sidelines, watching the whole thing play out. In Texas, we call this "playing possum."

In 2009, Michael Harold Patterson put together a deal that would have been the envy of any Wall Street titan. Over the course of ten months, Michael Patterson crafted an ingenious scheme that enabled him to purchase the entire inhabited shoreline of Possum Kingdom Lake for $50 million. Shortly thereafter, the Texas legislature unanimously passed House Bill 3031 which retroactively made Patterson's transaction legal. As a result of these two events, Michael Harold Patterson brags that he made $30 million in only 366 days.

While this may seem like a bold claim, I assure you it is not. Michael Harold Patterson made so much money off the deal in such a short period of time that he quickly earned a nickname around the Dallas/Fort Worth area: "The River Card."

The manner in which Patterson played the politicians and the bureaucrats was nothing short of amazing. In fact, it was a classic "Texas Miracle" that could only have been possible in a state that is "Wide Open for Business." What we are about to do is analyze whether Michael Harold Patterson's "Texas Miracle" was a hand well-played—or a crime against the state of Texas.

Chapter 3

HIGH CRIMES OR MISDEMEANORS?

Please allow me a moment of personal reflection:

> "I keep six honest serving-men (They taught me all I knew);
>
> Their names are *What* and *Why* and *When* and *How* and *Where* and *Who*.
>
> I send them over land and sea – I send them east and west;
>
> But after they have worked for me, I give them all a rest.
>
> I let them rest from nine till five, for I am busy then,
>
> As well as breakfast, lunch, and tea, for they are hungry men."

Rudyard Kipling penned those words in 1902 as the conclusion to his classic thesis on the principles of investigative journalism. This observation and others helped Rudyard win the Nobel Prize for Literature in 1907.[10]

I have been asking myself some probing questions after work and on the weekends for the better part of the past five years, leading me to fully appreciate Mr. Kipling's sentiments. It is now entirely possible that I have

---

[10] My interpretation of Rudyard Kipling's *"Just So Stories, An Elephant's Child."*

spent more time trying to unravel this deal than it took for the players to stitch it together.

The questions of "where" and "when" were the easiest to answer. Everything started in Austin and then headed north to Waco. From there, matters moved up to the Dallas and Fort Worth areas. If you drift west and northwest through a few other counties, you pretty much have the geography sewn up. As for the "when" of it, documenting every milestone down to the day, or the hour, or even the minute, was a simple matter of research.

Likewise, the question of "who" was thoroughly addressed by the players themselves. This occurred through public discourse and public communications. To say the least, the folks involved in this deal were more than willing to self-identify. If you supplement their disclosures with a modicum of *Freedom of Information* requests, you can also determine the players who chose to remain in the backroom. And then, you can also figure out what really happened. It was remarkable.

As for the "how" of it, the original strategy of brute force in *Round I* gave way to confidential negotiations, adversary elimination, and the illusion of competition in *Round II*. If you marinate the latter strategy with what is conveniently referred to as "enabling legislation," the end result was something called House Bill 3031.

The true challenge here is to determine *what* actually happened and *why*. You cannot answer the question of *why* without first answering the question of *what*. This will be our objective during *The Tale of the River Card, Round II*.

I would submit to you that there are three possible scenarios as to *what* actually happened here.

Scenario Number One holds that this was truly a case of collaborative commerce. A collection of strategic partners simply worked in unison to achieve a mutually beneficial outcome for all of the parties concerned. In other words, this could have simply been "business as usual" in the state of Texas. That would also make this an unpleasant reminder of what the phrase "Wide Open for Business" actually means.

Scenario Number Two is that this was a criminal conspiracy involving things like bribery, coercion, and bid-rigging. This activity might have reached from the highest public offices in Texas, down to the State Senate and the State House of Representatives—and down even further to the board and the staff of the Brazos River Authority.

Scenario Number Three is that this was a civil conspiracy that was executed by a few, for the benefit of more than a few, that resulted in a state asset worth approximately $1 billion being sold for a mere $50 million.

Scenario Number One is the position of the wealthy weekenders who wanted to force the Brazos River Authority to sell its shoreline for pennies on the dollar. I would suggest to you that these folks have already had their say. The weekenders now own their lakefront property and Michael Harold Patterson is now a very wealthy man. Moreover, the hydroelectric generator at Possum Kingdom Lake has been permanently shut down and the weekenders now own their property all the way to the water's edge. (We will be examining the demise of this renewable energy source as appropriate in due course.)

Scenario Number Two is obviously the extreme. Criminal activity must be proven beyond a reasonable doubt and this can be a difficult and expensive exercise. While circumstantial evidence can be persuasive in criminal proceedings, what one really needs in a deal like this is a smoking gun.

That brings us to *Scenario Number Three.*

A civil conspiracy, or collusion, is an agreement between two or more parties to deprive a third party of their legal rights, or deceive a third party, to obtain an illegal objective. A conspiracy is characterized by a group of people who make an agreement to form a partnership in which each participant becomes the agent—or partner—of the others. They then engage in planning or agreeing to commit some unlawful act. As will be demonstrated, there was a lot of planning and agreeing going on throughout this transaction.

To prove a civil conspiracy, it is not necessary that all of the conspirators be involved in all of the stages of the planning process. Nor is it necessary that all of the conspirators be aware of all of the details. Any voluntary agreement, followed by some overt act by one conspirator, in the furtherance of the plan, constitutes the main elements necessary to prove a conspiracy. A conspiracy may exist whether legal means are used to accomplish illegal results, or illegal means are used to accomplish something that is legal.

In the case of Possum Kingdom Lake, the taxpayers of Texas had a legal right to realize the fair market value of the state land that was sold to the weekenders. That means that those of us who reside in the Lone Star State represent the third party whose legal rights were deprived.

A civil conspiracy does not require proof beyond a reasonable doubt. Instead, a preponderance of the evidence is employed. In other words, if it is more likely than not that something happened, a jury can find for the plaintiff. As a member of the court of public opinion, I invite you to examine the evidence that is presented in the pages that follow.

Smoking Guns

In October 2009, a jury found the former Mayor Pro Tem of Dallas, Don Hill, guilty of conspiracy to commit bribery, two counts of bribery, conspiracy to commit extortion, extortion, conspiracy to commit deprivation of honest services, and conspiracy to commit money laundering. The judge in that case also ruled that Don Hill had lied on the witness stand. Don Hill was sentenced to eighteen years in prison.

In that same trial, the jury found former Dallas plan commissioner, D'Angelo Lee, guilty of conspiracy to commit bribery, two counts of bribery, conspiracy to commit extortion, extortion, conspiracy to commit deprivation of honest services, and conspiracy to commit money laundering. D'Angelo Lee was sentenced to fourteen years in prison.[11]

In addition to these sentences, a gentleman who worked as a consultant in the low-income housing development profession also received a fourteen-year sentence in a follow-on case. His name was Darren L. Reagan.

Reagan got busted by virtue of a smoking gun, which came in the form of *Government Exhibit 153D.*

Black State Employees Association of Texas
Community Development Corporation, Inc.
November 17, 2004
Attention: Bill Fisher

---

[11] Jason Trahan and Diane Jennings, "Three in Dallas City Hall Case Sentenced in a 'Betrayal of Our City," *Dallas Morning News*, February 27, 2010, accessed November 27, 2015. http://www.dallasnews.com/news/community-news/dallas/headlines/20100226-3-in-Dallas-City-Hall-case-6771.ece.

From: Darren L. Reagan (214) 207-xxxx (cell)

Re: Dallas West Village Mixed Use Contract

Transmitted Via Fax To (972) 255-xxxx

Dear Bill:

Please find attached the contract proposal for your signature (per Council Don Hill and Planning Commissioner De Angelo Lee); A copy of the SW Housing deed restriction as an example of what our show look like. [sic]

Please call me when I can come out and pick up the check ($12,500) this morning. I would like to compensate Allen for his hard work, dedication, loyalty and very long hours of service (last week's day long council hearing and various meetings held with Councilman Hill). I will be flying back out this afternoon, however, I will have my cell phone handy. You may leave a copy of the signed contract for our files at the receptionist desk.

Thanks and we look forward to expanding our mutually beneficial partnership.[12]

What a coincidence. The parties involved in the "Texas Miracle" at Possum Kingdom Lake also referred to their partnership as being "mutually beneficial." In the case of Darren Reagan, the jury determined that his mutually beneficial partnership was actually a criminal conspiracy.

Unfortunately for Darren Reagan, the recipient of his email, Mr. Bill Fisher, was a wired-up informant for the FBI who had already spent time in prison. Bill Fisher simply turned Darren Reagan's email over to the FBI and Reagan was cooked. The result was a fourteen year jail sentence.

By contrast, what might seem to be highly incriminating on the surface might actually prove to be a misfire, rather than a smoking gun.

A case in point is the following email from the same Bill Fisher to his business partner, Leon J. Backes, who owned a company by the name of

---

[12] United States of America v. Don Hill, et al., "Government Exhibit 153D," September 7, 2015, accessed November 27, 2015. https://web.archive.org/web/20150907061809/ http://coop.txnd.uscourts.gov/judges/hill/07-16-09/0153D.PDF.

Provident Realty. Together, Bill Fisher and Leon J. Backes had formed an offshoot company by the name of Provident Odyssey Partners. The purpose of this firm was to develop low income housing that targeted the same market controlled by Don Hill and D'Angelo Lee.

> 5/19/2004 9:22 PM
>
> From: Bill Fisher
>
> To: Leon Backes
>
> Subject: RE: CDC and upcoming meetings
>
> We have benefited from the CDC and Eugene's work for quite some time. They have been very patient due to their long relationship with me. I need to get them paid. They have been to many meetings with the councilmember's, neighbors and the other elected officials who are supporting our endeavors. We received letters and other support from them based upon their representation they were involved in the developments. Eugene is our HUB partner in the Dallas Hotel deal.
>
> Thanks,
>
> Bill[13]

What does "I need to get them paid" mean? And just so you know, the initials CDC stand for Community Development Corporation, as in the letterhead of the previous email from Darren Reagan to Bill Fisher.

   While these two emails might appear to be similar in content, Bill Fisher was an informant for the FBI who was never indicted in the Dallas City Hall corruption case. Nor was his business partner, Leon J. Backes. And while Mr. Backes may have been guilty of choosing his friends poorly, or of being in the wrong place at the wrong time, he was never charged with

---

[13] United States of America v. Don Hill, et al., "Government Exhibit BP-0076," September 7, 2015, accessed November 27, 2015. https://web.archive.org/web/20150907055901/http://coop.txnd.uscourts.gov/judges/hill/08-17-09/BP-076.pdf.

any crime. By the time the prosecution against the officials at Dallas City Hall was complete, the statute of limitations had expired for everyone else.

To be fair and balanced, Bill Fisher and Provident Realty enjoyed unusually strong support from some very prominent local politicians. On February 11, 2004, Dallas County Commissioner John Wiley Price addressed the Texas Department of Housing and Community Affairs.[14] Price testified glowingly about the work that Bill Fisher and Provident Realty had performed in his district. It is worth noting that this is the same John Wiley Price who was indicted on July 23, 2014, on multiple counts of public corruption.[15] (That trial is still pending).

The indictment against John Wiley Price stemmed from a three-year investigation that culminated with the FBI raiding Price's home and offices on June 27, 2011.[16] Price was charged with bribery and several other counts along with his business associate, Kathy Nealy. In a separate email from Bill Fisher to Leon Backes, Bill Fisher reminded Leon Backes that Kathy Nealy was representing their partnership.[17]

So, how are the events of the Dallas City Hall corruption case and the John Wiley Price indictment related to the "Texas Miracle" at Possum Kingdom Lake? Spoiler alert: Leon J. Backes was the only party to submit a competing bid against Michael Harold Patterson when the property at Possum Kingdom Lake was sold in 2009.

The records of Leon J. Backes and Provident Realty, as they were related to John Wiley Price, were also part of the search warrant when the FBI raided Mr. Price's offices in 2011. It should be noted here for the sake

[14] Texas Department of Housing and Community Affairs, "Board Meeting," February 11, 2004, accessed November 27, 2015. https://web.archive.org/web/20121023194116/http://www.tdhca.state.tx.us/board/docs/transcripts/040211-board.pdf.
[15] Dallas Morning News Research; Interactive by John Hancock, Breanna Dumbacher, Troy Oxford and Michael Hogue, "Breaking Down the John Wiley Price Indictment," *Dallas Morning News*, n.d., accessed January 3, 2015. http://res.dallasnews.com/interactives/john-wiley-price-breakdown.
[16] WFAA Staff, "FBI Raids Dallas Gallery Linked to Commissioner Price," *WFAA*, June 30, 2011, accessed July 18, 2012. http://www.wfaa.com/news/local/FBI-raids-Dallas-gallery-linked-to-Commissioner-Price-124817829.html.
[17] United States of America v. Don Hill, et al., "Government Exhibit BP-0300," September 7, 1015, accessed November 27, 2015. https://web.archive.org/web/20150907194755/http://coop.txnd.uscourts.gov/judges/hill/08-17-09/BP-300.pdf.

of the record that no allegations have been made against Leon J. Backes, or Provident Realty, in the John Wiley Price matter.[18]

Public Corruption

The Travis County District Attorney's office once held the primary responsibility for investigating and prosecuting public corruption in the state of Texas. This is because the state capitol of Texas, the city of Austin, is located in Travis County.

In the early 1980's, the Travis County District Attorney, Ronnie Earle, formed the Public Integrity Unit within his office for the specific purpose of investigating public corruption. Way back then, Ronnie Earle stated that the investigation of government crimes was "mostly left to the newspapers" because the Travis County District Attorney spent most of its time fighting street crime.[19] One of the Public Integrity Unit's most notable prosecutions was that of former U.S. House Majority Leader Tom DeLay in 2005. Congressman DeLay was convicted of money laundering and received a three-year prison sentence. That conviction has since been overturned.

The Public Integrity Unit had statewide jurisdiction and was consequently funded by the state of Texas, rather than the residents of Travis County. During the legislative session of 2013, the Texas legislature allocated $3,742,829 and $3,830,597 for the Public Integrity Unit for the following two budgetary years. On June 14, 2013, Governor Rick Perry exercised his constitutional line-item veto to eliminate this appropriation.

Governor Perry then issued the following statement:

> Despite the otherwise good work the Public Integrity Unit's employees, I cannot in good conscience support continued State funding for an office with statewide jurisdiction at a time when the person charged with ultimate responsibility

[18] Jason Trahan, " List of Items Sought by FBI Sheds More Light on Price Investigation," *Dallas Morning News*, July 7, 2011, accessed July 15, 2011. http://www.dallasnews.com/news/community-news/dallas/headlines/20110707-list-of-items-sought-by-fbi-sheds-more-light-on-price-investigation.ece.
[19] Staff, "TRIBPEDIA: Public Integrity Unit," *The Texas Tribune*, n.d., accessed January 23, 2015. http://www.texastribune.org/tribpedia/public-integrity-unit/about/.

of that unit has lost the public's confidence. This unit is in no other way held accountable to state taxpayers, except through the State budgetary process. I therefore object to and disapprove of this appropriation.[sic][20]

Please afford me another quick side note: If you are the governor of a state that is "Wide Open for Business," would it be too much to ask to have someone proofread the veto statement when you are eliminating funding for public corruption investigations? If the Governor's grammar is a product of the public education system, the opposition might start claiming that the system is underfunded. That could only lead to higher taxes and maybe even higher academic achievement. Higher academic achievement could lead to smarter voters and then what?

The "lost... public confidence" to which Governor Perry referred was in reference to the DWI conviction of Travis County District Attorney Rosemary Lehmberg earlier that year. Lehmberg pled guilty to the charges and received a forty-five day jail sentence. While she served this sentence, Rosemary Lehmberg also refused to resign from her office.

Despite Texas' environmental slogan being "Don't Mess with Texas," it seemed that things in Texas were in a bit of a mess already. Here was the rub:

Rosemary Lehmberg was a Democrat and there were three years remaining in her term as District Attorney. At the time of her DWI conviction, the Public Integrity Unit was investigating, among other things, the Cancer Prevention Research Institute of Texas (CPRIT). Under scrutiny were the methods utilized to award grants to cancer preventers.

As a result of the CPRIT investigation, CPRIT's chief commercialization officer, Mr. Jerald "Jerry" Cobbs, was indicted on a first degree felony count accusing him of "fraudulently causing another to sign a document affecting a financial interest." Specifically, Jerry Cobbs was indicted under Title 7 of the Texas Penal Code, *Offenses Against Property*, Chapter 32, *Fraud*, Section 32.46, *Securing Execution Of A Document By Deception*.

---

[20] Gov. Rick Perry, "Line-Item Vetos in SB 1, Article IV - The Judiciary," *Office of the Governor*, June 14, 2013, accessed July 10, 2013. https://wayback.archive-it.org/414/20130615153848/http://governor.state.tx.us/news/veto/18674/.

Obviously, someone did not get the memo that Texas was "Wide Open for Business." It was bad enough to have to constantly protect Texans from the overreaching federal government, without having to put up with local oversight at the same time.

Texas is the reddest of all red states. The Republican Party holds every statewide office and a significant majority in both the Texas House and the Texas Senate. If there is public wrongdoing going on, the odds suggest that a Republican will be involved. Conversely, Travis County is as blue as the Texas sky in August. A Democrat has held the Travis County District Attorney's office for decades. Were Rosemary Lehmberg to resign, Governor Perry would have certainly appointed a Republican to complete her term. The objective evidence here is Tarrant County District Attorney Joe Shannon.[21]

Here was another rub. Governor Rick Perry did not simply veto the funding for the Public Integrity Unit. He first *threatened* to veto the funding if Rosemary Lehmberg did not resign. It is alleged that Governor Perry then followed through on his threat. Moreover, it is alleged that he offered to reinstate the money after his line-item veto if Rosemary Lehmberg would simply resign. While Governor Perry's office characterized his actions as the constitutional execution of his veto authority, his critics and prosecutors characterized his actions as coercion and abuse of power. At the time of this writing, Governor Rick Perry remains under indictment for these charges.

In the absence of funding, the Travis County Commissioners were forced to vote on July 2, 2013, to send layoff notices to thirty-four employees of the Public Integrity Unit. In the absence of these investigators, it was not likely that the PIU would be scrutinizing the "sale by the Brazos River Authority of certain residential and commercial leased lots and other real property in the immediate vicinity of Possum Kingdom Lake." With the PIU being currently castrated, it is up to someone else to figure this deal out. That would be us.

---

[21] Eric Griffey, "Cut From the Same Cloth," *Fort Worth Weekly*, July 15, 2009, accessed February 1, 2014.
https://web.archive.org/web/20151129132118/http://www.fwweekly.com/2009/07/15/cut-from-the-same-cloth./.

Chapter 4

REMEMBER THE ALAMO

Following the debacle of Senate Bill 1326 in 2007, one might assume that the weekenders at Possum Kingdom Lake had shot their wad. The fact of the matter was that they were just warming up. The lessons learned in the failed attempt to pass Senate Bill 1326 in 2007 provided the ingenuity for House Bill 3031 in 2009.

The missteps of the weekenders were many. They had dramatically underestimated the extent to which their land grab would offend the sensibilities of others. They had also failed to properly address the overreaching issues related to the Texas Constitution. Moreover, they tried to make their case through public debate using poorly framed arguments that were virtually impossible to defend with a straight face. To make a bad hand even worse, they attempted to change the stakes one too many times while the hands were being played out.

Most importantly, the weekenders failed to properly stack the deck and they entered the legislative session in 2007 without having rigged the votes. Those mistakes would not be repeated in 2009.

The players seeking to force the Brazos River Authority to divest itself of its shoreline had learned their lessons and they took immediate corrective action. Less than one month after the end of the 2007 legislative session, the Possum Kingdom Lake Association held its annual membership meeting to discuss what went wrong and how to proceed. The weekenders had eighteen months until the next legislative session began and they would use the entirety of that time to ensure that their desired outcome was achieved.

The Possum Kingdom Lake Association's next annual meeting was held on June 23, 2007. During this meeting, the PKLA laid out their future strategy which included Governor Rick Perry's model for challenging a county's property assessments.[22]

The first order of business that day was to add Jay Turner from the Possum Kingdom Lake Preservation Association to the board of the Possum Kingdom Lake Association. This would create a single voice for those seeking to force the BRA to sell the shoreline. From this point forward, the big names from the Possum Kingdom Lake Preservation Association would go silent.

The next item of business at the PKLA's meeting was a status report concerning the lawsuits that had been filed against the Palo Pinto County Appraisal District. Following Governor Perry's example, five leaseholders had filed suit against the appraisal district claiming that the assessed values on their leased land were excessive. While the merits of their arguments were dubious, the Palo Pinto Appraisal District's annual budget for legal expenses was only $30,000.[23] Consequently, suing the Palo Pinto County Appraisal District into submission was not simply a theoretical possibility. It was, by all accounts, a key element of the Possum Kingdom Lake Association's strategy.

The next item on the agenda was a report from Mr. Lewis Simmons, who served as the chief of staff to State Senator Craig Estes. The official minutes of the annual meeting captured the following position statements from Mr. Simmons on behalf of the senator.

> a. Senator Craig Estes was unable to attend
> because of the very recent tragedy occurring

---

[22] John Marshall, "Playing Possum – The Tale of the River Card, Round I," *iUniverse*, April 29, 2014.

[23] John Marshall, "Playing Possum – The Tale of the River Card, Round I," *iUniverse*, April 29, 2014.

in Gainesville. Senator Estes arranged a victim's assistance program for the victims of the flooding which conflicted with the PKLA meeting.

b. Mr. Simmons emphasized that Senator Estes was already working toward another attempt to help lessees obtain divestiture in the next legislative session.

c. Mr. Simmons recognized the Lake Country Sun for its fair and thorough reporting on the divestiture issue. He thanked the PKLA and its sister organization, the Possum Kingdom Lake Preservation Association, for their invaluable resources and leadership.

d. Mr. Simmons complimented The Graydon Group [PKLPA lobbyist in Austin] and particularly their leading sled dog on this issue, Mr. Jay Propes.

"Jay Propes is a gentleman whose integrity is beyond question and without whom we could not have gotten as far as we did," stated Mr. Simmons. He further expressed the hope of Senator Estes that the relationship with the Graydon Group would continue into the future.

e. Lewis Simmons gave a very detailed explanation of SB 1326 (the divestiture bill) and its travels through the Senate and into the House.

f. Lewis Simmons stated that divestiture was "going to happen" and that it is hoped that the BRA will take a more pro-active posture

in arranging the divesture. He stated that with
the assistance of Governor Perry and Lieutenant
Governor Dewhurst, hopes are high that a
solution can be worked out before the next
session.[24]

Throughout the duration of this land grab, no one ever passed on
the opportunity to remind those who were watching that Governor Rick
Perry and Lt. Governor David Dewhurst were in support of this deal.
Invariably, those on the buy side of this equation asserted that they had the
full consent, and the active support, of Rick Perry and David Dewhurst.
For example, the president of the PKLA, Monte Land, claimed during this
same meeting that the Governor's office and the Lt. Governor's office had
been in contact with him during the previous three weeks.

The last person to speak that day at the annual meeting of the Possum
Kingdom Lake Association was Mr. Joe Shannon. (We examined Joe
Shannon in great detail during the first installment of this tale.)

We need to focus on Lewis Simmons' assertion that divestiture "was
going to happen" and his other remarks. While it was no surprise that
the parties pursuing divestiture wanted Jay Propes and the Graydon
Group to stay on the payroll in order to write the next bill, the optimism
projected during this annual meeting was a bit of a head-scratcher. One
month earlier, these people had gotten their asses handed to them in the
legislature. Now, they portrayed the forced sale of the shoreline at Possum
Kingdom Lake as a foregone conclusion.

One might suspect that these folks knew something that the rest of us
did not. The truth is that they knew something that almost every Austin
insider knows. You do not craft questionable special-interest legislation
in the middle of a session. You do so in between sessions and then you
walk your bill through the process like a champion steer at the local stock
show. Simultaneously, you publicly intimidate the opposition with a show
of strength.

---

[24] "Annual Membership Meeting Summary," *Possum Kingdom Lake Association*, June
23, 2007, accessed December 12, 2010.
https://web.archive.org/web/20151129132833/http://www.pklakeassn.org/June%20
23%20Annual%20Meeting.htm.

Shortly after the PKLA's annual meeting on June 23, 2007, the PKLA published the minutes of that meeting on their website. The content was direct and it put the opposition on notice. The true audience of this posting was not the membership of the PKLA that was absent that day. Knowing that the BRA's board and staff had as much access to the internet as anyone, the missive was aimed at them.

The directors of the Brazos River Authority had also learned a thing or two during Round One of the divestiture battle. For starters, they had learned through basic analysis that the Palo Pinto Appraisal District's assessed values were ridiculously low. They also understood that they were up against the kind of people who do not accept defeat on the first attempt, or even the second.[25] They further realized that they were fighting a war, as the leaseholders became fond of calling it, on multiple fronts.[26] They were more or less surrounded.

Given the opposition, it was nothing short of amazing that the BRA's board members put up a fight at all. When you have the Governor and Lt. Governor telling you that they want something done, a state senator and a state representative telling you how you are going to do it, and a cadre of wealthy benefactors funding the onslaught, surrender would have been an understandable course of action. But these people did not fold. Instead, many of them proved yet again that there is one thing that will never become extinct in the state of Texas: a duty-bound Texan.

Remember the Alamo?

On February 24, 1836, Lt. Colonel William Barrett Travis penned and dispatched the following message to whom he considered to be his fellow Texans. At the time of his writing, Texas did not yet exist, and it appeared highly unlikely that it ever would. His plea to the masses went like this:

---

[25] It took Governor Rick Perry three "Special Sessions' of the Texas Legislature in 2013 to pass his controversial abortion bill that made State Senator Wendy Davis famous.

[26] Libby Cluett, "War of Words" *Mineral Wells Index*, June 30, 2008, accessed February 1, 2012.
https://web.archive.org/web/20080820111131/http:/www.mineralwellsindex.com/local/local_story_182091601.html.

Commandancy of the The Alamo

Bejar, Feby. 24th. 1836

To the People of Texas & All Americans in the World -

Fellow Citizens & Compatriots -

I am besieged, by a thousand or more of the Mexicans under Santa Anna – I have sustained a continual Bombardment & cannonade for 24 hours & have not lost a man – The enemy has demanded a surrender at discretion, otherwise, the garrison are to be put to the sword, if the fort is taken – I have answered the demand with a cannon shot, & our flag still waves proudly from the walls – I shall never surrender or retreat. Then, I call on you in the name of Liberty, of patriotism & everything dear to the American character, to come to our aid, with all dispatch – The enemy is receiving reinforcements daily & will no doubt increase to three or four thousand in four or five days. If this call is neglected, I am determined to sustain myself as long as possible & die like a soldier who never forgets what is due to his own honor & that of his country –

Victory or Death.

William Barrett Travis.

Lt. Col. comdt.

P. S. The Lord is on our side – When the enemy appeared in sight we had not three bushels of corn – We have since found in deserted houses 80 or 90 bushels and got into the walls 20 or 30 head of Beeves.[27]

Travis

---

[27] The plural for beef is beeves. The mascot for the Texas Longhorns is appropriately named Bevo.

Being born and raised in Texas, I read Colonel Travis' letter for the first time in my sixth-grade Texas history class.[28] I have probably read it over one hundred times since. Almost every Texas school boy's ego would have him believe that if he had been inside that sorry excuse for a fort on March 6, 1836, his name would now be engraved on the list of those who crossed a line in the sand and were killed in battle.

My own ego would also like to believe that my footnote would read that there were a least a dozen of Santa Anna's men surrounding my corpse. But I was not there that day. And so, the Alamo was not my Alamo. It was theirs. If the Good Lord ever does decide to give me my own personal Alamo, I pray that I will perform up to His and Colonel Travis' standards. I also hope that He will be on my side.

For many of the board members of the Brazos River Authority, that is exactly what the war over the shoreline of Possum Kingdom Lake became—their own personal Alamo. These admirable defenders of the Texas Constitution dug in deep and prepared for the next assault. Unfortunately, those who chose to stand and fight would soon enjoy the same fate as Colonel Travis. Still, the taxpayers of the state of Texas can be extremely proud of the way that many of these people honored their duty and their respective oaths.

[28] In Texas, it is likely that you will take a class in Texas History before you take a class in U.S. History.

Chapter 5

VICTORY OR DEATH

After having successfully fended off Senate Bill 1326 in 2007, the board and the staff of the Brazos River Authority remained convinced that doing the right thing for their compatriots would win out in the end. Working together, they methodically attempted to shore up their defenses and prepare for the next assault from certain members of the Texas legislature.

On Monday, July 16, 2007—less than one month after the PKLA announced on the internet that divestiture was "going to happen"—the board of the Brazos River Authority met to hold a series of committee meetings. The first order of business was to consider a recommendation from the Executive Compensation Committee to award an annual bonus to General Manager Phil Ford in the amount of $75,000. After the committee voted 8-0 to recommend the bonus, the larger body voted 16-0 to approve the bonus.[29] The balance of the day was spent considering and adopting the 2008 fiscal budget and the water rates that would be charged to the BRA's customers.

On the following day, the board of the BRA reconvened and dedicated a special board meeting to the issues surrounding Possum Kingdom Lake. Ninety days prior to this, the board had met in an emergency meeting to

---

[29] Executive Compensation & Evaluation Committee "Agenda Items 1-8," *Brazos River Authority Board Meeting Minutes*, July 16, 2007, accessed November 10, 2014. http://www.brazos.org/Portals/0/board_audio/07162007_ECE.mp3.

address the threat of Senate Bill 1326. To say the least, the wounds from that emergency meeting were still raw.

While the meeting back in April had been highlighted by metaphors concerning rape, knives, and guns, the meeting on July 17, 2007, was subdued by comparison. In the absence of a quorum, the meeting got off to a clumsy start with those present trying to reach Director Martha Martin by cell phone to see if she would be attending the meeting.

Presiding Officer Steve Pena was absent due to illness. Assistant Presiding Officer Roberto Bailon asked the chief counsel if they should adjourn or wait for a quorum.[30] For the better part of five minutes, the open microphone captured an earful of hushed jokes and knowing laughter.

When Martha Martin finally arrived to establish a quorum, Director Bailon asked everyone to turn off their cell phones. He then read off a list of those directors who had indicated that they would not be present. This list included Suzanne Baker, Billy Wayne Moore, Robert Christian, Jacqueline Chaumet, John Skaggs, Fred Lee Hughes, Mark Carrabba, Ron Butler, and Steve Pena. It seemed that either battle fatigue was setting in for many of the board members or they simply had lives to lead with no spare time for facilitating a land grab. During the enumeration of those absent, two different cell phones went off in the background invoking both the ire and the tongue of Director Bailon.

At the outset of the meeting, three individuals from the public asked to speak to the board. Two of the three were entirely inconsequential. The middle speaker, however, was a fellow by the name of Vick Clesi, who presented the following resolution on behalf of the Possum Kingdom Lake Association.

> The membership of the Possum Kingdom Lake Association respectfully requests that the board of directors of the Brazos River Authority place a moratorium on their request for lessees to sign the newly adopted Cottage Site lease contract by October 1, 2007. This moratorium is being requested until the next legislative session so that

[30] Special Board Meeting "Agenda Items 1-8," *Brazos River Authority Board Meeting Minutes*, July 17, 2007, accessed November 10, 2014. http://www.brazos.org/Portals/0/board_audio/07172007_17SPL1.mp3.

Possum Kingdom Lessees, their representatives, and BRA can work on differences between the Possum Kingdom community and Brazos River Authority.

Monte Land

President Possum Kingdom Lake Association[31]

So with that, the board of the BRA was put on further notice that the leaseholders had no intention of going away and that they had every intention of exercising the full extent of their political clout.

After the comments from the public, the Board of Directors entered into an executive session at 8:18 that morning. At 11:40, the board emerged into open session and the tension in the room was striking. The following resolution was read into the record:

RESOLUTION OF THE BOARD OF DIRECTORS OF THE BRAZOS RIVER AUTHORITY
JULY 17, 2007

WHEREAS the Board recognizes that divestiture has received considerable legislative support and will continue to be an issue in the future; and

WHEREAS the Board has consulted with additional outside legal counsel regarding whether divestiture is a viable option under current law; and

WHEREAS the Board believes that if the Authority is to divest, the most favorable way for this to happen is under terms and conditions as set by the Board, so as to ensure that the divestiture process involves a willing buyer/willing seller scenario;

NOW, THEREFORE, BE IT RESOLVED that the Board of Directors of the Brazos River Authority hereby directs staff to develop a process for the sale of leased

---

[31] Special Board Meeting, "Agenda Items 1-8," *Brazos River Authority Board Meeting Minutes*, July 17, 2007, accessed November 10, 2014.http://www.brazos.org/Portals/0/board_audio/07172007_17SPL1.mp3.

residential properties at Possum Kingdom Lake to lessees, excluding property within the FERC project area, for subsequent consideration by the Board of Directors.

Within the text of this resolution, the board of directors of the Brazos River Authority committed a fatal error. In the third paragraph, the appointed members of the board stated that they intended to determine the terms and conditions of any eventual sale of the property. This was nothing short of blasphemy to the Republican hierarchy.

Director Wade Gear moved that the resolution be adopted and Director Carolyn Johnson seconded the motion. When the eleven members present were polled for the vote, the result provided a clue as to who the first turncoat would be.[32]

Director Bailon? "Yes."

Director Ellison? "Yes."

Director Adams? "Yes."

Director Blum? "Yes."

Director DeCluitt? *"No!"*

This was stated rather emphatically and was followed by a long and awkward pause.

Director Garcia? "Yes."

Director Gear? "Yes."

Director Johnson? "Yes."

Director Kilgore? "Yes."

[32] Special Board Meeting, "Agenda Items 5-7," *Brazos River Authority Board Meeting Minutes*, July 17, 2007, accessed July 10, 2013. (Fast forward to 02:11). http://www.brazos.org/Portals/0/board_audio/07172007_17SPL2.mp3.

Director Martin? "Yes."

Director Zaccagnino? "Yes."

Following this vote, the board recessed for lunch. When they returned, Phil Ford assumed the persona of a humble bureaucrat who had just received a $75K bonus from the taxpayers. He also acted like a man who had learned some lessons about how the legislature worked.

Phil Ford explained to the board that certain state legislators had made it abundantly clear that they were in favor of a forced sale. Ford further stated that the BRA's staff had spent hundreds of hours working on draft legislation and had gone to great lengths to explain to the legislators that there were many challenges related to the process.[33]

Phil Ford enumerated those challenges as FERC, the Texas Constitution, environmental issues, and public services. The first challenge that he brought to the board's attention was the topic of granting discounts and freezes on lease rates to those leaseholders who were sixty-five years of age or older. At the heart of the issue was whether or not the practice was in violation of the Texas Constitution. To that end, the BRA had hired the law firm of Scott, Douglass, and McConnico to analyze the situation and provide a recommendation.

In summary, Jennifer Knauth, an attorney with Scott, Douglass, and McConnico, advised that the Texas Constitution prevented a public agency from granting public funds, *or anything of value*, to private individuals. Consequently, it was the opinion of her firm that the BRA had no legal authority to grant a discount to the senior citizens as this would be "a thing of value."

Jennifer Knauth further explained that in those cases where such discounts were granted elsewhere, there was a specific Constitutional Amendment that created the authority to do so. She then reminded the board that the only way to amend the Texas Constitution was to put a proposition on the ballot that would be decided upon by the voters of Texas. To conclude, Jennifer Knauth recommended that the board repeal

---

[33] Special Board Meeting, "Agenda Items 8-10," *Brazos River Authority Board Meeting Minutes*, July 17, 2007, accessed July 10, 2013. (Fast forward to 03:18). http://www. brazos.org/Portals/0/board_audio/07172007_17SPL3.mp3.

the rental discounts that were currently being granted to the older crowd. She then recommended that these same questions be put to the Attorney General of Texas.[34]

These recommendations were presented to the Board in the following resolution.

RESOLUTION OF THE BOARD OF DIRECTORS OF THE BRAZOS RIVER AUTHORITY
July 17, 2007
Agenda Item 8
Possum Kingdom Senior Homestead Lease
Rate Reduction/Rate Freeze

The following resolution is presented for consideration to the Board of Directors of the Brazos River Authority for adoption at its July 17, 2007 meeting.

WHEREAS, the Board of Directors of the Brazos River Authority, previously approved and for a number of years have applied a ten percent (10%) discount to the residential lease rate for lessees sixty-five (65) years old and older who qualify for a homestead exemption; and

WHEREAS, the Authority has recently retained outside legal counsel to conduct a comprehensive legal review of leasing policies at Possum Kingdom Lake; and

WHEREAS, in the course of reviewing overall leasing policies, outside legal counsel has called into question the practice of offering the ten percent (10%) discount and proposed rate freeze for lessees sixty-five (65) years old and older who qualify for a homestead exemption, and is of the opinion that this practice violates Article III, Section 52 of the Texas Constitution; and

---

[34] Special Board Meeting, "Agenda Items 8-10," *Brazos River Authority Board Meeting Minutes*, July 17, 2007, accessed July 10, 2013. (Fast forward to 07:19). http://www.brazos.org/Portals/0/board_audio/07172007_17SPL3.mp3.

WHEREAS, outside legal counsel recommends that the Brazos River Authority discontinue granting discounts for lessees sixty-five (65) years old and older who qualify for a homestead exemption;

NOW, THEREFORE BE IT RESOLVED that the Board of Directors of the Brazos River Authority hereby discontinues any reduced lease rate to lessees sixty-five (65) years old and older who qualify for a homestead exemption; and

BE IT FURTHER RESOLVED that the Board of Directors of the Brazos River Authority hereby requests its Presiding Officer to seek an opinion from the Texas Attorney General regarding the constitutional, statutory, and legal constraints on the Brazos River Authority's ability to grant lease rate discounts or lease rate freezes to lessees sixty-five (65) years old and older who qualify for a homestead exemption;

The aforementioned resolution was approved by the Board of Directors of the Brazos River Authority on July 17, 2007, to certify which witness my hand and seal.

Roberto Bailon

Assistant Presiding Officer[35]

Jennifer Knauth's legal arguments made it intuitively obvious that the BRA's past practice of granting discounts to the older residents was a violation of Article III, Section 52 of the Texas Constitution. When the board was polled to eliminate the practice, the resulting vote was unanimous at 11-0.[36]

[35] BRA Staff, "Senior Rate Freeze Resolution," *Brazos River Authority*, July 17, 2007, accessed July 10, 2013.
https://web.archive.org/web/20141107072121/http://www.brazos.org/generalPdf/pk_07-17-2007_SeniorHomesteadLeaseRateReduction-RateFreeze.pdf.
[36] Special Board Meeting, "Agenda Items 8-10," *Brazos River Authority Board Meeting Minutes*, July 17, 2007, accessed July 10, 2013. (Fast forward to 17:15). http://www.brazos.org/Portals/0/board_audio/07172007_17SPL3.mp3.

In hindsight, this might have been the pivotal moment as everyone in the room could now connect the dots. If leasing the property at a discount violated the Texas Constitution, then certainly selling the property at a discount would do the same. If the property were to be sold, it would have to be sold at fair market value.

The next order of business was to consider two other resolutions also related to Possum Kingdom Lake. The first resolution would discontinue the practice of basing the rental rates on the county appraisal district's assessed values. Beginning in 2010, all lease rates would be based on a fair market appraisal of the land.[37] The second resolution would decrease the length of the term of each lease from fifty years to twenty years with a ten-year extension option.[38]

As the resolution to shift from assessed values to appraised values was being introduced, Martha Martin quietly walked out of the room. Only she and God will ever know why, but this left only ten members present and eliminated the board's quorum. No further business could be conducted.

To the disgust of those remaining, the meeting had to be adjourned before they could vote on the last two resolutions.[39] Director Wade Gear closed the meeting by expressing his disdain for the number of members who were absent and stated that he hoped that the governor would appoint new members who would be more faithful in their attendance of meetings. Unfortunately for the taxpayers of Texas, Director Gear would soon get his wish.

Thirteen days later, on July 30, 2007, the board of the BRA held its next regularly scheduled meeting. As was becoming the norm, the meeting

[37] BRA Staff, "Lease Rate Methodology Resolution," *Brazos River Authority*, July 17, 2007, accessed July 10, 2013. https://web.archive.org/web/20141107072214/http://www.brazos.org/generalPdf/pk_07-30-2007-PossumKingdomResLeaseRateMethodology.pdf.
[38] BRA Staff, "Residential Lease Term Resolution," *Brazos River Authority*, July 17, 2007, accessed July 10, 2013. https://web.archive.org/web/20141107002051/http://www.brazos.org/generalPdf/pk_10-29-2007-Residentail_Grnd-Lease-Term-Form.pdf.
[39] Special Board Meeting, "Agenda Items 8-10," *Brazos River Authority Board Meeting Minutes*, July 17, 2007, accessed July 10, 2013. (Fast forward to 18:20). http://www.brazos.org/Portals/0/board_audio/07172007_17SPL3.mp3.

was front-loaded with issues related to Possum Kingdom Lake. To begin the proceedings, Presiding Officer Steve Pena announced that Suzanne Baker, Christopher DeCluitt, Sal Zaccagnino, and Martha Martin would not be in attendance. Pena then advised that there were no members from the public who wished to speak.

At 9:00 AM, the board entered into executive session to consult with outside legal counsel. At 10:19 AM, the board returned to open session and took up the issues that were postponed due to Martha Martin having walked out two weeks earlier.[40]

For the next twenty minutes, the board discussed a new rental methodology that would tie the lease rates at Possum Kingdom Lake to the fair market value of the land. This valuation would be determined by an independent appraisal. The tone of the discussion was academic, and the vote to adopt the resolution was unanimous at 16-0.[41] A subsequent vote to reduce the term of the leases from fifty years to thirty years was also unanimous.

During the first attempt at a forced divestiture, the directors of the Brazos River Authority had learned that ambiguity was not their friend. Immediately after this meeting's conclusion, Presiding Officer Steve Pena followed the advice of Jennifer Knauth and crafted a Request for Opinion that was sent to Attorney General Greg Abbott.[42] The desire of the BRA was simply to have the attorney general ratify the findings of Scott, Douglass, and McConnico. This request was stamped as having been received by the attorney general's office two days later.

July 30, 2007

Hon. Greg Abbott

---

[40] Board Meeting, "Agenda Items 1-4," *Brazos River Authority Board Meeting Minutes*, July 30, 2007, accessed July 10, 2013. (Fast forward to 03:05). http://www.brazos.org/Portals/0/board_audio/07302007_BRD1.mp3.

[41] Board Meeting, "Agenda Item 8," *Brazos River Authority Board Meeting Minutes*, July 30, 2007, accessed July 10, 2013. (Fast forward to 15:39). http://www.brazos.org/Portals/0/board_audio/07302007_BRD3.mp3.

[42] Steve Pena, "Request for Opinion," *Office of the Attorney General*, August 1, 2007, accessed May 1, 2011. https://www.texasattorneygeneral.gov/opinions/opinions/50abbott/rq/2007/pdf/RQ0611GA.pdf.

Office of the Attorney General

Opinions Committee

P.O. Box 12548

Austin, TX 78711-2548

Re: Request for an Opinion

Dear General Abbott:

The Brazos River Authority (the "BRA") owns substantial property surrounding Possum Kingdom Lake, and much of that property is subject to long-term residential leases to private individuals. Many of the residential lessees have held their leases for decades. In the past, the leases have reflected very low lease rates, and the BRA has recently begun a process of transitioning to lease rates that more accurately reflect current market value. Because of the low lease rates in the past, the transition to a current market value rate will result in rate increases for many lessees over time.

Rate increases have a disproportionate adverse impact on lessees over the age of sixty-five (65), who are more likely to live on fixed incomes. In addition, many of the over-65 lessees have held their leases for decades, resulting in the benefit of stable occupancy and use of the property and administrative continuity for the BRA regarding those leases. The BRA is also concerned that if the over-65 lessees are forced to leave due to higher lease rates, their departure will be a loss to the Possum Kingdom community

For these reasons, the BRA desires to minimize the adverse impact of the lease rate increases on lessees over 65. To this end, the BRA wishes to grant a ten percent (10%) discount off of current lease rates for lessees over 65 who would qualify for a homestead exemption, and also to freeze the discounted lease rate for such lessees on a going-forward basis.

BRA'S outside counsel has advised that such a discount or freeze would violate Article III, Section 52 of the Texas Constitution, as there is no specific amendment allowing such a discount or freeze. The BRA therefore respectfully asks the Attorney General to issue an opinion as to whether the BRA is authorized to give such a lease rate discount and lease rate freeze to lessees over 65 who qualify for a homestead exemption on their leased property at Possum Kingdom Lake. In particular, the BRA requests that the opinion address the question whether that discount or freeze would violate the provisions of Article III, Section 52 of the Texas Constitution.

Sincerely,

Steve Pena

Presiding Officer

Brazos River Authority

cc: Board members, Brazos River Authority

Roughly two months earlier, the leaseholders had been defeated in their attempt to force the BRA to sell the land beneath their lakefront homes at a ten percent discount. Now, the board was officially introducing the concept of fair market value into the equation. Even more alarming was the fact that independent appraisals would be used to determine what the land was actually worth.

Monte Land wasted no time in notifying the membership of the Possum Kingdom Lake Association of these developments. On the following day, Monte posted an alert on the PKLA's website.

BRAZOS RIVER AUTHORITY DIRECTOR'S
MEETING 30 JULY 2007

The Brazos River Authority Board resolutions on divestiture and canceling the 10 percent discount for seniors on July 17, and the new residential lease rate methodology and residential lease revisions resolutions on July 30, will have

significant short and long term impacts on all of us at
Possum Kingdom. Plus, there will be more to come as a
result of the Board requesting the Staff to develop plans
to sell leased residential properties at Possum Kingdom to
lessees "under terms and conditions as set by the board"
and to establish rental rates starting January 1, 2010,
based on a percentage of the actual appraised land value.[43]

Monte Land and the membership of the PKLA had just learned that
their free ride was over. They now knew that, unless they brought the full
force of their political power to bear on the situation, they would soon
be paying fair market value to either rent or purchase the dirt beneath
their homes. They also knew that avoiding that outcome would require a
concerted effort that would last for almost two full years.

Three months later on October 29, 2007, the Brazos River Authority
held its next quarterly meeting. It began, as usual, with comments from the
public. This, of course, meant that Monte Land would spend another six
minutes explaining to the world that he and his wife would not be able to
realize their taxpayer-subsidized dream retirement if the BRA introduced
fair market rates.[44] If poor-mouthing was an art form, Monte Land would
have been a Rembrandt.

Following the public comments, the board entered into executive
session for a little over one hour. After this, Matt Phillips introduced the
Draft Divestiture Policy that the staff of the BRA had been instructed to
create earlier in the year. Phillips opened his remarks by stressing that
the policy that was being presented was merely a draft, and that it would
remain so for quite some time. Phillips went on to explain that the reasons
for this were three-fold.

[43] PKLA Staff, "Notes: Brazos River Authority Director's Meeting, 30 July 2007,"
Possum Kingdom Lake Association, August 1, 2007, accessed July 10, 2013.
https://web.archive.org/web/20141106060934/http://www.pklakeassn.org/
BRAB_%208_1_07a.html.
[44] Board Meeting, "Agenda Items 1-4," *Brazos River Authority Board Meeting
Minutes*, October 29, 2007, accessed July 10, 2013. http://www.brazos.org/Portals/0/
board_audio/10292007_BRD1.mp3.

The first reason offered was to give the general public a chance to see the policy and to digest it. The second reason was simply that the policy was not yet complete. The third reason was that State Senator Kip Averitt had recently submitted his own Request for Opinion to Attorney General Greg Abbott seeking to determine how the shoreline property should be valued were the BRA to sell out to the individual leaseholders.[45]

Matt Phillips then explained that the staff of the BRA had used Dan Branch's *Hail Mary* amendment to Senate Bill 3 in 2007 as the template for the draft policy. He further stated that they had "taken some things out, that they had put some things in, and that they had changed a few things." But, by and large, this was the foundation of the draft policy being presented. The end result would be what Matt Phillips referred to as the "dueling appraisal" process that Senator Estes had championed during Senate Bill 1326.[46]

Matt Phillips ended his presentation by informing the audience that the draft policy would be posted on the BRA's website for the public's review. Later that evening, the BRA issued the following press release.

FOR IMMEDIATE RELEASE

CONTACT: Judi Pierce

Public Information Officer

(254) 761-3103

BRA BOARD CONSIDERS DIVESTITURE POLICY

October 29, 2007 - A draft policy for divestiture of Brazos River Authority-owned property at Lake Possum Kingdom has been presented to the BRA Board of Directors. The Board will consider the policy to divest leased residential properties excluding properties within the Federal Energy Regulatory Commission (FERC) project area at their

[45] Senator Kip Averitt, "Request for Opinion," *Office of the Attorney General*, August 16, 2007, accessed May 1, 2011. https://www.texasattorneygeneral.gov/opinions/opinions/50abbott/rq/2007/pdf/RQ0639GA.pdf.
[46] Board Meeting, "Agenda Items 5-7," *Brazos River Authority Board Meeting Minutes*, October 29, 2007, accessed November 10, 2014. (Fast forward to 05:50). http://www.brazos.org/Portals/0/board_audio/10292007_BRD2.mp3.

regular quarterly meeting in January. To view the full draft Divestiture Policy, please click here.[47]

Within the referenced ten-page policy was the following paragraph defining the purchase price. This language was intended to document one last time that the BRA intended to sell the property at fair market value in compliance with Article III, Section 52 of the Texas Constitution.

> (e) Purchase Price. Once an application is deemed complete, the determination of a purchase price shall commence. A-Leased Lot sold under this Policy must be sold for not less than the fair market value of the fee simple estate (the "Fair Market Value"). An appraisal of the Fair Market Value of a Leased Lot under this Policy may not (i) include consideration of a freeze or other suspension of lease rate increases for the homestead of a person who is 65 years of age or older, (ii) take into account the value of any improvements constructed on the Leased Lot or over the water or (iii) take into account any leasehold interest.[48]

This was the final board meeting of the Brazos River Authority in 2007. At that point, a reasonable person might have concluded that the BRA had managed to preserve the taxpayers' interest in a premium state asset. The members of the board of directors of the Brazos River Authority had indeed drawn a line in the sand—not unlike Lieutenant Colonel William Barrett Travis.

Remember the Alamo indeed.

---

[47] Judi Pierce, "BRA Board Considers Divestiture Policy," *Brazos River Authority*, October 29, 2007, accessed July 10, 2013.
http://wayback.archive-it.org/414/20141117024314/http://www.brazos.org/newsPdf/10-29-2007 BRA %20Board Considers PKDivestiture.pdf.
[48] Staff, "Divestiture Policy," *Brazos River Authority*, January 28, 2008, accessed August 1, 2013.
http://wayback.archive-it.org/414/20080602155247/http://www.brazos.org/generalPdf/Divestiture Policy 01-28-08.pdf.

Chapter 6

THE CALL TO GENERAL ABBOTT

Gregory Wayne Abbott was born in Wichita Falls, Texas on November 13, 1957. At the beginning of this tale, he was the fiftieth attorney general of Texas. He is now the Governor of Texas, having defeated Democratic challenger Wendy Davis. Governor Abbott's hometown is also the political epicenter of State Senator Craig Estes.

Greg Abbott was only the second Republican to serve as Attorney General of Texas since Reconstruction and was sworn into office on December 2, 2002. Prior to assuming the office of attorney general, Greg Abbott was a justice on the Texas Supreme Court. He was appointed to that position by none other than Governor George W. Bush in 1995. This appointment made Greg Abbott a full-fledged Republican insider.

On July 14, 1984, when Greg Abbott was twenty-six years old, he was struck by a falling oak tree while jogging in the River Oaks section of Houston. That accident left him partially paralyzed and he has been constrained to a wheelchair ever since. Greg Abbott sued the property owner who owned the tree and they ultimately settled. Details of that settlement were eventually leaked to the press and it seems that Greg Abbott will receive more than $10 million from this settlement over a prolonged period of time. That fact is neither here nor there.

Greg Abbott's political career began nine years later, in 1993, with a three-year term as a trial judge on the 129th District Court. In 1995, Governor George W. Bush appointed him to the Texas Supreme Court.

Greg Abbott was subsequently re-elected twice, first in 1996, and then again in 1998.

In 2001, Abbott resigned from the court to run for Texas attorney general. This office was vacated when John Cornyn was elected to the U.S. Senate. In the 2002 general election, Abbott defeated the former mayor of Austin, Kirk Watson, by almost 800,000 votes. In 2006, he beat Democratic opponent David Van Os by almost a million votes. In 2010, he destroyed Democrat Barbara Ann Radnowsky, winning by a margin of 1,495,205 votes.

As state attorney general, Greg Abbott built a reputation as a staunch conservative and an aggressive litigator. In March 2005, he appeared before the U.S. Supreme Court in the case of Van Orden vs. Perry arguing that a monument of the Ten Commandments on the north grounds of the state Capitol should be allowed to remain in place. The justices ruled in his favor in a 5-4 decision.[49]

Greg Abbott has also been an outspoken proponent of tort reform. In light of Abbott's own personal injury case, this stance has raised accusations of hypocrisy. Abbott rejects the charge, stating that he is against frivolous lawsuits and that his own lawsuit was not frivolous.

Abbott has shown up repeatedly on the national radar. He has sued the federal government twenty-seven times since 2010. The topics of these lawsuits have ranged from the regulations of the Environmental Protection Agency to those of the Women's Health Program.

Critics have often accused Greg Abbott of political posturing to further his career. These same critics always point out that he only sued the federal government three times while George W. Bush was President. Greg Abbott's response to this accusation is that the federal government has dramatically increased its overreaching activities since that time.

Greg Abbott often described his typical day at the office as attorney general in the following fashion:

---

[49] Staff, "Governor Greg Abbott," *The Texas Tribune*, circa 2014, accessed November 27, 2015.
http://www.texastribune.org/directory/greg-abbott/#ui-tabs-1.

I go into the office in the morning, I sue Barack Obama, and then I go home.[50]

By contrast, the state of Texas describes the attorney general as the lawyer for the State of Texas. According to the state's website, the attorney general is charged by the Texas constitution to do the following:

1. Defend the laws and the Constitution of the State of Texas,

2. Represent the State in litigation, and

3. Approve public bond issues.

To fulfill these responsibilities, the Office of the Attorney General serves as legal counsel to all boards and agencies of state government, issues legal opinions when requested by the Governor, heads of state agencies and other officials and agencies as provided by Texas statutes, sits as an ex-officio member of state committees and commissions, and defends challenges to state laws and suits against both state agencies and individual employees of the State.[51]

An attorney general's opinion is a written interpretation of existing law. Attorney General opinions cannot create new provisions in the law or correct unintended or undesirable effects of existing laws. Furthermore, attorney general opinions cannot resolve factual disputes. Courts have stated that attorney general opinions are highly persuasive and are entitled to great weight. However, the ultimate determination of a law's applicability, meaning, or constitutionality is left to the courts.[52]

---

[50] Jennifer Rios, "Greg Abbott Shares Views with Local Republicans," *Standard-Times*, February 19, 2013, accessed March 3, 2014. http://www.gosanangelo.com/news/abbott-shares-views-with-local-republicans.

[51] "Duties and Responsibilities of the Office of Attorney General," *The office of the Attorney General of Texas*, circa 2015, accessed November 27, 2015. https://www.texasattorneygeneral.gov/agency/duties-responsibilities-of-the-office-of-the-attorney-general.

[52] "About Attorney General Opinions," *The office of the Attorney General of Texas*, circa 2015, accessed November 27, 2015. https://www.texasattorneygeneral.gov/opinion/about-attorney-general-opinions.

In other words, if a state agency becomes concerned that it is running afoul of the Texas Constitution, it can request an opinion from the attorney general before any harm is done. This is exactly what Presiding Officer Steve Pena was attempting to do when he submitted his Request for Opinion on July 30, 2007.

The same was true eleven weeks later when State Senator Kip Averitt submitted a subsequent Request for Opinion on October 16, 2007. While Director Pena had simply asked about the constitutionality of granting discounts to senior citizens, Senator Averitt went to the heart of the matter and asked Attorney General Greg Abbott about the constitutionality of selling the shoreline of Possum Kingdom Lake below fair market value.

As the chairman of the Senate committee on Natural Resources, Senator Averitt had served as the last line of defense for the taxpayers of Texas during the 2007 legislative session. Expecting a repeat of that exercise in 2009, Senator Averitt was no doubt hoping that Attorney General Greg Abbott would provide the legal protection, and clarity, that the taxpayers would need during the next confrontation.

To this end, Senator Averitt posed the following Request for Opinion to Attorney General Greg Abbott.

> October 16, 2007
>
> The Honorable Greg Abbott
>
> Attorney General of Texas
>
> P.O. Box 12548
>
> Austin, Texas 78711-2548
>
> Re: Request for an Opinion
>
> Dear General Abbott:
>
> The Brazos River Authority (the "BRA") owns substantial property surrounding Possum Kingdom Lake, and much of that property is subject to long-term residential leases to private individuals. A majority of the existing leases reflect a below-market rate, and many of the below-market leases have a number of years remaining in their terms. Legislation proposed in the last session would have

required the BRA to sell the leased property to the lessees. In response to that proposed legislation, the BRA is in the process of formulating processes and procedures to offer to sell the leased property to the lessees, and one substantial question presented is the legal requirements governing valuation of the property as part of any sell to the lessees.

Certain lessees contend that the property should be valued as though encumbered by the remaining term of the existing leases. This method of valuation would result in a substantial discount from fair market value of the fee simple interest, because of the below market lease rates. Outside counsel for the BRA, however, has advised the BRA that any sale of leased property to a lessee for a price that reflects the existing lease would result in a windfall to the lessee, who would acquire the full fee simple interest in the property for a price discounted by a below-market lease that would cease to exist the moment the property is sold. Counsel advises that such a windfall is prohibited by article III, section 52 of the Texas Constitution, which prohibits grants of public funds or things of value to individuals. Enclosed is an opinion letter to the BRA from its outside counsel containing their legal analysis of this issue.

Because this is a matter of vital interest to the BRA, and to other constituents of mine, I respectfully request the Attorney General to issue an opinion as to whether leased property at Possum Kingdom Lake should be valued as though unencumbered by the existing leases where the sale is to the lessee, or whether the sales price should be discounted to reflect the remaining term of the existing leases, although the lease would cease to exist the moment the property is sold. In particular, I request that the opinion address whether using the discounted sales price would violate the prohibitions of article III, section 52 of the Texas Constitution. The Attorney General has previously addressed this issue in a Letter Opinion. Tex. Att'y Gen. L.O. 98-082 (Sept. 28, 1998).

Sincerely,

Kip Averitt

Cc: The Honorable David Dewhurst, Lt. Governor of Texas

Mr. Phil Ford, General Manger/CEO, Brazos River Authority

Enclosure[53]

Call me slow, but does Senator Averitt's question not answer itself? In other words, should these people get a discount on the purchase price of their lake lots because of something that will disappear at the time of the purchase? And by definition, is a discount not a thing of value?

Not wanting to leave anything to chance, Senator Averitt enclosed the nine pages of analysis that had been prepared by the outside legal counsel of Scott, Douglass, and McConnico. This comprehensive document was entitled *"Opinion Letter Regarding Sales of Property to Lessees at Possum Kingdom Lake"* and was signed by Jennifer Knauth.

Pursuant to an earlier request, this analysis was delivered to the BRA on August 16, 2007 and contained the following conclusion:

IV. CONCLUSION

Under both the merger doctrine and the prohibition against granting public funds to individuals, the valuation of property to be sold to the lessees should reflect the fact that the lease will terminate upon closing and the lessee will acquire the entire fee title to the property. The sales price therefore should not give any discount to the lessee

---

[53] Senator Kip Averitt, "Request for Opinion," *Office of the Attorney General*, August 16, 2007, accessed May 1, 2011. https://www.texasattorneygeneral.gov/opinions/opinions/50abbott/rq/2007/pdf/RQ0639GA.pdf.

for any portion of lease burden, because that burden will no longer exist after the sale. The only Texas authority directly on point so provides, and the constitutional prohibition against the grant of public funds operates here to prohibit any windfall to lessees by allowing them to acquire the full fee title in the property without paying for the full fee title.

Sincerely yours,

Jennifer Knauth[54]

Eureka! Everyone was now in possession of a common sense answer to a common sense question. And, it was from a prestigious law firm nonetheless. All that was needed now was to have Attorney General Greg Abbott agree with the findings and the matter would be put to rest.

Unfortunately, Senator Averitt would be disappointed on all counts. As the months passed by, Attorney General Greg Abbott would provide more confusion than clarity. Simultaneously, Lieutenant Governor David Dewhurst would ensure that Senator Averitt was not a party to the next legislative battle over Possum Kingdom Lake. And, since the "Three Amigos" worked in unison, Governor Rick Perry would likewise eliminate the opposition to the forced divestiture on the board of the Brazos River Authority.

If you thought that Rick Perry's indictment related to the Rosemary Lehmberg saga was somewhat "sketchy," you will love what happens next.[55]

---

[54] Jennifer Knauth, "Request for Opinion, Analysis," *Office of the Attorney General*, August 16, 2007, accessed May 1, 2011.
https://www.texasattorneygeneral.gov/opinions/opinions/50abbott/rq/2007/pdf/RQ0639GA.pdf.
[55] This is a shout-out to @DavidAxelrod whose first Twitter observation of the Rick Perry indictment became a Rick Perry defense point.

Chapter 7

RICK PERRY'S MASSACRE

No, this chapter is not about the "Oops" moment. What follows is an example of one of the few real political powers that the Texas Constitution grants to the governor of Texas.

As noted earlier, the board of directors of the Brazos River Authority consists of twenty-one members who are appointed by the governor. These appointments are made subject to the advice, consent, and confirmation of the Texas Senate. However, because the Texas legislature meets only once every two years for roughly five months, the ability for a sitting governor to temporarily stack the board of an agency such as the BRA through recess appointments— without the consent of the Senate—is readily available.

It has also been noted that these directors serve a six-year staggered term, with one-third of them being either replaced or reappointed each odd-numbered year. This is intended to prevent a single governor from doing irreparable harm to the state of Texas. This model breaks down, however, if a single governor serves for twelve years and winds up appointing every nonelected public servant in the state of Texas. If that same governor then serves long enough to replace any appointee who does not satisfy his will, he has the ability to stack the deck in a way that will guarantee any desired outcome.

On January 28, 2008, the Brazos River Authority held its first meeting of the year.[56] For many of the board members who were adamantly opposed to the forced divestiture, it would also be their last.

Presiding Officer Steve Pena announced that Martha Martin and Wade Gear had informed him that they would not be present for the meeting. Pena then offered a heartfelt tribute to Roberto Bailon who had passed away two weeks earlier. There was a flower placed on the table where Director Bailon usually sat.

Steve Pena then shared that there had been a few announcements from Austin during the past week. Director Ron Butler had been replaced by Grady Barr and Director Fred Lee Hughes had been replaced by Leroy Bell. Grady Barr and Leroy Bell were both from Abilene. Coincidentally, Director Fred Lee Hughes had replaced Leroy Bell's wife Deborah on the board back in 2001.

Steve Pena also informed those present that Director Sal Zaccagnino had been reappointed by the governor. He then stated that Director Christopher DeCluitt would be replacing him as the new Presiding Officer effective February 1. He further advised that he would be staying on the board for a while longer, but that he would then be moving on. Steve Pena neglected to comment, however, as to exactly *where* he would be moving on.[57]

The first order of business that day was to grant General Manager Phil Ford the authority to contract for legal services with Scott, Douglass and McConnico, LLP, for the Possum Kingdom divestiture project. The price of the contract was not to exceed $250,000.[58] This was in addition to the money that had already been spent to secure the firm's legal opinion as

---

[56] Board Meeting, "Agenda Item 8," *Brazos River Authority Board Meeting Minutes,* January 28, 2008, accessed November 10, 2014. (Fast forward to 05:50). http://www.brazos.org/Portals/0/board_audio/01282008_BRD3.mp3.
[57] Board Meeting, "Agenda Items 1-4," *Brazos River Authority Board Meeting Minutes,* January 28, 2008, accessed November 10, 2014. http://www.brazos.org/Portals/0/board_audio/01282008_BRD1.mp3.
[58] Staff, "Board of Directors Quarterly Board Actions," *Brazos River Authority,* January 28, 2008, accessed July 3, 2011. http://wayback.archive-it.org/414/20090705213303/http://www.brazos.org/board_actions/Board_Synopsis_01-08.pdf.

to the proper method for valuing the shoreline if it were to be sold. The resulting vote was unanimous at 16-0.[59]

The next order of business was related to the draft divestiture policy being developed by the staff of the BRA. The BRA's manager of governmental affairs, Matt Phillips, explained that the appraisals that would be used to determine the new lease rates would also be used to value the property in the event that it was sold. Phillips also stated that the divestiture policy was still designated as a *draft,* and that the issues surrounding the FERC buffer zone were being reviewed by outside counsel.[60]

After that came the death knell for the weekenders. The ninth item on the agenda was cited as *Appraisal Procedure for Possum Kingdom Lake* which lasted for eleven minutes and twenty-one seconds.[61] During this discussion, a staffer by the name of Mr. Baker explained that a Request for Proposal had been issued for appraisal services and five responses had been received. From these five responses, there were three firms who were selected for interviews. Mr. Baker also informed those present that Director Christopher DeCluitt had been invited to sit in on those interviews. Perhaps this was intended to give the process an air of legitimacy, or perhaps it was intended to signal that Director DeCluitt was now in charge of the process.

As a result of those interviews, Integra Realty Resources was chosen to create and implement a new appraisal procedure that would be used for establishing rental rates and pricing for any subsequent sale of the property. This selection was presented to the board for ratification in the following resolution.

---

[59] Board Meeting, "Agenda Items 5-7," *Brazos River Authority Board Meeting Minutes,* January 28, 2008, accessed November 10, 2014.
http://www.brazos.org/Portals/0/board audio/01282008 BRD2.mp3.
[60] Board Meeting, "Agenda Item 8," *Brazos River Authority Board Meeting Minutes,* January 28, 2008, accessed November 10, 2014.
http://www.brazos.org/Portals/0/board audio/01282008 BRD3.mp3.
[61] Board Meeting, "Agenda Item 9," *Brazos River Authority Board Meeting Minutes,* January 28, 2008, accessed November 10, 2014.
http://www.brazos.org/Portals/0/board audio/01282008 BRD4.mp3.

RESOLUTION OF THE BOARD OF DIRECTORS OF THE BRAZOS RIVER AUTHORITY
January 28, 2008
Agenda Item 9
Appraisal Procedure for Development and Implementation of Possum Kingdom Lake Residential Properties

"**BE IT RESOLVED** that the Board of Directors of the Brazos River Authority hereby authorizes the General Manager/CEO to negotiate and execute a contract with Integra Realty Resources DFW L.L.P. to develop a new appraisal determination procedure for Brazos River Authority property at Possum Kingdom Lake, for an amount not to exceed $495,000 for Phase One; and

BE IT FURTHER RESOLVED that the Board of Directors of the Brazos River Authority hereby authorizes the General Manager/CEO to negotiate and execute as part of the contract to provide individual appraisals for approximately 300 properties transitioning to a market value rental basis in 2010, at a cost not to exceed $225,000 for Phase Two; and

BE IT FURTHER RESOLVED that the Board of Directors of the Brazos River Authority hereby authorizes the General Manager/CEO to negotiate and execute as part of the contract to provide individual appraisals for properties, as needed on an interim basis for divestiture at a cost not to exceed $2,000 per tract, unless contested, in which case the cost per tract will not exceed $2,250."

The aforementioned resolution was approved by the Board of Directors of the Brazos River Authority on January 28, 2008 to certify which witness my hand and seal.

Steve Pena
Presiding Officer[62]

---

[62] Staff, "Board of Directors Quarterly Board Actions," *Brazos River Authority*, January 28, 2008, accessed July 3, 2011.http://wayback.archive-it.org/414/20090705213303/http://www.brazos.org/board_actions/Board_Synopsis_01-08.pdf.

The vote to adopt the resolution related to *Agenda Item 9* that would introduce a formal appraisal process was both unanimous and incendiary.

It should be obvious by now that Governor Rick Perry's office was intimately involved in the process to force the BRA to sell its lakefront property to the wealthy weekenders at Possum Kingdom Lake. It should be equally obvious that the BRA's board members were not satisfying the will of the governor who had appointed them.

Governor Perry's Director of Appointments, Mr. Ken Anderson, would remedy that in short order. Ken Anderson was one of the key players in the nine-hour Austin meeting that had been held less than one year earlier and he was acutely aware of which board members needed to be eliminated. And, he would see to it that this occurred before the next board meeting.

The seven board members who had been appointed in 2001 and whose terms were set to expire in 2007 were:

1. Martha Stovall Martin,
2. Ronald D. Butler,
3. Fred Lee Hughes,
4. John Skaggs,
5. Suzanne Alderson Baker,
6. Pamela Jo Ellison, and
7. Salvatore A. Zaccagnino.

On April 1, 2008, Governor Rick Perry's office issued a press release announcing an overhaul of the board of the Brazos River Authority. This announcement was Governor Perry's April Fools' Day Massacre.

AUSTIN – Gov. Rick Perry named Christopher DeCluitt of Waco as chair of the Brazos River Authority Board of Directors. He also appointed 10 members to the board, which is responsible for developing and conserving the surface water resources of the Brazos River Basin.[63]

Within the full text of that announcement, six of the expiring members were replaced and one was reappointed. The lone survivor of the expiring class of 2007 was Salvatore A. Zaccagnino who was reappointed to serve through 2013.

Salvatore Zaccagnino was first appointed to the board of the BRA in 2001. At that time, his daughter-in-law, Lia Zaccagnino, served as a Deputy Appointments Director for Rick Perry. During Governor Perry's run for the White House in 2012, Lia served as the Senior Advisor to the First Lady of Texas, Anita Perry.[64] It might be safe to assume that Governor Perry could rely on Salvatore to see things his way regarding Possum Kingdom Lake.

The same cannot be said for the other six members of the 2007 expiring class. Ron Butler and Martha Martin both had conflicts of interest and would be obligated to abstain on all votes related to the sale of the property. This fact made Butler and Martin useless to the cause. The other four members were insisting that the property be sold for fair market value. These six members were replaced by Governor Rick Perry in the following fashion.

Martha Martin was replaced by Richard L. Ball from Mineral Wells.[65] This small hamlet is the closest real town to Possum Kingdom Lake. It might be safe to assume that Mr. Ball would be sympathetic to the leaseholders' position given that many of them were his neighbors. Mr. Ball was also the President and Chief Executive Officer of Wes-Tex Vending

---

[63] Governor Rick Perry, "Gov. Perry Names DeCluitt Chair of Brazos River Authority Board of Directors," *Office of the Governor*, April 1, 2008, accessed August 13, 2010. http://wayback.archive-it.org/414/20141117185953/http://governor.state.tx.us/news/appointment/4067/.

[64] Lia Zaccagnino, "Events and Logistical Manager," *LinkedIn*, n.d., accessed July 13, 2012. http://www.linkedin.com/pub/lia-zaccagnino/6/504/817.

[65] Staff, "Richard Ball Bio," *Brazos River Authority*, January 6, 2009, accessed July 3, 2011. http://web.archive.org/web/20090106221427/http://www.brazos.org/board_bios/Richard_Ball_Final.pdf.

Company of Mineral Wells. (I have been thinking all along that what this situation really needed was someone with some serious vending machine expertise. Evidently, Governor Perry was thinking the same thing).

In an interview with Libby Cluett, who covered politics for the Mineral Wells Index, Richard Ball described his appointment as follows on April 3, 2008:

> "I'm very honored," said Ball of being asked to serve on the authority board.
>
> "It's been three weeks since I was approached," he said, adding that he received materials to help familiarize him with the issues facing the board.
>
> Ball has been reviewing materials sent by the governor's office, which include two notebooks dealing with rules and regulations of being part of a state agency, audio recordings of BRA meetings for the past two years, and a book covering the history of the Brazos River.
>
> He said that prior to his most recent study of the BRA and Brazos River, he did not know other than what he read in the local papers.
>
> "There is so much more involved than I imagined," said Ball.

Somewhere there is a village looking for its idiot. Richard Ball might as well have stated that he was totally unqualified to serve on the board of the Brazos River Authority. He concluded the interview with the following quote:

> There are a number of men from Mineral Wells who have been involved with the Authority. I'm honored to be among them.[66]

---

[66] Libby Cluett, "Ball Named to River Authority Board," *Mineral Wells Index*, April 3, 2008, accessed July 10, 1010 (since removed). http://mineralwellsindex.com/local/x154979383/Ball-named-to-river-authority-board/print.

In a subsequent interview five months later, Libby Cluett reported that Richard Ball's primary purpose for serving on the board of the BRA had nothing whatsoever to do with the issues surrounding the availability of water in the state of Texas.

> He said his number one concern since he joined the BRA board last spring has been, "How do we protect leaseholders?"[67]

I will never again be able to feed eight one-dollar bills into a cigarette machine without thinking about Richard Ball and how this deal went down. It would not appear that Richard Ball applied to serve on the board of the BRA out of an insatiable desire to provide for the water needs of the state of Texas. Rather, it would appear that he was recruited by the governor's office to serve a specific purpose.

That takes us to Ron Butler. In 2008, Ronald D. Butler was the president and chief executive officer of First Financial Bank. This bank had locations in Abilene, Stephenville, Granbury, and Glen Rose. Butler was also the state chairman for the American Bankers Association and an active member of the Texas Bankers Association.

To pull this deal off, Mike Patterson would need a cartel of banks to underwrite his deal and First Financial Bank would be part of that syndicate. If Ron Butler were still on the board while Mike Patterson was making his play, Butler would have been constantly conflicted out. Governor Perry replaced Ron Butler with Grady Barr of Abilene.[68] Mr. Barr was the former mayor of Abilene and the retired president of Barr Roofing. I will resist the urge to comment on how bad this situation was in need of a good roofer; but, I will acknowledge that Grady Barr had political experience.

---

[67] Libby Cluett, "One Man's Divestiture Plan Becomes That of Another," *Mineral Wells Index*, September 24, 2008, accessed July 10, 1010. https://web.archive.org/web/20080928121904/http://www.mineralwellsindex.com/local/local_story_268100313.html.

[68] Staff, "Grady Barr Bio," *Brazos River Authority*, January 6, 2009, accessed July 3, 2011. http://wayback.archive-it.org/414/20121026210020/http://www.brazos.org/board_bios/Grady_Barr_bio.pdf.

Turning to those who were opposed to divestiture, Fred Lee Hughes[69] was replaced by Leroy Bell.[70] Mr. Bell was the President of Compass Financial Strategies in Abilene. That makes two replacements from a city that is almost one hundred miles removed from the Brazos River.

John R. Skaggs of Amarillo was replaced by Peter G. Bennis of Fort Worth[71]. Peter Bennis was the President and Chief Executive Officer of Pinnacle Bank in Keene, Texas. Pinnacle Bank, by the way, would also be part of Mike Patterson's banking syndicate. According to his biography on the BRA's website, Peter Bennis and his wife live in Fort Worth and Possum Kingdom Lake.

Hmm, I wonder how Mr. Bennis is going to vote.

Suzanne Alderson Baker from Lubbock was replaced by an attorney from Lubbock by the name of Zachary S. Brady.[72] Zachary Brady did not even serve long enough to be rubber-stamped by the Texas Senate. Eighteen days after Governor Perry submitted Brady's name for confirmation, the governor sent the following Message to the Senate.

TO THE SENATE OF THE EIGHTY-FIRST LEGISLATURE, REGULAR SESSION:

On January 22, 2009, I submitted the name of Zachary S. Brady for appointment to the Brazos River Authority Board of Directors for a term to expire February 1, 2013.

---

[69] Staff, "Fred Hughes Bio," *Brazos River Authority*, November 20, 2007, accessed July 3, 2011.
http://wayback.archive-it.org/414/20071120004914/http://www.brazos.org/board_bios/fred_hughes_bio.pdf.

[70] Staff, "Leroy Bell Bio," *Brazos River Authority*, June 14, 2013, accessed July 3, 2011.
http://wayback.archive-it.org/414/20071120004914/http://www.brazos.org/board_bios/bell-2013-bio.pdf.

[71] Staff, "Peter Bennis Bio," *Brazos River Authority*, June 14, 2013, accessed July 3, 2011.
http://web.archive.org/web/20130614194130/http://www.brazos.org/board_bios/Bennis-2013-bio.pdf.

[72] Staff, "Zachary Brady Bio," *Brazos River Authority*, August 21, 2008, accessed July 3, 2011.
http://www.brazos.org/board_bios/Brady_Final.pdf.

Because he resigned, I hereby withdraw his nomination
and request that the Senate return the appointment to me.

Respectfully submitted,

/s/Rick Perry

Governor

February 10, 2009

Austin, Texas[73]

After his resignation from the board of the BRA, Zachary Brady ran
for the Texas House seat for District 83 in 2010. He lost by a wide margin
even though Mike Patterson donated $1,000 to his campaign.

The last of the class of 2007 who needed to be eliminated was Pamela
Jo Ellison.

P.J. Ellison's famous comment, "It's not whether you're going to be
raped or not—it's just at what extreme are you going to?" ensured that
she would not be reappointed. Instead, that appointment would go to
Mr. John A. Brieden, who was an insurance agent from Brenham.[74] With
this appointment, Governor Perry hit the trifecta as this situation would
obviously be enhanced appreciably by the addition of a good insurance
salesman.

John Brieden was a native of south Texas who graduated from Calallen
High School before he headed off to Texas A&M University. While
studying at Texas A&M, John Brieden served in the prestigious Corps of
Cadets. He was also the college roommate of a future governor of the state
of Texas by the name of James Richard "Rick" Perry.

---

[73] "Senate Journal," Eighty-First Legislature, Regular Session, Texas Senate, February
11, 2009.
http://www.journals.senate.state.tx.us/sjrnl/81r/html/81RSJ02-11-F.HTM.
[74] Staff, "John Brieden Bio," *Brazos River Authority*, August 21, 2008, accessed July
3, 2011.
http://web.archive.org/web/20080821225157/http://www.brazos.org/board_bios/
Brieden_III_John.pdf.

Well, I'll be a tied up goat.[75]

In a story presented by Lauren French on August 8, 2011 on MySanAntonio.com, John Brieden recounted the days when he and Rick Perry sold Bibles together door-to-door. This interview occurred during the early stages of Rick Perry's failed bid for the White House in 2012. To say the least, Brieden was one of Perry's major supporters. Lauren French characterized the relationship between the two men as follows:

> Now Brieden, with contacts around the nation as past American Legion National Commander, is on the steering committee of a veterans-based super PAC designed to boost a presidential bid by Perry, an Air Force veteran. Brieden noted that Perry has done favors for him as well, such as flying to St. Louis in 2003 to nominate him for the Commander's post and, while fending off his own re-election challenge last year, doing a fund-raiser for Brieden's county judge race.[76]

John Brieden served on the board of the BRA just long enough to vote yes on every vote in 2008 and 2009 related to the sale of the lakefront property. He then resigned to run for County Judge in Washington County. And yes, Governor Perry did indeed campaign for him. Brieden was replaced by William A. Masterson of Guthrie, Texas on March 18, 2010.[77]

---

[75] As a reminder from *Round I*, that is a reference to the scene in *Jurassic Park* (Amblin Entertainment, 1993) where they tied that poor little goat to a post and fed him to Tyrannosaurus Rex.

[76] Lauren French, "Who is Rick Perry?" *MySA.com*, August 8, 2011, accessed August 3, 2011.
http://blog.mysanantonio.com/texas-on-the-potomac/2011/08/who-is-rick-perry-his-days-as-a-door-to-door-bible-reference-book-salesman/.

[77] Staff, "William Masterson Bio," *Brazos River Authority*, July 25, 2010, accessed July 3, 2011.
http://web.archive.org/web/20120220001007/http://www.brazos.org/board_bios/Masterson-Bio.pdf.

We have covered seven of the ten appointments to the Brazos River Authority that Rick Perry announced on April Fools' Day, 2008. That obviously leaves three board members whose terms had not yet expired.

The first of the three non-expiring members that had to go was the presiding officer of the board, Mr. Steve Pena.[78] During the first legislative attempt to force the BRA to sell its property in 2007, Steve Pena was arguably one of the most persistent and persuasive opponents of doing so.

Mr. Pena was first appointed to the board of the Brazos River Authority in 1999. On May 6, 2005, Governor Perry reappointed Pena and designated him as the Presiding Officer. So how do you fire someone whom you had chosen as the person to run the whole show only thirty-six months earlier?

It is simple: You promote them. On April 1, 2008, Governor Rick Perry appointed Steve Pena to the Texas State Board of Public Accountancy. As Pena was a practicing CPA in real life, this was an extremely prestigious appointment for both Steve and his firm. Pena accepted the promotion without public objection. Steve Pena was replaced by Jon Sloan of Round Rock for a term that would expire on February 1, 2011.[79]

The second outspoken opponent of divestiture to be dealt with was Roberto "Bob" Bailon. Bob was Steve Pena's assistant presiding officer and was appointed to the board in 2004.[80] Roberto Bailon had testified vigorously against the forced sale in both chambers of the legislature in 2007 and his sway over the rest of the board was substantial. Sadly, removing Bob would be easy as he had passed away on January 14, 2008. He was replaced by his wife, Patricia Bailon, in what would prove to be a gracious and yet ceremonial appointment.

---

[78] Staff, "Steve Pena Bio," *Brazos River Authority*, August 18, 2006, accessed July 3, 2011.
http://web.archive.org/web/20060818122232/http://brazos.org/board_bios/steve_pena_bio.pdf.

[79] Staff, "Jon Sloan Bio," *Brazos River Authority*, October 26, 2010, accessed July 3, 2011.
http://web.archive.org/web/20101026153044/http://brazos.org/board_bios/Sloan-Jon-E.pdf.

[80] Staff, "Roberto Bailon Bio," *Brazos River Authority*, February 16, 2007, accessed July 3, 2011.
http://web.archive.org/web/20070216201726/http://www.brazos.org/board_bios/Roberto_Bailon_bio.pdf.

On February 2, 2009, the Senate Journal recorded the following *Message from the Governor.*

TO THE SENATE OF THE EIGHTY-FIRST
LEGISLATURE, REGULAR SESSION:

I ask the advice, consent and confirmation of the Senate with respect to the following appointments:

BRAZOS RIVER AUTHORITY BOARD OF
DIRECTORS

Patricia S. Bailon - Belton

Appointment Date: March 13, 2008

Expiration Date: February 1, 2009[81]

Please note that Mrs. Bailon's term of service on the board of the BRA had expired the day before her name was submitted to the Texas Senate for confirmation. In fact, of the eleven BRA Board appointments made by Governor Rick Perry that were submitted to the Texas Senate on February 2, 2009, four of the appointees' terms had expired the day before. I am no expert, but the entire process of senate confirmation of the governor's appointees strikes me as pure bullshit. Mrs. Bailon served less than twelve months on the board and would be gone when the crucial votes in the spring of 2009 occurred.

The last to be sent packing early was Rodolfo "Rudy" Garcia.[82] Rudy was first appointed to the BRA board in 1997 and was reappointed in 2004 for a term to expire in 2009. By all accounts, Rudy had served the board of the BRA admirably throughout his tenure. His sin was stating repeatedly that "We are not encumbered—the people that want to buy the land are the ones that are encumbered." Based on his years of debate on the matter

---

[81] "Senate Journal," Eighty-First Legislature, Regular Session, Texas Senate, February 2, 2009, p. 75.
http://www.journals.senate.state.tx.us/sjrnl/81r/pdf/81RSJ02-02-F.PDF.
[82] Staff, "Rudy Garcia Bio," *Brazos River Authority*, February 16, 2007, accessed July 3, 2011.
http://web.archive.org/web/20070216201749/http://www.brazos.org/board_bios/rudy_garcia_bio.pdf.

and his voting record, there was no reason to think that Rudy would not strongly oppose divestiture in 2009.

Rudy Garcia was replaced by Scott D. Smith of Cedar Park.[83] At the time of his appointment, Scott D. Smith was a Vice President of Investments with Wachovia Securities in Austin. Scott Smith was also a past president of the Capital City A&M Club.

I am going to have to assume that Scott D. Smith served the governor well. Fourteen months after his temporary assignment to the BRA, Governor Perry appointed Smith to the State Pension Review Board for a term to expire on January 31, 2015.[84] This board assesses pension funds in need of corrective action before the problems become critical. Hopefully, I don't have to point out that this is a very prestigious appointment if you earn your living in the capital markets. Scott Smith's temporary service on the board of the BRA ended on April 9, 2009. This was the day after Mike Patterson submitted his bid to purchase the entire shoreline of Possum Kingdom Lake.

The single most important aspect of Rick Perry's April Fools' Day Massacre was the designation of Christopher D. DeCluitt as the new Presiding Officer. The promotion of Steve Pena from the board of the BRA to the Texas State Board of Public Accountancy had left the presiding officer's position vacant. Governor Perry filled this role with a serial appointee and chronic supporter. During Rick Perry's 2006 reelection campaign, Christopher DeCluitt had also served as a member of the Rick Perry Reelection Steering Committee.

Christopher DeCluitt was born and raised in Waco, Texas. He attended Waco High School, received an electrical engineering degree from Texas A&M, and then went on to receive a law degree from the University of Tulsa, College of Law. He is a hardcore Republican and a hardcore Aggie.

---

[83] Staff, "Scott Smith Bio," *Brazos River Authority*, August 21, 2008, accessed July 3, 2011. http://web.archive.org/web/20080821225103/http://www.brazos.org/board_bios/Smith_Final.pdf.
[84] Governor Rick Perry, "Gov. Perry Appoints Three to State Pension Review Board," *Office of the Governor*, June 23, 2009, accessed August 13, 2010. http://wayback.archive-it.org/414/20100820085424/http://governor.state.tx.us/news/appointment/12658/.

Christopher's father was Douglas R. DeCluitt, who ran for Lieutenant Governor in 1968 against Ben Barnes. Running as a Republican, when the state was dominated by the Democratic Party, Doug DeCluitt polled less than 28% of the statewide votes. From 1987 to 1993, Douglas DeCluitt was also a member of the Board of Regents of Texas A&M University.

While Governor Perry's April Fools' Day massacre was a good start, his overhaul of the noncompliant board of the Brazos River Authority was by no means complete. On June 20, 2008, the Governor's Office issued another press release announcing three more replacements.[85] These appointments would seal the deal for Mike Patterson.

The first new appointee was Nancy Porter[86] of Sugar Land who replaced Jacqueline Baly Chaumette[87] to complete her term that would expire on February 1, 2009. Ms. Chaumette had resigned.

Nancy Porter was the Director of Communications for the Fort Bend Independent School District and a member of Rick Perry's Reelection Steering Committee. On April 9, 2009, Governor Perry issued a press release announcing that he had reappointed Ms. Porter for a term to run through 2015. Thirteen months later on May 28, 2010, Governor Perry issued yet another press release announcing that Nancy Porter had resigned.[88]

[85] Governor Rick Perry, "Gov. Perry Appoints Three to Brazos River Authority Board," *Office of the Governor*, June 20, 2008, accessed August 13, 2010. http://wayback.archive-it.org/414/20100820090426/http://governor.state.tx.us/news/appointment/5134/.

[86] Staff, "Nancy Porter Bio," *Brazos River Authority*, August 21, 2008, accessed July 3, 2011. http://web.archive.org/web/20080821225131/http://www.brazos.org/board_bios/Porter_Nancy_bio.pdf.

[87] Staff, "Jacqueline Chaumette Bio," *Brazos River Authority*, February 16, 2007, accessed July 3, 2011. http://web.archive.org/web/20070216201653/http://www.brazos.org/board_bios/Jacqueline_Chaumette_bio.pdf.

[88] Texas Register, Volume 35, Number 25, Page 5131, June 18, 2010. http://texashistory.unt.edu/ark:/67531/metapth101192/m2/1/high_res_d/0618is.pdf.

The second appointee announced on June 20, 2008, was Mr. John Steinmetz[89] of Lubbock. Steinmetz replaced Jere M. Lawrence[90] to complete his term that would expire on February 1, 2009. Jere Lawrence had also resigned.[91]

John Steinmetz was the Lubbock President of Vista Bank. On April 9, 2009, he was reappointed to the Board of the BRA for a term to expire on February 1, 2015. On February 1, 2011, Governor Perry also appointed then thirty-two-year-old John Steinmetz to the Board of Regents of Texas Tech University.

That was one helluva thank-you note by Governor Perry and the appointment caused a bit of a stir in the Lubbock area. Shortly after Steinmetz was added to the Board of Regents at Texas Tech, it was learned that he had claimed to possess a graduate degree from Texas Tech on his appointment application that did not actually exist. Steinmetz eventually resigned from the BRA's board but managed to retain his seat on the Texas Tech Board of Regents. Go figure.

Last, but by no means least, the third new appointee announced on June 20, 2008 was Ms. Mary Ward of Granbury.[92] Mary Ward would be

---

[89] Staff, "John Steinmetz Bio," *Brazos River Authority*, August 21, 2008, accessed July 3, 2011.
http://web.archive.org/web/20080821225022/http://www.brazos.org/board_bios/Steinmetz_John.pdf.

[90] Staff, "Jere Lawrence Bio," *Brazos River Authority*, February 16, 2007, accessed July 3, 2011.
http://web.archive.org/web/20070216201849/http://www.brazos.org/board_bios/Jere_Lawrence_bio.pdf.

[91] Texas Register, Volume 33, Number 24, Page 4583, June 13, 2008.
http://texashistory.unt.edu/ark:/67531/metapth90826/m2/1/high_res_d/0613is.pdf.

[92] Staff, "Mary Ward Bio," *Brazos River Authority*, Jan 6, 2009, accessed July 3, 2011.
http://web.archive.org/web/20090106221331/http://www.brazos.org/board_bios/Mary_Ward.pdf.

replacing the former mayor of Clifton, Mr. Truman Blum.[93] You guessed it. Truman Blum had resigned.[94]

The term that Mary Ward inherited from Truman Blum would run through February 1, 2011 and this was all the time that Mike Patterson would need. At the time of her appointment, Mary Ward served as the Regional President of Southwest Securities, FSB, in Granbury. Simultaneously, Mike Patterson served on the Board of Directors of that bank.

Over the course of eighty days, Governor Rick Perry had announced twelve new recess appointments to the Brazos River Authority. Of these twelve, only four would serve a full term. Most of the others served less than twenty-four months. Along the way, Governor Perry had also reappointed the father-in-law of one of his employees. These thirteen votes created the majority needed to get the Brazos River Authority to reverse its position and support the forced sale of the shoreline of Possum Kingdom Lake.

"The Texas Miracle" was in the making.

---

[93] Staff, "Truman Blum Bio," *Brazos River Authority*, February 16, 2007, accessed July 3, 2011.
http://web.archive.org/web/20070216201704/http://www.brazos.org/board_bios/Truman_Blum_bio.pdf.
[94] Texas Register, Volume 33, Number 24, Page 4583, June 13, 2008.
http://texashistory.unt.edu/ark:/67531/metapth90826/m2/1/high_res_d/0613is.pdf.

Chapter 8

CAPITULATION & SURRENDER

He did not care for the lying at first. He hated it. Then later he had come to like it. It was part of being an insider but it was a very corrupting business.[95]

The impact of Rick Perry's April Fools' Day massacre was immediate. On April 28, 2008, the board of the Brazos River Authority met for the first time with Christopher DeCluitt serving as the presiding officer. One year and one day earlier, on April 27, 2007, the board of the Brazos River Authority had held an emergency meeting to fend off a forced divestiture. During that meeting, Christopher DeCluitt had referred to the process surrounding Senate Bill 1326 as "obscene."[96]

Capitulation

With Christopher DeCluitt now at the helm, the opposing position of the board of the Brazos River Authority was immediately reversed. It would appear that someone had gotten the memo.

---

[95] Ernest Hemingway, "For Whom the Bell Tolls," *Charles Scribner's Sons*, October 21, 1940.

[96] Emergency Board Meeting "Agenda Items 5-6," *Brazos River Authority Board Meeting Minutes*, April 27, 2007, accessed November 10, 2014. http://www.brazos. org/Portals/0/board_audio/04272007_EME2.mp3.

Since the introduction of the *Staubach Report* in 2006, the board of the
BRA had spent countless hours deliberating the issues surrounding Possum
Kingdom Lake. Each agenda item related to the topic during the board
meetings was typically lengthy and laced with passionate debate. For the
balance of the battle, there would never again be an agenda item related
to the forced sale of the shoreline that lasted for more than thirty minutes.

That is, except for one.

The meeting on April 28, 2008, began with newly appointed Presiding
Officer Christopher DeCluitt informing those present that Zachary Brady,
Jacqueline Chaumet, and Sal Zaccagnino would not be present. DeCluitt
then welcomed all of the new board members and asked everyone to
introduce themselves so that they could all become acquainted. He then
asked if there was anyone from the public who wished to speak. There was
only one. The former presiding officer of the Brazos River Authority, Mr.
Steve Pena, asked to address the board as a private citizen. Pena's comments
were magnanimous. And yet, they revealed that both his heart and his
conscience were bothered.

> Mr. Chairman, uh, Board Members, last January when
> I had the privilege of sitting on this Board, some of us
> knew that our time would be short, but we didn't know
> just exactly when we would be replaced by other board
> members. And as such I didn't have the opportunity to
> say thank you which I wanted to try to do today without
> taking too much time.
>
> To the Board members that I've had the privilege to
> work with for many years, thank you very much for your
> support. We had some tough times together. We faced
> some tough issues, but it was always very good for me
> to know that I had your support and your backing and I
> appreciate it very much.[97]

[97] Board Meeting "Hear Comments from Members of the Public," *Brazos River Authority Board Meeting Minutes*, April 28, 2008, accessed November 10, 2014. http://www.brazos.org/Portals/0/board_audio/04282008_BRD1.mp3.

Steve Pena closed his remarks by thanking Phil Ford for his service as the general manager of the BRA. Pena received a heartfelt ovation and there was a sense in the room that a page had been turned. Indeed it had.

After several other agenda items related to the core business of the Brazos River Authority, the board entered into yet another executive session related to Possum Kingdom Lake. When they emerged at 12:07 that afternoon, *The Texas Miracle* was put into perpetual and irrevocable motion.[98]

At the beginning of *Agenda Item 9*, Christopher DeCluitt asked Matt Phillips to provide an update on the divestiture process. For the next six minutes, Phillips explained that the BRA's staff had spent hundreds of hours working on the divestiture policy and that to date, less than ten comments had been received from the public. He also pointed out that the BRA had already spent hundreds of thousands of dollars on legal fees and "we haven't even been sued yet." Phillips used the term "doom-and-gloom" multiple times and the tone of his voice reflected that sentiment.

Presiding Officer DeCluitt then asked General Manager Phil Ford to tell the Board about a letter that had recently been received. Phil Ford explained that he had received an unsolicited inquiry from an unnamed real estate developer that raised the question of an all-inclusive sale of the BRA's property holdings at Possum Kingdom Lake. Ford stated that the BRA's outside legal counsel had advised that the BRA could not deal exclusively with a single party, and that such a sale would have to occur through a public bidding process.

Phil Ford's comments on the topic of an all-inclusive sale lasted for exactly two minutes and fifteen seconds. Christopher DeCluitt took it from there. After a forty-five second introduction, DeCluitt stated the following:

> I move that Staff is directed to develop a proposed request for bids to purchase all of the Brazos River Authority's land at Possum Kingdom Lake, outside the FERC project area, and that the request for bids include protection for the

---

[98] Board Meeting "Agenda Item 9," *Brazos River Authority Board Meeting Minutes*, April 28, 2008, accessed November 10, 2014. http://www.brazos.org/Portals/0/board_audio/04282008_BRD10.mp3.

lessees' existing rights and provide a right for the lessees to purchase their lots, excluding property necessary for present and future Brazos River Authority operations."[99]

Newly appointed director Grady Barr seconded the motion and DeCluitt then asked if there were any questions. Director Wade Gear responded with the following:

And that's all of the land in total, correct?

To which Presiding Officer DeCluitt replied,

DeCluitt: That is all of the land. Leased, un-leased, and again, excluding what may be determined – may be necessary for the operations of the BRA.

Gear: So in doing this, we would also be divesting ourselves of the responsibility of the road maintenance.

DeCluitt: Exactly.

And then, Director Jean Kilgore asked the single most important question that would be raised during the entire attempt to force the BRA to sell its shoreline to the weekenders:

I have a question. This couldn't be construed as a way of getting around the fact that we can't sell to individuals? That we might have a sham company or something take this over?[100]

---

[99] Board Meeting "Agenda Item 9," *Brazos River Authority Board Meeting Minutes*, April 28, 2008, accessed November 10, 2014. (Fast forward to 09:15). http://www.brazos.org/Portals/0/board_audio/04282008_BRD10.mp3.

[100] Board Meeting "Agenda Item 9," *Brazos River Authority Board Meeting Minutes*, April 28, 2008, accessed November 10, 2014. (Fast forward to 11:34). http://www.brazos.org/Portals/0/board_audio/04282008_BRD10.mp3.

To which DeCluitt replied with what would prove to be the biggest damn lie that was told along the way.

No. That's where the bidding process comes into play.

To my way of thinking, there are three types of bidding processes. The first would be a competitive bidding process. The second would be a non-competitive bidding process. And the third would be a rigged bidding process. From this point forward, I would challenge you to be on the lookout for anything that even remotely resembles a competitive bidding process. Here is another spoiler alert. You are not going to find one.

Shortly thereafter, Presiding Officer DeCluitt was asked if an all-inclusive sale would be at fair market value. In hindsight, his response was chilling.

In the bidding process, it's going to be what the market will bear. So it will be a competitive bid process of which – we will – we're not going to have our finger in it. It's going to be what the market will bear.

Please focus on the phrase "we're not going to have our finger in it." I will concede this point to Presiding Officer Christopher DeCluitt. From April 28, 2008, until the day that Mike Patterson won the bid to purchase the shoreline of Possum Kingdom Lake, Director DeCluitt did not have his finger in it. He had his whole hand up in there.

When the vote was taken on DeCluitt's motion, the result was unanimous at 17-0.

There is a very important point to keep in mind here. DeCluitt's motion stated that *all* of the land would be sold, which would include the raw land that was not leased out. This would later prove problematic to Mike Patterson when he went to finance his transaction with bank debt. And, like all of the other problems, this minor complication would also disappear.

Surrender

On the following day, the Brazos River Authority issued a press release that might as well have been entitled "Unconditional Surrender." This press release also read like a tell-all story conceding that the weekenders had been enjoying a sweetheart deal at the expense of the taxpayers for decades. This chronicle also explained that the Texas legislature had attempted to "force the BRA to sell the property to the current lease holders at a price greatly below market levels" in 2007.

In terms of historical records, this press release was probably one of the most important. It provided an excellent recap of how things had gotten to the point that they had and provided a foreshadowing of what would happen next. Consequently, it is important to read this item in its entirety.

> FOR IMMEDIATE RELEASE
>
> CONTACT: Judi Pierce
>
> Public Information Officer
>
> (254) 761-3103
>
> BRAZOS RIVER AUTHORITY BOARD VOTES TO TAKE PUBLIC BIDS FOR AN ALL INCLUSIVE SALE OF PROPERTIES AT POSSUM KINGDOM LAKE
>
> **Waco, Texas - April 29, 2008** -- Years of uncertainty and turmoil regarding the Brazos River Authority's (BRA) management of property at Possum Kingdom Lake (PK) are one step closer to a potential solution. The BRA Board of Directors voted to investigate an alternative form of property divestiture through an all-inclusive sale of the majority of BRA land holdings at the lake.
>
> "The Board of Directors would like to investigate the possible all-inclusive sale of the Brazos River Authority holdings at Possum Kingdom Lake through a bid process as an alternative to sales of individual leaseholds," said Christopher DeCluitt, presiding officer of the BRA Board. "As a river authority, our primary responsibility is providing water resources to the people of the Brazos basin. We feel it is prudent and necessary that we explore

every option for divestiture of property in order to remove the Authority from the burden of land management."

More than 65 years ago, the BRA began leasing tracts of land at PK for camping, fishing and other recreational activities. As time went on, individuals leasing these tracts constructed small cabins that were eventually replaced with more permanent structures ranging from cottages to multi-million dollar homes.

Over the years, lease rates for the tracts of land were increased minimally and arbitrarily beginning at as little as $1 per acre annually in 1944 and reaching an average price of $808 annually in 2007. There are currently 1,560 residential lessees at PK; about 16 percent of them make the lake their fulltime home while the remaining 84 percent have built second or weekend homes at PK.

A land-use study conducted by the Tennessee Valley Authority in 1998 examined the leasing process at PK and encouraged the BRA to continue offering lease contracts. The same study advised that the leases were greatly undervalued in comparison to property at other Texas lakes and recommended raising lease rates to six percent of the property's value. For the last eight years, the BRA Board of Directors and staff have worked diligently to accomplish this goal while attempting to balance the need for fiscal responsibility and the expectations of our lessees. Each attempt was met with greater consternation and opposition from lessees. As a result, in 2006, a group of PK lessees sought legislation that would force the BRA to sell the property to the current lease holders at a price greatly below market level.

Though the mandatory divestiture bill was not made law, the Authority Board of Directors acknowledged the legislature's urging to remove the organization from the property management business. In July 2007, the Board directed BRA staff to determine if it would be possible to create a divestiture process similar to the one outlined in the failed legislation.

The BRA staff began creating a "to do" list of items that must be accomplished in order to sell the leased property. The list includes numerous issues such as platting and dedication of road ownership and maintenance, property surveys, appraisals and legal costs for the development and implementation of a policy.

As the list continued to grow, it became apparent to the Board that in attempting to extract the BRA from land management, the process would, in fact, require an expansion of property management duties.

As a self-funded, public entity whose main goal is to provide water for the Brazos basin, the BRA does not have the expertise or manpower necessary for real estate management and development. Moreover, the potential expenses required, with no guaranteed method of cost recovery from sales, could affect the rates that the BRA would need to charge customers for water throughout the Brazos basin.

With this in mind, the Board noted that it would be prudent and necessary to explore every option for divestiture and passed a resolution directing the staff to investigate the option of an all-inclusive sale of the BRA-owned properties at PK through a public bid process.

The proposed bid will include all BRA-owned properties outside the Federal Energy Regulatory Commission (FERC) project areas and exclude any properties necessary for future operations at the lake. The Board also stipulated that the public bid should include protection for the current lessees' existing rights and provide a right for the lessees to purchase their leasehold. Once the proposed bid process is complete, the BRA Board will evaluate whether it wishes to further engage in the bid process.

An all-inclusive sale of BRA holdings at the lake could prove to be a win-win for all involved. Lessees would be protected and those interested in purchasing would be allowed to do so. Further, the sale of leased properties would then be streamlined and managed by real estate professionals knowledgeable in property sales and capable of working toward the positive growth of the community. Finally, the BRA would fulfill the will of the legislature by eliminating property management responsibilities.

Should an all-inclusive sale be completed, revenues would be used toward the implementation of the more than $3 billion of water storage and infrastructure needed within the Brazos basin in the next 50 years to meet the projections set by the State Water Plan.

The BRA Board of Directors will keep the public informed throughout the information gathering process of alternative divestiture opportunities. The goal is to protect current lessees while allowing the Brazos River Authority to manage its core purpose – providing water resources to the people of the Brazos basin.[101]

One might surmise that the leaseholders at Possum Kingdom Lake were overjoyed to learn that years of uncertainty and turmoil were one step closer to a potential solution. One might also assume that the leaseholders at Possum Kingdom Lake would have been extremely grateful for the gift that they had just received from Governor Perry's hand-selected presiding officer. This presumption would be entirely incorrect.

The Possum Kingdom Lake Association's lack of immediate enthusiasm is somewhat understandable. The prospect of having to deal with a professional real estate firm, rather than a state agency that could be bullied by certain members of the state legislature, was a wild card that

---

[101] Judi Pierce, "BRA Board Votes to Take Public Bids for an All Inclusive Sale of Properties at Possum Kingdom Lake," *Brazos River Authority*, April 29, 2008. http://web.archive.org/web/20080602151429/http://www.brazos.org/newsPdf/PK_Open_Bid_Process.pdf.

could not be predicted. Moreover, the PKLA remained convinced that Attorney General Greg Abbott had a better gift in store. The same was true of House Speaker-wannabe Jim Keffer and Attorney General-wannabe Dan Branch. The forced divestiture of the shoreline of Possum Kingdom Lake was turning into a Texas version of a white elephant Christmas party.

One month after the BRA's Surrender Meeting, on May 17, 2008, the PKLA met to discuss their current strategy and the latest developments. The pertinent parts of the published minutes of that meeting read as follows.

Board of Directors' Meeting Minutes

May 17, 2008

The Possum Kingdom Lake Association directors met at 9:30am in Bryan Insurance conference room in Graham at 623 Elm Street on May 17, 2008. [...]

A meeting with Senator Estes was held in Wichita Falls. The theme for the meeting was a return to Austin to pass a divestiture bill. Senator Estes agreed to sponsor and work for passage of a bill.

John Connally reported on a recent meeting in Austin with Matt Phillips, BRA public relationship manager, and Trent Thomas, from Representative Keffer's office. The discussion at this meeting included a Divestiture Bill for '09 Legislation, county taxes and 3rd party sell of all BRA land.

Greg Fitzgerald and Robert Aldrich gave the directors an update on the tax case. A trial was held on April 21 & 22, 2008. Judge Ray has yet to issue his ruling on the case. [...]

Third party Sale of the land around PK was considered not acceptable and not in the best interest of the lessees. Directors decided that a position statement to that effect should be read at the next BRA board meeting which is scheduled for Tuesday, May 20, 2008.

Directors discussed a return to Austin in January '09 to pass a divestiture bill. Robert Aldrich and Jay Turner will work on the bill with completion scheduled by September. Kerry Groves agreed to set up an appointment with Rick Hardcastle to discuss support and sponsorship of the bill in the house. Paul Pulliam will visit with Dan Branch about the same issues. Jim Lattimore agreed to set up meetings with representatives in the Metroplex.

Talking points will be outlined and sent to directors.

The Annual meeting will be Saturday, June 21, 2008 at the Chamber of Commerce on the east side at 10am. Pulliam asked that the agenda and printed materials that would be passed out at the meeting be provided to the directors before the meeting. Lattimore offered help in formatting a positive presentation that can be sent out for publicity and educating membership on upcoming issues.

The meeting adjourned at 12:00 Noon.[102]

As if in response to the PKLA's board meeting, Presiding Officer Christopher DeCluitt called a Special Meeting of the BRA three days later dedicated solely to the issues surrounding Possum Kingdom Lake. If you had been in the room that day, you would have left wondering who the directors of the BRA were appointed to serve. All of the talk about preserving the interests of the taxpayers of Texas was now gone. That vacuum was filled by conversations that focused on protecting the investments of the leaseholders.

Presiding Officer DeCluitt began the special meeting on May 20, 2008, by announcing that Chris Adams, Grady Barr, Truman Blum, Nancy Porter, and Jon Sloan had informed him that they would be absent. DeCluitt went on to announce that Truman Blum had submitted his resignation to the governor's office. He then felt compelled to recite several points related to the *Texas Open Meetings Act*.

---

[102] PKLA Staff, "Board of Directors' Meeting Minutes May 17, 2008," *Possum Kingdom Lake Association*, May 17, 2008, accessed July 10, 2011. https://web.archive. org/web/20151129202103/http://www.pklakeassn.org/Minutes%205-17-08.htm.

After that, it was time to hear from the public. And God help me if Monte Land was not the first guy in front of the microphone again. Monte introduced himself to the new board members as the president of the PKLA. Surprisingly, he skipped his usual dissertation about how the BRA was threatening his retirement plans and instead stated that the PKLA was adamantly opposed to a third party sale.

Monte Land then read a letter from the PKLA that asked how the BRA intended to protect the "millions of dollars of investments" that the leaseholders had made. He went on to lecture the new board members about their responsibilities related to protecting the leaseholders. He then asked the BRA to resume its work on a lot-by-lot divestiture plan.[103]

After Monte's remarks, Presiding Officer Christopher DeCluitt became the gift that kept on giving. During the first agenda item, a resolution was presented and approved to complement the resolution that had been passed three weeks earlier. This resolution, entitled *Agenda Item 1A – Executive Session,* introduced the concept of leaseholder protections in the event of a bulk sale to a third party. Within the resolution, five "protections" were enumerated for any subsequent Request for Bids to sell the property. These were:

> 1. A third-party purchaser must acknowledge and accept the terms and conditions of all existing leases on lands that are part of the sale,
>
> 2. The third-party purchaser must maintain the lease rate methodology adopted by the BRA Board in July of 2007 for eight (8) years. Rates may be based upon assessed rather than appraised values, at the option of the third party purchaser,
>
> 3. The third-party purchaser must provide each lessee a period of eight (8) years to purchase

---

[103] Special Board Meeting "Notice of Meeting," *Brazos River Authority Board Meeting Minutes,* May 20, 2008, accessed November 10, 2014. http://www.brazos.org/Portals/0/board_audio/05202008_BRD1.mp3.

their leasehold property from the third-party purchaser, or its successor,

4. The purchase price of any sale to the lessee will be for the value of the leased land only and will not include the value of improvements such as homes, docks and patios. The cost of the land purchase will be for no more than the fair market value of the unencumbered fee simple estate, and,

5. The third-party purchaser will extend the term of any lease as necessary to allow each lessee the full eight-year (8) period of time to purchase their leased lot.

Less than 120 days earlier on January 28, 2008, the board of the Brazos River Authority had voted to tie lease rates to the fair market value of the land as determined by a fair market appraisal. With this simple resolution on May 20, that earlier decision was rescinded by virtue of Lessee Protection #2. The impact of Rick Perry's April Fools' Day massacre was indeed immediate.

To further the inertia for an all-inclusive sale, the new board of the BRA then voted to hire a firm to market the property. This decision was captured in a resolution entitled *Agenda Item 1B – Executive Session*. The text of that resolution read as follows:

BE IT RESOLVED that the Board of Directors of the Brazos River Authority hereby authorizes the General Manager/CEO to seek proposals from firms having the professional expertise to assist the Brazos River Authority in managing, marketing, and evaluating bids for the sale of the Brazos River Authority real property interests at Possum Kingdom Lake.

On the surface, this resolution appears to be nothing short of an extremely prudent course of action on the part of the board. In reality, it represented one of the most convincing pieces of evidence that this was a whorehouse deal in the making.

To wrap things up that day, the board also voted to suspend the work being performed by Integra Realty Resources related to appraising the properties.[104] This appraisal work had been authorized on January 28 and awarded to Integra Realty as a result of Christopher DeCluitt's interviewing process. Those appraisals were immediately halted. The BRA reported its progress on the forced divestiture that evening in the form of a press release.[105] The days of sending a status report to anyone in the governor's office were over.

Here is another spoiler alert: Even though the board of the BRA voted to hire someone to market the shoreline of Possum Kingdom Lake on May 20, 2008, they would not actually do so until ten months later on March 19, 2009. This was exactly seventy days after the BRA put the property up for sale and exactly twenty days before the deadline to submit a bid. This makes me wonder if the newly constituted board of the BRA actually wanted this to be a competitive bidding process.

[104] BRA Staff, "Board Actions–Special Meeting," *Brazos River Authority*, May 20, 2008, accessed June 14, 2013. https://web.archive.org/web/20080602151438/http://www.brazos.org/generalPdf/05-20-08_Quarterly_Board_Actions.pdf.

[105] BRA Staff, "BRA Board Passes Resolutions for Lessee Protections at Possum Kingdom Lake," *Brazos River Authority*, May 20, 2008, accessed October 14, 2013. https://web.archive.org/web/20080602151242/http://www.brazos.org/generalpdf/pk_protections.pdf.

Chapter 9

GENERAL ABBOTT'S
SMOKE SIGNALS

Editor's Note: This chapter is appropriately titled and is admittedly swollen with legalese. Every possible effort has been made to mitigate the minutiae while presenting the requisite information.

As we discussed earlier in Chapter 6; the presiding officer of the Brazos River Authority, Mr. Steve Pena, and the key state senator in this deal, Senator Kip Averitt, individually petitioned attorney general Greg Abbott for his official opinions related to the matters at Possum Kingdom Lake.

One of the primary questions in *The Texas Miracle* is whether or not the sale of the shoreline of Possum Kingdom Lake violated the Texas Constitution. That is not to say that the other questions regarding bid rigging and conspiracy are unimportant—only that they are secondary.

Article III, Section 52 of the Texas Constitution prevents the Texas legislature from granting a gratuitous gift to any individual, or group of individuals. Specifically, the text of this article states:

> The Legislature shall have no power to authorize any county, city, town or other political corporation or subdivision of the State to lend its credit or to grant public money or thing of value in aid of, or to any individual, association or corporation whatsoever.

The purpose of this grammatically questionable sentence is simple. The citizens of Texas do not want the Texas legislature to have the authority to give things away. This public sentiment is the same reason that the Texas legislature is only allowed to meet and pass new laws once every two years. And, both of these limitations are intended to limit the damage that the legislature can do.

During the failed attempt to force the BRA to sell the property to the weekenders in 2007, an emergency meeting had been held to discuss the situation. Director John R. Scaggs made the following observation during that meeting:

> The legislature passes laws all of the time that hurt people. They do it *all* of the time – and they are about to do it to us![106]

Roughly three months later, in the immediate aftermath of the first attempt to force the BRA to sell its shoreline at a discount, the BRA had held a Special Meeting on July 17, 2007. During this meeting, the law firm of Scott, Douglass, and McConnico had advised the BRA that its practice of granting discounts to the senior citizens at Possum Kingdom Lake violated the prohibitions of Article III, Section 52. Jennifer Knauth, who spoke on behalf of the outside counsel, further recommended that the BRA put the question of discounts to Attorney General Greg Abbott. The former presiding officer of the BRA, Mr. Steve Pena, did exactly that on July 30, 2007.

Attorney General Greg Abbott replied to Steve Pena's request almost six months later on January 25, 2008. The summary of Greg Abbott's Opinion, numbered GA-0599, served as a reminder to the weekenders that laws are what you make of them. Sometimes laws are made to be broken, and sometimes you simply have to find the loophole. The summary of Greg Abbott's first Opinion on the issues at Possum Kingdom Lake took the latter tack.

---

[106] Emergency Board Meeting, "Agenda Items 5–6," *Brazos River Authority Board Meeting Minutes*, April 27, 2007, accessed July 11, 2013. (Fast forward to 37:23). http://www.brazos.org/Portals/0/board_audio/04272007_EME2.mp3.

SUMMARY

We find no statutory provision in either the Brazos River Authority's enabling legislation or applicable general laws that specifically prohibits a discounted lease rate and freeze for certain lessees.

As to Article III, Section 52(a) of the Texas Constitution, it does not preclude offering discounted lease rates and rate freezes to certain lessees if the lease terms do not constitute the gratuitous application of public funds for a private purpose and if the governing body reasonably determines, in the first instance, that: (1) the lease terms have as their predominant purpose the accomplishment of a public, rather than a private, purpose of the BRA; (2) the BRA retains sufficient control to ensure accomplishment of the public purpose and to protect the public's investment; and (3) the public receives a return benefit.[107]

Attorney General Greg Abbott's opinion started off by saying "There is no law on the books that specifically says that you cannot offer a discount to the older folks—so perhaps you can." This was in direct contradiction to the analysis that was performed by the law firm of Scott, Douglass, and McConnico.

Greg Abbott's opinion then provided both a warning and a roadmap for navigating around the prohibition of the Texas Constitution. The key word, in Greg Abbott's opinion, was the term "gratuitous." He explained this in the body of his decision.

We cannot definitively answer your question because whether the proposed lease discount and freeze are gratuitous is a fact question for the governing body in the first instance, and ultimately for the court.

---

[107] Atty. Gen. Greg Abbott, "Opinion No. GA-0599," *Office of the Attorney General*, January 25, 2008, accessed May 1, 2011. https://www.texasattorneygeneral.gov/opinions/opinions/50abbott/op/2008/pdf/ga0599.pdf.

In other words, the attorney general was informing the BRA that it was up to them to decide if granting a discount to the senior citizens was gratuitous.

Additionally, the attorney general was informing the BRA that if they decided to offer a discount to the older crowd, it would be up to someone else to file a lawsuit objecting to the practice. A lawsuit of this nature would then have to be adjudicated in a court of law. During a period of economic downturn, the line of folks who were eager to sue the BRA over renting property to old people was rather short.

Attorney General Abbott also declined to comment on the analysis that was performed by the law firm of Scott, Douglass, and McConnico. The explanation for this was buried in the seventh footnote of his Opinion.

> You explain that your "outside counsel has advised that such a discount or freeze would violate Article III, Section 52 of the Texas Constitution, as there is no specific amendment allowing such a discount or freeze."
>
> We have not been provided any details regarding this analysis and thus, do not address that analysis.

Please understand that even though Attorney General Greg Abbott had chewed on this topic for almost six months, he was under no obligation to request a copy of the ignored analysis from the BRA. And so he didn't. Please also understand that the assertion that the Attorney General and his office had not been provided with that analysis was entirely untrue. In fact, it was a damn lie.

Ten weeks after Presiding Officer Steve Pena submitted his initial Request for Opinion, State Senator Kip Averitt had followed up with a request of his own. This request was submitted on October 16, 2007, and specifically asked Greg Abbott how the property should be valued if the BRA was forced to sell its shoreline to the weekenders.

> Because this is a matter of vital interest to the BRA, and to other constituents of mine, I respectfully request the Attorney General to issue an opinion as to whether leased property at Possum Kingdom Lake should be

valued as though unencumbered by the existing leases where the sale is to the lessee, or whether the sales price should be discounted to reflect the remaining term of the existing leases, although the lease would cease to exist the moment the property is sold. In particular, I request that the opinion address whether using the discounted sales price would violate the prohibitions of Article III, Section 52 of the Texas Constitution. The Attorney General has previously addressed this issue in a Letter Opinion. Tex. Att'y Gen. L.O. 98-082 (Sept. 28, 1998).

Senator Averitt's request was directly on point and included the legal analysis that had been performed by the law firm of Scott, Douglass, and McConnico. This was over three months before Greg Abbott issued the Opinion recited above, which claimed that the analysis had not been received.

Senator Averitt's request also pointed out that former Attorney General Dan Morales had already addressed an identical issue in 1998. This came in the form of Opinion 98-082.

SUMMARY

Under Local Government Code section 272.001(h), the fair market value of a municipality's interest in land is the amount that a willing buyer, who desires but is not obligated to buy, would pay a willing seller, who desires but is not obligated to sell. Unless evidence to the contrary is produced, the leasehold estate merges into the fee simple estate when the lessee purchases the land that he or she currently leases. A lessee who purchases the whole of the city's interest in a lakeside lot under section 272.001(h) must pay for both the city's right to future rent payments and the city's reversionary interest.[108]

---

[108] Asst. Atty. Gen. Kymberly K. Oltrogge, "Opinion No. 98-082," *Office of the Attorney General*, September 28, 1998, accessed May 1, 2011. https://www.texasattorneygeneral.gov/opinions/opinions/48morales/lo/1998/htm/lo1998082.htm.

Obviously, Dan Morales' earlier opinion agreed completely with the legal analysis that had been performed by Scott, Douglass, and McConnico. It also agreed with common sense. Nonetheless, Attorney General Greg Abbott chose to ignore this previous opinion when he rendered his own.

SUMMARY

The Brazos River Authority (the "Authority"), a special law conservation and reclamation district under Texas Constitution Article XVI, Section 59, owns real property surrounding Possum Kingdom Lake that is leased to private parties at below-market lease rates. The Authority is formulating procedures to offer to sell the property to the lessees of the property. [...]

The first question presented is whether the leased property must be valued as unencumbered by the leases or encumbered by the unexpired terms of the existing leases for the purposes of determining the sales price if the property is offered for sale to the lessees. If the property is offered for sale to the lessees, the Authority would sell the property pursuant to Water Code section 49.226. Section 49.226(a) generally provides that surplus real or personal property owned by a water district may be sold in a private or public sale or be exchanged. Section 49.226(a) requires that the surplus property be exchanged for "like fair market value." The Authority and the lessees assume that this fair market provision applies to the sale of the Authority's property.

The lessees contend that the fair market value provision in section 49.226 requires the Authority to value the property as encumbered by the leases. Because section 49.226(a) does not explicitly state that a lease may not be considered, fair market value as used in the statute has the meaning established by the Texas courts, which meaning includes the value of a lease. Thus, application of the established judicial definition of fair market value requires the Authority to value the property as encumbered by the leases.

The second question presented is whether using the discounted sales price resulting from valuing the Authority's property as encumbered by the leases would violate Texas Constitution Article III, Section 52(a), which prohibits gratuitous transfers of public funds to individuals or private parties. Using a discounted sales price – resulting in this particular instance from valuing the property as encumbered by the existing leases – would not violate Article III, Section 52(a).

Very truly yours,

GREG ABBOTT

Attorney General of Texas[109]

I suppose that it is possible that Attorney General Greg Abbott, and his entire staff, did not realize that the two requests that had been received from Presiding Officer Steve Pena and State Senator Kip Averitt were related. However, I do not find this possibility to be highly plausible. Both of the Opinions rendered in regard to the property at Possum Kingdom Lake were co-signed by the following highly-placed members of Greg Abbott's staff:

KENT C. SULLIVAN

First Assistant Attorney General

ANDREW WEBER

Deputy Attorney General for Legal Counsel

NANCY S. FULLER

Chair, Opinion Committee

---

[109] Atty. Gen. Greg Abbott, "Opinion No. GA-0634," *Office of the Attorney General*, June 5, 2008, accessed May 1, 2011. https://www.texasattorneygeneral.gov/opinions/opinions/50abbott/op/2008/htm/ga-0634.htm.

Moreover, the second Opinion referenced the first opinion in its statutory analysis. To add further insult to sensibilities, the Attorney General's office invited the Possum Kingdom Lake Association to submit a brief in response to the second request from Senator Averitt and provided a copy of the analysis in question.[110] This invitation occurred almost three months before the Attorney General's office claimed not to have "been provided any details regarding this analysis."

As the saying goes, the wheels of justice turn slowly. State Senator Kip Averitt would not receive a response to his Request for Opinion, which was submitted on October 16, 2007, for almost eight months. This occurred on June 5, 2008. During this eight month waiting period, Governor Rick Perry had executed his April Fools' Day Massacre. Likewise, the newly appointed presiding officer of the BRA, Christopher DeCluitt, had placed a final halt on anything that would introduce fair market value into the equation at Possum Kingdom Lake.

When the wheels of justice finally did turn, Attorney General Greg Abbott provided a response to Senator Averitt that defied all logic. Amazingly, Abbott and his staff concluded that the property should be discounted to reflect the value of the leases even though the leases would cease to exist the moment that the property was sold. Within his analysis, General Abbott cited multiple Texas statutes. Predominant among these was chapter 49 of the Water Code.

> By its terms, section 49.226(a) authorizes a district's board of directors to determine the fair market value of land or an interest in land to be exchanged: "land or interest in land … must be exchanged for like fair market value, which value may be determined by the district."
>
> The statute does not directly state that a water district board must or must not, in arriving at the fair market value of the land or interest in land, consider any leases on the land.

[110] PKLA Staff, "Divestiture History During 2007 - 2008," *Possum Kingdom Lake Association*, circa June 2008, accessed July 10, 2011.
https://web.archive.org/web/20110701042812/http://pklakeassn.org/Divestiture%20History.html.

In other words, the board of directors of the BRA held the responsibility for determining the fair market value of the land. This does not mean that the board's determination could not be challenged in court, only that the board should be the first to act. Moreover, the Attorney General pointed out that this prevailing statute did not directly address the issue of the existing leases, and there was no existing case law relative to chapter 49 of the Water Code.

In the absence of any legal precedents related to the Water Code, Greg Abbott turned his attention to a case in Dallas that involved two private parties and a commercial building. This was referred to as the Petula case. Greg Abbott's analysis stated several reasons why the Petula case was different from the situation at Possum Kingdom Lake. He then stated that he was going to rely on the outcome of that case, nonetheless.[111]

In the closing of his analysis, Greg Abbott offered his final loophole to the weekenders at Possum Kingdom Lake.

> Moreover, in this instance, the "windfall" or "discount" the Authority's lessees may receive is not the direct result of valuing the property as encumbered by the lease, but the result of the previously granted discounted or below-market lease rates.

To summarize, Greg Abbott was stating that the inevitable windfall that the weekenders would receive was simply the fault of the BRA for having given them such a sweetheart deal for over sixty years. God save Texas.

As I have mentioned before, the state of Texas frowns upon those who practice law without a license. Consequently, I will not attempt to challenge the arguments and findings in Greg Abbott's opinions. I will point out, however, that in the second paragraph of the *Summary* of GA-0634, Greg Abbott stated the following:

---

[111] "Petula Associates, Ltd. v. Dolco Packaging Corporation, No. 99-11375, at 13," *United States Court of Appeals, Fifth Circuit*, February 12, 2001. http://openjurist. org/240/f3d/499/petula-associates-ltd-v-dolco-packaging-corporation.

If the property is offered for sale to the lessees, the Authority would sell the property pursuant to Water Code section 49.226.

In fact, the entire analysis and opinion that Attorney General Abbott rendered is predicated on this premise. Conversely, paragraph 12 of House Bill 3031, which was signed by Governor Rick Perry on May 27, 2009, states the following:

(12) The following laws do not apply to sale of an individual Leased Tract under this subsection:

(A) Chapter 272, Local Government Code;

(B) Section 49.226, Water Code; and

(C) Section 8502.013 of this code.

Oops.

I am no legal scholar but it would appear to me that Attorney General Greg Abbott failed to examine the appropriate laws. This makes me wonder what else he might have gotten wrong.

If you think it disrespectful to refer to the official actions of the Attorney General of Texas as a smokescreen, give some thought to this. On April 17, 2013, fifteen people lost their lives in what became known as the West Texas Fertilizer Explosion. Most of those killed were volunteer firemen. Roughly one year later, Attorney General Greg Abbott issued an Opinion that stated that the location of hazardous chemicals in the state of Texas was no longer public information.

During a press conference that can only be described as bizarre, Greg Abbott explained the position that he took in the following manner.

Additional Editor's Note: The following exchange contains a certain degree of Hooptedoodle.[112]

---

[112] Elmore Leonard, "Easy on the Adverbs, Exclamation Points and Especially Hooptedoodle," *The New York Times*, July 16, 2001. http://www.nytimes.com/2001/07/16/arts/writers-writing-easy-adverbs-exclamation-points-especially-hooptedoodle.html.

Q: General, why did you rule that people shouldn't be able to see the dangerous chemicals in their communities?

Abbott: Very important to understand: I did not rule that. If you read the Opinion, you'll find that there are two rulings in there. Under the Communities Right to Know Act, I ruled that under that law everyone in the state of Texas has a right to see any chemical held by any plant anywhere in the state of Texas, and they have a right to get that information within 10 days.

In a separate statute under the Texas Homeland Protection law, I ruled that information that is gathered by the state of Texas, if it contains information that falls in the category of homeland security, that type of information cannot be received by the public. There is a clear reason why that law exists, that was demonstrated in Austin, Texas, last week, and that is because we have ongoing terroristic activity here in central Texas.

My office worked with federal authorities and others to arrest two terrorists who were working on schemes that could have proven dangerous for people here as well as dangerous for people in other areas. And anyone is mistaken to think that these are the only examples of terrorism; these are just the most recent examples of terrorists working actively here in Texas.

So the ruling was a win-win. It allowed the state of Texas to not disclose information that could make it more risky for the state of Texas by exposing information to terrorists, but it also upheld the law that insures that every single mom and dad, every single parent, every single teacher, every single business owner, every single homeowner, every single person in the state of Texas will have access to information stored in any plant in their neighborhood.

Q: General, on the Tier II question, what information is available? What can we see, and how do we do that?

Abbott: You, as a reporter, you, as a community member of the state, can go to any chemical facility in the entire state of Texas and say, "Identify for me all chemicals you "have on your facility," and you are entitled to get that information within 10 days.

Q: Do you have to know where the facility is?

Abbott: Well, it's helpful. I mean, you wouldn't just want to say, "Well, I wonder if there's one up in Andrews, Texas." You know where they are, if you drive around. Let's bear this down. If you're living in West, Texas, you know that there is some facility there and you have the right to ask the people in West, Texas, "Hey, what chemicals do you have in there?" Same thing as you drive from here back to your office, you may see any kind of plant or facility, you don't have to know whether or not they do or do not have anything in there whatsoever, you can ask every facility whether or not they have chemicals, you can ask them if they do, and they can tell you, "Well, we do have chemicals" or "we don't have chemicals," and if they do, they tell which ones they have.

Q: So we ask the facility, not (the Department of State Health Services)?

Abbott: Right. That's the way that law works to protect homeland security. DSHS has the right to not disclose this information for homeland security purposes. However, to ensure that those living in neighborhoods, those who live in areas where they want to make sure that things are safe, or those who are thinking about buying a home, when you buy a home you don't just target on the internet and move in the next day, you drive around the neighborhood. You're going to know everything that exists in the neighborhood in which you move, and you have the right to inquire before you move in there, every single facility along the way, whether or not they're storing any kind of chemical whatsoever.

> **Q:** You can just walk on their private property and say, "I have a right to be on your private property and ask you what you have?"
>
> **Abbott:** Absolutely.

Attorney General Abbott realized almost instantly that he was making a fool of himself. He attempted to walk back from his previous comments with little success.

> **Abbott:** Just to make clear, I mean, you may not be able to walk on private property, but you can send an email or letter or notice to anyone who owns any kind of private property or facility saying that under the Community Right to Know law, you need to tell me within 10 days what chemicals you have, so it doesn't matter who you are or where you are, you're obligated under that law to respond.[113]

I am fairly comfortable in my position that Attorney General Greg Abbott provided a smokescreen for Mike Patterson's "Texas Miracle."

Before we turn our attention away from Greg Abbott, let's revisit the question that was asked by BRA Director Jean Kilgore on April 28, 2008.

> I have a question. This couldn't be construed as a way of getting around the fact that we can't sell to individuals, that we might have a sham company or something take this over?[114]

This is yet another example of a key problem that needed to be resolved. How can we get these unruly board members to stop burdening the

---

[113] Jay Root, "Abbott: Ask Chemical Plants What's Inside," *The Texas Tribune*, July 1, 2014, accessed July 15, 2014. http://www.texastribune.org/2014/07/01/abbott-ask-chemical-plants-whats-inside/.

[114] Board Meeting "Agenda Item 9," *Brazos River Authority Board Meeting Minutes*, April 28, 2008, accessed November 10, 2014. (Fast forward to 11:34). http://www.brazos.org/Portals/0/board_audio/04282008_BRD10.mp3.

public record with embarrassing questions about legalities or inflammatory statements about rape? The answer to that problem was simple: take the issues surrounding Possum Kingdom Lake off of the board's agenda and thus off of the public record.

For the next four months, the board of the Brazos River Authority would have no agenda item related to the divestiture of the shoreline of Possum Kingdom Lake. Everything would occur via email, telephone, or invitation-only meetings.

Chapter 10

THE QUEEN OF GRANBURY

If you want to make thirty million dollars selling state property to wealthy folks over the course of one year and one day, you will probably need to have an ace up your sleeve. If you can't manage that—perhaps a queen will do.

Cue the Queen of Granbury.

During the events that produced "The Texas Miracle", a woman by the name of Mary Ward was serving on the board of directors of the Texas Bankers Association. Ms. Ward was also serving as one of eight members on the TBA's Executive Committee and was the Chair of the TBA's Government Relations Council. Suffice it to say that Mary Ward was not lacking for connections in the banking industry, or within the political circles of Texas.

Being a champion of the greater good, Mary Ward simultaneously served on the board of the Granbury Economic Development Council. Unfortunately, such selfless sacrifice does not pay the bills and Mary was required to keep her day job. In June of 2008, Mary Ward held the position of Regional President for Southwest Securities, Federal Savings Bank. Given that Mike Patterson was on the board of directors of this bank, it seems reasonable to assume that he and Mary Ward had met.

On June 2, 2008, Governor Rick Perry announced that he had appointed Mary Ward to the board of the Brazos River Authority.[115] Ms. Ward would be replacing Truman Blum of Clifton who had resigned. At 6:34 PM that evening, Mike Patterson sent an email to the board of the Brazos River Authority in the care of Judy Pierce.

> Dear Brazos River Authority Board of Directors,
>
> I think many, if not most, BRA PK lessees, wish we could return to the days before the Staubach Report. However, I understand that the BRA is intent on getting out of the land management business to focus on its primary purpose, "provide water resources to the people of the Brazos basin." We thank you for your excellent stewardship of the area for so many years.

Mike Patterson opened his email to the BRA by acknowledging that it was the *Staubach Report* that had led to the weekenders' efforts to force the BRA to sell the property. He then immediately attempted to head off an open bidding process and tendered an offer to purchase the property.

> It is not uncommon for companies to first offer themselves for sale to their employees and management before going outside to seek 3rd party bids. Giving the PK BRA lessees an opportunity to control their own destiny, although perhaps not legally required, would go a long way in helping to make a smoother transition, even if the lessees were not ultimately successful with a buyout. The Staubach Company on April 11, 2006, suggested that "the price which the BRA could reasonably expect to achieve in a lump sum payment is somewhere between $60 and 75 million" for a discounted lump sum sale (Source: Staubach Company April 11, 2006 Phase III Report-Lease Portfolio Strategy-page 10).

---

[115] Texas Register, Volume 33, Number 24, Page 4583, June 13, 2008. http://texashistory.unt.edu/ark:/67531/metapth90826/m2/1/high_res_d/0613is.pdf.

Before the BRA goes to the time, expense, and trouble, caused by a traditional 3ʳᵈ party RFP bid process, we respectfully request the opportunity to put together an ownership group to raise the suggested $75,000,000 to purchase those referenced BRA properties. We request your review and consideration of our proposal instead of the RFP process, because of the timing and other logistics associated with creating a new BRA PK lessee owned entity. In the alternative, if we are forced into a traditional RFP process and time line we respectfully request a process and time line that is logistically possible for us to organize, evaluate, and effectively bid for the properties. We would also additionally request the opportunity to better any other 3ʳᵈ party bid exceeding our $75,000,000 offer.

Mike Patterson accurately observed that the Staubach Company had stated that the BRA could reasonably expect to achieve "between $60 and $75 million" if they chose to sell the property to a single third party. Conveniently, however, Patterson neglected to include the following four critical sentences in that same report:

> **Staubach Report:** Using these assumptions, the price which the BRA could reasonably expect to achieve in a lump sum payment is somewhere between $60 and $75 million. This value is substantially lower than the estimated market value of the underlying land.
>
> A baseline land valuation was completed in Phase II. According to this valuation, the underlying land is estimated to be worth at least $100,000 per lot on average. This totals approximately at least $158 million and as much as $200 million.[116]

---

[116] BRA Staff, "Staubach Report, Section 6, page 10" *Brazos River Authority*, May 6, 2006, accessed July 5 2013.
https://web.archive.org/web/20060506223913/http://www.brazos.org/generalPdf/Staubach_PIII_Section6.pdf.

Patterson also neglected to observe that for the reasons stated above, the Staubach Company had advised against selling the property in a bulk sale and instead recommended that the lease rates be raised to market levels.

Mike Patterson's email then offered an ill-advised observation that is difficult to explain.

> In addition to creating the obvious morale/good will advantages associated with a "member owned" ownership entity this land company" could:
>
> > a) Negotiate discounts to sell lots/land to the existing BRA PK lessees. I understand that the BRA is presently legally prohibited from discounting land sales to their lessees.[117]

Why would you point out that you were proposing a property laundering scheme that might possibly enable the BRA to circumvent Article III, Section 52?

It is impossible to know whether the timing of this email was another example of a hand well played or merely one of Mike Patterson's many fortuitous coincidences. At the exact same time that Mike Patterson was talking to his fellow weekenders about putting a deal together to take the BRA out, the governor of Texas was appointing one of his subordinates to the board of the BRA. Even more fortunate was the fact that Mike Patterson's subordinate was the landlord for two of the principal politicians in this deal.

Mary Ward's office was located on Highway 377 in Granbury, Texas. At the time of her appointment to the BRA, her bank building in Granbury had two tenants in the office suites that fronted the building. Those tenants were State Representative Jim Keffer and State Senator Kip Averitt. During

---

[117] Mike Patterson, "Patterson to Lender Clients Request for Consideration," *Patterson Equity Partners*, June 3, 2008, accessed July 23, 2011. https://web.archive.org/web/20151128180538/http://www.pklandpartnership.com/downloads/6-3-2008%20Patterson%20to%20Lender%20Clients%20Request%20for%20Consideration.pdf.

The Tale of the River Card, Round I, Keffer carried the water for Senate Bill 1326, while Averitt did everything within his power to kill it.

Far be it for me to suggest that Mary Ward served as a liaison between these two legislators during *Round II* while Mike Patterson was making his play. But, I will say this: I have found no evidence that she in any way hindered the process that converted the humiliating defeat of Senate Bill 1326 in 2007 into the virtually unchallenged passage of House Bill 3031 in 2009. I will also point out that the walk from Mary's office—down the sidewalk of her bank—to the doorsteps of the politicians' offices was a mere fifty steps.

Raise your hand if you want to go to Vegas with this lucky son of a gun.

What is important to understand is that Mike Patterson's initial offer was $75 million and that he was willing to go higher. Equally important is Mike Patterson's observation that the BRA could not sell the individual properties to the individual homeowners at a discount. His solution to the problem at hand was simple. Let's sell the property in bulk to an ownership group formed by the weekenders so that they can turn around and sell the property to themselves at a discount. This makes perfect sense, does it not?

The response from the staff of the Brazos River Authority followed the letter of the law. On the next day, June 3, 2008, the manager of Government and Customer Relations sent an appropriately courteous reply to Mike Patterson.

> Mr. Patterson,
>
> Thank you for your email regarding the BRA's current exploration of a third-party sale of property at Possum Kingdom Lake. This reply will serve as acknowledgement of receipt of your email dated June 2, 2008.
>
> Per Board direction, staff is currently in the process of working to obtain real estate expertise to assist us in developing a global sale option package for the Board's consideration. We are not currently in a position to accept bids or offers for BRA property; therefore we cannot act on your request at this time. However, we are certainly

pleased with your interest and are encouraged to see a proposal that might be amenable to the lessees.

Attached is the list of lessees along with their mailing addresses per your request.

Please let me know if you have any further questions.

Matt

Matt S. Phillips

Government and Customer Relations Manager

Brazos River Authority

254-761-xxxx office

254-424-xxxx cell[118]

Two days later, Matt Phillips sent an official rejection letter to Mike Patterson on the stationery of the BRA declining his offer. He also returned a check for $100,000 that Mike Patterson had sent to the BRA as "evidence" of his confidence that he could put his deal together. Within the official rejection letter, Matt Phillips informed Mike Patterson on behalf of the BRA that, "We hope you will continue to participate in the bid process."[119]

And then the lights went out. For the next four months, there would not be a single agenda item considered by the Brazos River Authority related to the sale of the shoreline. Likewise, the next time that Mike Patterson would be seen in a public setting related to the sale of the shoreline, he would be pitching his plan to the Brazos River Authority in the fall of 2008. In the interim, Mike Patterson would be meeting with the politicians and the bureaucrats who would enable and consecrate his deal.

---

[118] Mike Patterson, "BRA Response," *Patterson Equity Partners*, June 3, 2008, accessed July 23, 2011. https://web.archive.org/web/20151129202959/http://www.pklandpartnership.com/downloads/6-3-2008%20BRA%20Response.pdf.

[119] Mike Patterson, "Return of Patterson Earnest Money," *Patterson Equity Partners*, June 5, 2008, accessed July 23, 2011. https://web.archive.org/web/20151129203052/http://www.pklandpartnership.com/downloads/6-5-2008%20BRA%20Return%20of%20Patterson%20Earnest%20Money.pdf.

Chapter 11

THE PATTERSON PLAN

On September 8, 2008, State Senator Kip Averitt, the chairman of the Senate Committee on Natural Resources, hosted a meeting in Waco to discuss the situation at Possum Kingdom Lake. The meeting lasted for two hours and the reported purpose of the meeting was to review Mike Patterson's plan to buy the entire inhabited shoreline of Possum Kingdom Lake. The guest of honor was none other than Mike Patterson himself.

Representatives of the Brazos River Authority were in attendance that day. These included members of the staff, some of the BRA's lawyers, and the BRA's presiding officer, Christopher DeCluitt.

Joining the contingency from the BRA were several legislators. These included Senator Chris Harris, Representative Charlie Geren, Representative Jim Keffer, Keffer's chief of staff Trent Thomas, and Senator Craig Estes' chief of staff, Lewis Simmons. Carmen Cernosek, who served as the natural resources director for Lieutenant Governor David Dewhurst, was present as well.

The guest list also included Jay Propes and Jay Brown from the Graydon Group. Jay Propes had crafted Senate Bill 1326 during the failed attempt at a forced divestiture in 2007. At this point in the tale, Propes was serving as Mike Patterson's lobbyist. Here is how Mike Patterson described Mr. Propes:

Jay was the lobbyist (The Graydon Group) in Austin that helped navigate me through the political landmines. I hooked on to Jay's wagon and just held on. Initially working for free until I could afford to hire him, and after I hired him still significantly underpaid, Jay deserves much of the credit. I have promised him, if ever given the opportunity, I will name something after him. That scares him a little bit.[120]

The final two attendees were Lance Byrd and Dennis Cannedy, who were both leaseholders at Possum Kingdom Lake. Mike Patterson credited Lance Byrd as being his inspiration for getting involved while Mr. Cannedy was State Senator Craig Estes' campaign treasurer.[121]

Whether or not this meeting violated the Texas Open Meetings Act is a matter for the experts. What is important to realize is that no competitors to Michael Patterson were invited to discuss their plan for laundering the property. The reason for this may simply have been that there was no true competition, only the illusion of competition. Selling the property to the weekenders for less than fair market value required a straw man, and expedience required the absence of any competition for this role. Expedience also required that the straw man be someone who was capable of mixing politics with business while putting the proper spin on the deal.

Everyone who was needed to put a deal together was in the room that day on September 8, 2008. The question is whether they were collaborators or conspirators. What is certain is that they left with an agreement that immediately became known as the *Patterson Plan*. What is also known is that the Patterson Plan was set in motion sixteen days later during a Special Board Meeting called by presiding officer Christopher DeCluitt.

To put the meeting that Senator Averitt hosted into historical context, the S&P 500 index closed at 1267 on September 8, 2008. Exactly one

[120] Mike Patterson, "Unsung Heroes," *Patterson Equity Partners*, n.d., accessed February 1, 2010. https://web.archive.org/web/20090718210202/http://www.pklandpartnership.com/Heroes.aspx.
[121] Libby Cluett, "One Man's Plan," *Mineral Wells Index*, September 22, 2008, accessed July 10, 2010. https://web.archive.org/web/20080927030255/http:/www.mineralwellsindex.com/local/local_story_266091033.html.

week later, on September 15, Lehman Brothers filed for bankruptcy and the financial meltdown that became known as the Great Recession was underway. During the seventy-five day period that began on September 8, the S&P 500 lost forty percent of its value and real estate prices were collapsing. In a move that defies all comprehension, the Brazos River Authority decided that this was the perfect time to sell its shoreline.

On September 22, 2008, the Brazos River Authority convened with nine agenda items on the schedule. Five of the items on the agenda related to Possum Kingdom Lake, the first of which was the *Notice of Meeting and Announcements, Hear Comments from Members of the Public.*[122]

Presiding Officer DeCluitt read several written statements from members of the public who did not wish to testify. Each of these statements expressed support for what each person referred to as *The Patterson Plan.* Afterwards, other individuals rose to speak in favor of what each of them also referred to as *The Patterson Plan.*

The first to speak was one of Mike Patterson's "friends in need," Mr. Jim Maibach.[123]

Jim Maibach stated that his wife's family had known the Patterson family for over fifty years. He pointed out that Mike Patterson was not merely a lawyer, but that he had also grown up around the banking business and served as a board member for a bank in Dallas. Maibach did not mention, however, that he and Mike Patterson were both board members of the bank to which he referred—Southwest Securities, FSB. Maibach also neglected to disclose that he would be investing in Mike Patterson's deal.

Jim Maibach spoke about the various civic activities that he and Mike Patterson had participated in together, which included gathering toys for children at Christmas. Maibach did not bother to mention that the name of the organization that gathered those toys was the Margarita Society of

---

[122] Special Board Meeting "Notice of Meeting," *Brazos River Authority Board Meeting Minutes*, September 22, 2008, accessed November 10, 2014. http://www.brazos.org/Portals/0/board_audio/09222008_SP-BRD1.MP3.

[123] Mike Patterson, "Unsung Heroes," *Patterson Equity Partners*, n.d., accessed February 1, 2010. https://web.archive.org/web/20090718210202/http://www.pklandpartnership.com/Heroes.aspx.

Arlington.[124] Many of the members of this society would also be investing money in *The Patterson Plan*.

The next to speak that day on the topic of *The Patterson Plan* was Dennis Cannedy. Mr. Cannedy stated that he represented the Possum Kingdom Lake Association and made several comments regarding the fairness of the BRA's plan to increase the lease rates at Possum Kingdom Lake. He also stated that the PKLA had not yet established a position on the concept of a third-party sale, except to say that they feared having a New York hedge fund own the land beneath their homes. Mr. Cannedy chose not to bore the public in attendance with certain details i.e. that he was the campaign treasurer for State Senator Craig Estes *and* that he was a leaseholder at Possum Kingdom Lake.

After the comments from the public, the board moved to *Agenda Item 1: Presentations from Parties Interested in Purchasing Lands at Possum Kingdom*. Not surprisingly, Mike Patterson was the first to act.

If you really want to understand how Mike Patterson pulled this deal off, listen to the audio recording of his presentation.[125] His "aw-shucks" persona was masterful, and he convinced everyone in the room that day that he was simply a good old boy trying to help solve a problem.

As you would expect, Mike Patterson opened his pitch by asking "How 'bout those Cowboys?"

Ok, maybe you didn't see that coming but I swear that he did. After that, Patterson got back on script and recited a list of the Texas legislators "that really helped open doors and encourage a conversation and dialogue." He called some of these politicians out by name.

[124] Staff, "Directors," *Arlington Margarita Society*, February 6, 2007, accessed November 20, 2010.
https://web.archive.org/web/20070206050925/http://www.arlingtonmargaritasociety.org/directors.aspx,
https://web.archive.org/web/20080821132042/http://www.arlingtonmargaritasociety.org/directors.aspx,
https://web.archive.org/web/20130731113037/http://arlingtonmargaritasociety.org/Directors.aspx.
[125] Special Board Meeting "Agenda Item 1," *Brazos River Authority Board Meeting Minutes*, September 22, 2008, accessed November 10, 2014. http://www.brazos.org/Portals/0/board_audio/09222008_SP-BRD2.MP3.

> And I'd be remiss if I didn't say a big thank you to Senator
> Kip Averitt, Senator Craig Estes; and a special big hug
> and thanks to Chief of Staff Lewis Simmons, so helpful,
> Senator Kim Brimer, Senator Chris Harris, Representative
> Charlie Geren, Representative Jim Keffer, and many,
> many other legislators."

It is impossible not to notice that Mike Patterson basically read off the roll call for the lawmakers who had attended the meeting sixteen days earlier on September 8.

Mike Patterson then stated that he was not totally comfortable with the fact that his laundering plan for selling the property to the weekenders was being called *The Patterson Plan*. He summed up his discomfort with the following statement:

> "If it works, I would love for it to be called *The Patterson
> Plan*. But, if it doesn't, I'd rather it be called somebody
> else's plan."[126]

That statement received a nice round of laughter and put everyone at ease.

Mike Patterson put all of his cards on the table that day. He acknowledged that the board of the BRA had a duty to protect the state's assets. He also admitted that he wanted to avoid a competitive bidding process. And, he flat out stated that he wanted FERC to go away. Mike Patterson outlined the precepts of his proposal and claimed that his primary ambition was to avoid having the BRA sell the property under his home to a hedge fund in New York. In fact, he invoked the term "New York Hedge Fund" multiple times over the course of fifty-five minutes.

Mike Patterson explained to the board of the BRA that approximately 199 leaseholders had informed him that they would be willing to invest $100,000 in an investment fund constructed to purchase the property in question. In other words, fifteen percent of the leaseholders were not

---

[126] Special Board Meeting "Agenda Item 1," *Brazos River Authority Board Meeting Minutes*, September 22, 2008, accessed November 10, 2014. (Fast forward to 02:00). http://www.brazos.org/Portals/0/board_audio/09222008_SP-BRD2.MP3.

merely interested in gaining title to the property under their weekend homes—they were also interested in creating a Texas Hedge Fund that would enable them to profit off of their less wealthy neighbors.[127]

To complement the Texas Hedge Fund, Mike Patterson asserted that he had eight banks lined up to loan him between forty and fifty million dollars. He stated emphatically that his proposal was economically viable, and then he introduced his silver bullet—the ultimate protection for the leaseholders.

Mike Patterson explained that he had asked all of the leaseholders the following question:

> Would they buy their lot, at either 90 to 100 percent, of not fair market value, but the 2008 assessed value? One of the problems out there is the uncertainty of fair market value. There are people out there that are buying, paying so much for some properties, and it is a little bit of a distortion, I think, of what fair market value is – if not a distortion, at least a fear of it – the uncertainty of it.
>
> So our proposal is based on the 2008 assessed value. That is something that is very certain. It is very easy to determine and it was arrived at by a third party, by Donna Rhoades.

Donna Rhoades was the chief appraiser for the Palo Pinto Appraisal District who was responsible for determining the property tax values for the weekender's homes. Mike Patterson then informed those in attendance that ninety-three percent of the leaseholders had replied "You bet. I'll do that in five minutes!"

What he failed to mention was that there were so many protests and lawsuits filed against Donna Rhoades that the Palo Pinto Appraisal District had already rolled the 2008 assessments back to the 2007 values. On average, the original 2008 assessments were almost double those of 2007.[128]

---

[127] Precious few of them would actually get the opportunity to do so.

[128] Mike Patterson, "2008 Tax Assessment," *Patterson Equity Partners*, May 7, 2009, accessed July 23, 2011. https://web.archive.org/web/20151121224538/http://www.pklandpartnership.com/downloads/PK%20BRA%205.pdf.

On another historical note, a significant portion of the Q&A that followed Mike Patterson's presentation dealt with the topic of incorporating unincorporated areas, the need for strategic zoning, and the possible need to create one or more homeowners associations. Mike Patterson remarked that many in the area did not want to incur any new taxes for any reason. He then made this observation:

> "When you're house is burning, and you don't have the kind of fire equipment that you need to put it out, you're going to say 'well, gosh dog, you know—a little bit of new fire equipment sure would have been nice right about now."

Karma is a bitch. Less than three years later, a series of massive wildfires broke out around Possum Kingdom Lake and over two hundred homes burned to the ground.

What happened next during Mike Patterson's presentation is extremely difficult to explain. In what sounded like a confession, presiding officer Christopher DeCluitt informed his fellow board members about the meeting that Senator Averitt had held in Waco sixteen days earlier.

> "For the Board's edification, Senator Averitt invited us to a meeting. I attended that meeting, and it is what resulted in this agenda item today."[129]

At this point, the topic of conversation turned to the FERC buffer zone. As long as the hydroelectric power plant at the Morris Sheppard Dam was in existence, the Federal Energy Regulatory Commission was in control of the first twenty-five feet of the land surrounding the entire lake. As a result, the Brazos River Authority could not sell this property to the weekenders. Moreover, any U.S. citizen had the right to traverse this land if they desired.

---

[129] Special Board Meeting "Agenda Item 1," *Brazos River Authority Board Meeting Minutes*, September 22, 2008, accessed November 10, 2014. (Fast forward to 42:26). http://www.brazos.org/Portals/0/board_audio/09222008_SP-BRD2.MP3.

Imagine that you have a weekend home on Possum Kingdom Lake, and that you have gone to a lot of time and trouble to force the Brazos River Authority to sell you the property beneath your home through a straw-man transaction. Imagine further that you are having your first backyard barbeque to celebrate the transaction, and that you have invited 175 friends over to hear Cross Canadian Ragweed play some Country & Western music. Now imagine that a group of Texans are walking back and forth along the water's edge in your backyard carrying picket signs that read the following:

> "These people just screwed the taxpayers of Texas like a tied-up goat!"

And then, finally, imagine that the presence of the protestors in your backyard would be totally legal and there would not be one damn thing that you could do to stop it. Would that be an acceptable outcome? Neither the presiding officer of the BRA, Christopher DeCluitt, nor the president of the PKLA, Monte Land, seemed to think so.

At roughly forty-five minutes into Mike Patterson's presentation, Christopher DeCluitt stated his position on the FERC boundary:

> "We can't sell the FERC land because of our license. But, should FERC ever go away, I would be in favor of a remainder right."

To which Mike Patterson quickly replied,

> "Thank you! That's exactly, exactly – if you would do that for us..."

Before Mike Patterson could finish his sentence, Christopher DeCluitt asked Monte Land if the PKLA was taking a position on *The Patterson Plan*, or any other proposal.

> So Monte, my question is, you've represented that you represent a majority of the leaseholders. Mr. Cannedy

said earlier that y'all aren't taking a position. What is the position of the PKLA?

Monte Land walked up to the podium, cleared his throat, and stated the following for the record.

> Well, our position is—I hope that I can say this where everybody can understand it. We really appreciate what he is trying to do, and the efforts he's made. But for us to come out and totally support the positions that he has made, or his proposal, without knowing some of the unanswered questions— and primarily the main question is the one that you posed having to do with FERC—and what's going to happen to that FERC land.
>
> Uh, for example, right now I feel like I'm leasing a lakefront property. I don't want to buy a lakefront property and have it turn in to a lake-view property—not being able to at least control, or have some kind of control, over my water front.
>
> Right now, we really haven't gotten together as a board. And we really haven't set a position. We are waiting to see exactly what this proposal is going to do. Our position is we want to buy the property. But we also want some protection as far as that front, that FERC property that's on our waterfront.

As the conversations continued, a spirit of agreement developed that the leaseholders should be entitled to receive the FERC property for free if FERC should ever go away. Would anyone care to guess what is going to happen to FERC and the hydroelectric plant at Possum Kingdom Lake?

Eventually, a few of the board members got up the courage to ask a few hard questions. The first of these was Jean Kilgore. Given that *The Patterson Plan* was predicated on reselling the property to the weekenders at 90% of the 2008 assessed values, Jean Kilgore had only one question to ask:

I have a question. I have been reading in the paper about PK and I understand that the county appraisal district is having a lot of problems. And, all of these hands went up and everybody would buy their land at the county appraised value now.

How many of you have protested your land value and had it lowered?[130]

This question resulted in ten long seconds of dead silence that was broken only by Christopher DeCluitt asking the following question, "Any further questions?"

There was one. Carolyn Johnson asked Mike Patterson about the part of his proposal that requested a right of first refusal to beat any superior bid to his offer.

When you were talking, you were saying something about "if we went ahead with the third party open bidding," which I think we are required to do—I'm not sure, but I think we are—you wanted the right of first refusal. Would that still be open bidding?

In response, Mike Patterson put the rest of his cards on the table:

I don't think that you have to go through open bidding. I think that you are subject to the Water Code. And, I think this is surplus property. And, I think you have to get a fair value for it. But, I don't think you have to put us through the open bid process. That puts us at a big disadvantage.

I'm not telling you we won't try to pony up and come do what we can do. But, it puts us at a big disadvantage, just because it costs so much money to organize 199 people or however many there are.

[130] Special Board Meeting "Agenda Item 1," *Brazos River Authority Board Meeting Minutes*, September 22, 2008, accessed November 10, 2014. (Fast forward to 56:20). http://www.brazos.org/Portals/0/board_audio/09222008_SP-BRD2.MP3.

I know that $82.2 million works. It works with eight banks. They say "Patterson, if you'll guarantee it, and you'll get $30 or $40 million into it—we'll bank it."

I'm confident about that.

In response to this, Director Johnson then added her usual pragmatic observation: "The money seems to be coming down."

She was right. During the legislative battle in 2007, the argument was whether the total price should be $100 million or $200 million. Now the offer on the table was $82.2 million and the opposition was fading away.

Prior to his presentation, Mike Patterson had granted an interview to the Mineral Wells Index regarding the proposal that he would be offering to the Brazos River Authority that evening. The resulting article that was written by Libby Cluett was appropriately entitled "One Man's Plan." The article ended with the following quotes from Mike Patterson:

"When I started out I was told this wouldn't work out and nobody would listen. I've been pleasantly surprised that there have been a lot of people wanting to listen," said Patterson.

"We won't make everyone happy," he added, but said this proposal is "a balance of four things—it gives lessees what they need most, gives the BRA a reasonable exit strategy, and gives investors and lenders a sound vehicle to do the deal."

If anything, Patterson claims, "I am guilty of good intentions. Let's just try to solve a problem. What we can't do is nothing. We'll just end up fighting with each other. What we need to do is leave egos at the door and treat everybody fairly—BRA and lessees."

"I don't fault anybody. It has evolved into what it is," Patterson said. "Change is inevitable. You have to decide if you can control a soft landing."

"I don't want to look back in two years from now and say, 'I could have done something,'" he added.

"We want an opportunity to buy whatever they're selling, especially as it relates to land under our houses. We're doctors and lawyers and bankers and bakers, not developers," said Patterson, who said he wants to make "a more palatable option."[131]

It seems odd that Mike Patterson would highlight the fact that his pool of investors consisted of a bunch of rich guys who were not actual real estate developers. This is especially intriguing considering that, for approximately thirty minutes on September 22, 2008, there was actually a modicum of competition.

---

[131] Libby Cluett, "One Man's Plan," *Mineral Wells Index*, September 22, 2008, accessed July 10, 2010.
https://web.archive.org/web/20080927030255/http://www.mineralwellsindex.com/local/local_story_266091033.html.

Chapter 12

THE COMPETITION

Following Mike Patterson's presentation, a gentleman by the name of Craig Walker, who owned a company known as Clearview Capital, addressed the crowd at the BRA's meeting on September 22, 2008.

Craig Walker was an accomplished developer at Possum Kingdom Lake. Mr. Walker had the developments of The Ranch and The Harbor to his credit and this made him a serious competitor. Five years earlier, he had made an unsolicited cash offer to buy all of the BRA's real estate holdings at Possum Kingdom Lake. Since that time, he had been monitoring the topic of divestiture and was prepared to participate in the process.

During his opening remarks, Walker took the newly constituted board of the BRA through his professional pedigree. It was substantial.

> We have a long term interest in the lake. We are heavily invested and we have been for 13 years. And, we continue to invest. We work next door to the Brazos River Authority's office there at the lake. We border their property.
>
> We have a track record of over 70 acquisitions all over the country – close to $700 million worth of acquisitions, in excess of 18,000 acres of residential development, over six million feet of commercial buildings, four golf courses, two hotels, 900 marina slips, and a ski resort.

Um, we will not go to Wall Street. We don't go up there. That is not how we fund our current business. We more than likely will go to just a few private individuals with private equity for this transaction.

With the credit crisis, you know, naming off a bank that will give you a commitment letter to close today, um, may not be worth the paper that it's written on. It is a very difficult market, and that is our specialty – structuring transactions with heavy private individual equity.[132]

Unfortunately for Craig Walker, he was not politically connected. While Mike Patterson had opened his remarks by thanking a great many politicians "that really helped open doors," Craig Walker stated, "I am not a lawyer and I am not very political. I have not contacted any congressmen regarding this issue." That might have been strike one for Craig Walker.

In essence, what Craig Walker did was simply take Mike Patterson's proposal and increase the offering price by $5 million. The pot was now up to $87.2 million and it appeared that a bidding war was breaking out. The primary difference between Craig Walker's proposal and that of Mike Patterson was the source of funds. Mike Patterson was touting a syndicate of bankers while Craig Walker stressed that he would be relying primarily on private equity. This might have been strike two.

One of the key elements of Mike Patterson's proposal that was repeated by Craig Walker was the rental rate that would be offered to any leaseholder who chose not to purchase their lot. In both proposals, the annual rental rate went immediately to 6% of the assessed value of the property.

Director Wade Gear took exception to this. He posed the following question to both Craig Walker and Mike Patterson:

This is a question for both you and Mike. One of your options is the lease modification option and both of y'all go straight to 6% of the currently assessed value with an annual CPI increase. We've gotten lambasted for a proposal that gets us to 6% in 25 or 30 years.

Mixed laughter and snickers floated across the room.

How do you address that to these folks? Because, that is what has gotten up the fervor down in Austin?

Everyone ran down to Austin and said we can't afford this. But, yet, this is an option that both of you guys have presented.

And, what that tells me is – it gives the folks who have the ability to buy, the option to buy, and the folks who can't buy and have to keep on leasing are kind of S.O.L.[133]

This drew a nice round of applause.

Roughly ten more minutes of general discussion ensued and then BRA director Billy Wayne Moore put the last question on the table. He directed his observations to Craig Walker regarding the notion of granting Mike Patterson a right of first refusal.

Moore: Mr. Patterson has asked for the right of first refusal to come back and beat you by a buck. I notice that your offer is already $6 million over his.

Walker: It's really a net $5 [million].

Moore: I understand, but my point is, if the right of first refusal is granted, you have three options.

One is, continue with the bid as written. Two, throw up your hands and say it doesn't make any difference what I bid so I'm going home. Or three, push it as high as possible. Uh, have you considered your position if that right of first refusal is given?

---

[133] Shit out of luck.

Walker: I would ask you not to. My mama taught me to not give away rights of first refusal and get them whenever you can. But, uh, you know, that's a handy thing.

This comment invoked a room full of belly-laughs and more than a few "Amens."

> Um, but I think it would be – uh, a first right of refusal for a buck over would prevent our team from engaging. I would probably have to go to the bench. So...[134]

The tension in the room was inflating. Presiding Officer Christopher DeCluitt attempted to let some of pressure out of the balloon by asking yet again, "Any other questions?"

After the presentations were complete, Presiding Officer DeCluitt informed those in attendance that he had been remiss in not informing the audience of the relationship between Mary Ward and Mike Patterson. At 1:35:39 in the audio minutes, DeCluitt yielded the floor to Ms. Ward who made the following statement:

> Yes, I do have a statement. Because I'm employed as a Regional President with Southwest Securities, FSB, and Mike Patterson serves on the Board of Directors for that bank; although I've been advised by BRA counsel that I am not required by law to abstain; I feel that in order to avoid any appearance of impropriety, that I would, uh, abstain from any discussion or voting on any proposal that Mr. Patterson is involved in.[135]

---

[134] Special Board Meeting "Agenda Item 1," *Brazos River Authority Board Meeting Minutes*, September 22, 2008, accessed November 10, 2014. (Fast forward to 01:33:00).
http://www.brazos.org/Portals/0/board_audio/09222008_SP-BRD2.MP3.
[135] Special Board Meeting "Agenda Item 1," *Brazos River Authority Board Meeting Minutes*, September 22, 2008, accessed November 10, 2014. (Fast forward to 01:35:39).
http://www.brazos.org/Portals/0/board_audio/09222008_SP-BRD2.MP3.

Pay close attention to how Mary Ward votes in the future.

As she had done with Mike Patterson, Libby Cluett interviewed Craig Walker for the Mineral Wells Index and provided a balanced article on Mike Patterson's primary competitor.

> Walker's experience includes 20 years in the real estate business, including 13 years at PK Lake.
>
> "Thirteen years ago we purchased almost 1,800 acres of land, with about 5 miles of shoreline. We developed about 1,500 acres into The Ranch on Possum Kingdom," said Walker. "It's been very successful. We are currently developing 300 acres of that original land into The Harbor."
>
> Walker explained that The Harbor is a combination of lots, condos, real log cabins, cottages, a full-service marina and a restaurant. He added that Clearview has control of building the units and said they just sold their first condominium building.
>
> "We're developers; we're developers there," he said, citing that Clearview's projects are "high quality and sensitive to the shoreline."

A reasonably prudent person in the room that day would likely have concluded that Craig Walker had the upper hand. Mike Patterson was fronting a startup investment group that had not even been formed yet. Craig Walker and Clearview Capital had a stellar track record, and they had substantial experience developing property around Possum Kingdom Lake. Since this is the *Tale of the River Card*, and not the tale of *Walker: Possum Ranger*, would anyone care to guess how this competition is going to turn out?

Libby Cluett also interviewed Jim Keffer's chief of staff, Trent Thomas, for her article entitled "One Man's Plan Becomes That of Another."

> Trent Thomas, aide for State Rep. Jim Keffer, said the issue is, "Very complicated." He said that the goals are

to protect residential lessees whether or not they become landowners as well as protect the lake.

He said lessees at the meeting were concerned about what will happen to the undeveloped BRA-owned areas and the Federal Energy Regulatory Commission land, which the BRA manages along the lake shoreline.

Members of the PKLA have concerns about the FERC "buffer zone," which cannot be deeded to a potential landowner, nor can it be developed or controlled with fencing or structures, according to Thomas.

"People want to own their property down to the water, which is understandable, but our federal regulations preclude an individual from owning that property," he said.

Thomas said he and Representative Keffer advised Patterson Monday to get together with the PKLA and their board of directors to discuss third-party divestiture and their concerns related to his proposal. He said Patterson has been very open and Thomas applauds his efforts at taking the lead in seeking a divestiture solution.

"There's been a lot of discussion between lessees and other elected officials. We will all need to be on the same page when we go into session in January 2009," said Thomas.[136]

I cannot help but notice that Trent Thomas was not quoted as having said the he and his boss, Representative Jim Keffer, had advised both Mike Patterson *and* Craig Walker to get with the leadership of the PKLA and get on the same page. But then again, I am reminded that Jim Keffer was renting his office from Southwest Securities, FSB and not from Clearview Capital.

---

[136] Libby Cluett, "One Man's Divestiture Plan Becomes That of Another," *Mineral Wells Index*, September 24, 2008, accessed July 10, 1010. https://web.archive.org/web/20080928121904/http://www.mineralwellsindex.com/local/local_story_268100313.html.

While Monte Land of the PKLA had declined to take a public position on Mike Patterson's proposal during the open meeting, the PKLA met five days later to discuss the topics at hand. Later that evening, the minutes from their meeting were posted on the PKLA's website.

September 27, 2008

Possum Kingdom Lake Association Board of Directors Meeting

On Saturday, September 27, 2008, the Directors met in Bryan Insurance office at 9:30am in Graham.

Directors present at the meeting were Monte Land, Dennis Cannedy, Greg Fitzgerald, Scott Wheatley, Vic Clesi, Jay Turner, Mike Veresh, Paul Pulliam, Tom Harris and John Connally. Visitors present were Robert Aldrich, George Gault, Jim Hamlett, and Jim, Linda and Hank Lattimore. Not present was Kerry Groves.

President Monte Land called the meeting to order. Membership of the Association is at an all-time high of 867. A financial report of the general funds and the Property Protection fund were provided.

Agenda

> 1. Report on the BRA Board meeting September 22, 2008 was brief since we had six directors in Waco attending this meeting.

> 2. Third party proposal presentations made by Mike Patterson and Craig Walker were discussed. Directors appreciated Patterson's efforts in developing his proposal. Questions arose about the FERC project area regarding how this footage would be handled after a 3rd party sale and exactly what land was being considered for this sale. There was concern why some land was being removed from the all-inclusive sale, example commercial leases.

The board voted to take no position on a third party sale. There were too many unanswered questions.

3. Legislative Report was given by all the Directors that have had meetings with Legislators. Senators Kip Averitt, Craig Estes and Chris Harris have all been in meetings with PKLA directors. Representatives Dan Branch, Rick Hardcastle, Joe Hefllin, David Farabee, and Jim Keffer have all been approached about legislation in the next session. Directors were encouraged to keep sharing names and information with other legislators. Membership will be asked to help contact legislators in the future to achieve momentum. Directors' position is to actively pursue a legislative solution for divestiture. The Membership of this Association has indicated that 90% of them support the sale of leases to each leaseholder. PKLA member David George will be in charge of membership efforts at reaching the State legislators about forthcoming legislation.

A motion was made to adjourn. Motion passed. The meeting adjourned at 11:45am.[137]

In essence, the Possum Kingdom Lake Association was posting a position statement to the Brazos River Authority regarding Mike Patterson's proposal. They were also advertising the roster of legislators who would be championing their cause. And most important, they were putting the BRA on notice that the FERC buffer zone was still a major point of contention.

The Brazos River Authority got the message.

---

[137] PKLA Staff, "Possum Kingdom Lake Association Board of Directors Meeting," *Possum Kingdom Lake Association*, September 27, 2008, accessed July 10, 2011. https://web.archive.org/web/20151122002009/http://pklakeassn.org/Minutes%20 9-27-08.htm.
http://pklakeassn.org/Minutes%209-27-08.htm.

Chapter 13

THE IMMACULATE RESOLUTION

Thirty-five days after Mike Patterson and Craig Walker presented their competing proposals to the Brazos River Authority, the board of the BRA reconvened to take the next step. On October 27, 2008, the Board held a regularly scheduled meeting that included *Agenda Item 13: Possum Kingdom Bid Document*.

Matt Phillips, the BRA Manager of Government and Customer Relations, addressed the board to explain *Agenda Item 13*. He stated that he was presenting a resolution for adoption by the board that "would give staff the authority to issue an RFB" for the sale of the lakefront property.[138] He also asserted that, "some, if not all, of the conditions" contained in *the Patterson Plan* had been incorporated into the resolution.

Matt Phillips further explained exactly what was being offered for sale.

> First of all, let's talk about what we're selling. At this time, what we would propose that this RFB include is just the developed property – just the leased residential property and *some* commercial property which is located wholly outside of FERC. We have about 19 of those properties.
>
> Un-leased, or the undeveloped property, would not be included in what we're proposing today. Uh, there are a lot of different issues associated with that property that kind

---

[138] RFB: Request for Bids.

of set it apart from the developed land. And so, we would hold it out at this time.

As to lessee protections, the RFB will require any purchaser to ratify any current leases, which is an obvious thing, and, also as far as options for lessee protections.

Um, it would include all of the options that are laid out in the Patterson and Walker proposals. I believe there were five of those. There were two purchase options, and there were two lease options, and there was a fallback option which was the eight-year protection that the board adopted.[139]

Within these two minutes of testimony, Matt Phillips eliminated any competition to Mike Patterson in the form of a developer. If there was no undeveloped land being sold, there was nothing to develop. If there was nothing to develop, why would Craig Walker or his development company be interested? Evidently he wasn't. The public record never heard from Craig Walker again and Mike Patterson's primary competitor disappeared from the process.

Moreover, the only parties who would be interested in responding to the RFB would be limited to someone willing to serve as a conduit for the wealthy weekenders who wanted to purchase their property. At the same time, any such third-party purchaser would have to be willing to serve as a slum lord for those inhabitants who could not afford to purchase the dirt beneath their fishing cabins.

Matt Phillips also reversed the assertions that Presiding Officer Christopher DeCluitt had made six months earlier when he first proposed that the BRA pursue a third party sale of the property. As a reminder, here is how the newly appointed Presiding Officer, Christopher DeCluitt, had framed his motion back in April 2008:

---

[139] Board Meeting "Agenda Item 13," *Brazos River Authority Board Meeting Minutes*, October 27, 2008, accessed November 10, 2014. (Fast forward to 02:00). http://www.brazos.org/Portals/0/board_audio/10272008_BRD10.MP3.

I move that Staff is directed to develop a proposed request for bids to purchase all of the Brazos River Authority's land at Possum Kingdom Lake, outside the FERC project area, and that the request for bids include protection for the lessees' existing rights and provide a right for the lessees to purchase their lots, excluding property necessary for present and future Brazos River Authority operations."[140]

At that time, Director Wade Gear had sought to clarify DeCluitt's position.

And that's all of the land in total, correct?

To which Presiding Officer DeCluitt had replied,

That is all of the land. Leased, un-leased, and again, excluding what may be determined, may be necessary, for the operations of the BRA.

In response to this statement, Director Jean Kilgore had asked her incredibly uncomfortable, yet most prescient of questions:

I have a question. This couldn't be construed as a way of getting around the fact that we can't sell to individuals, that we might have a sham company or something take this over?[141]

To which DeCluitt had replied at the time,

No. That's where the bidding process comes into play.

[140] Board Meeting "Agenda Item 9," *Brazos River Authority Board Meeting Minutes*, April 28, 2008, accessed November 10, 2014. (Fast forward to 09:15). http://www.brazos.org/Portals/0/board_audio/04282008_BRD10.mp3.
[141] Board Meeting "Agenda Item 9," *Brazos River Authority Board Meeting Minutes*, April 28, 2008, accessed November 10, 2014. (Fast forward to 11:34). http://www.brazos.org/Portals/0/board_audio/04282008_BRD10.mp3.

With any potential land developers taken out of the equation, the bidding process that Presiding Officer DeCluitt had been touting would indeed become critical. Fortunately for the taxpayers of Texas, the board had authorized the CEO of the BRA to hire a firm to market the property five months earlier on May 10, 2008. As a reminder, the text of that resolution read as follows:

> **BE IT RESOLVED** that the Board of Directors of the Brazos River Authority hereby authorizes the General Manager/CEO to seek proposals from firms having the professional expertise to assist the Brazos River Authority in managing, marketing, and evaluating bids for the sale of the Brazos River Authority real property interests at Possum Kingdom Lake.[142]

Unfortunately for the taxpayers of Texas, no one had gotten off of their lazy ass and actually done so. Even more unfortunate is the fact that the BRA did not actually hire a firm to market the property until there were only twenty days left for someone other than Mike Patterson to submit a bid. I would suggest to you that, by the time they did so, it was way too late.

Matt Phillips went on to discuss the issues surrounding the FERC-regulated property that surrounded the shoreline. He informed the board that the BRA had asked FERC for permission to sell that property along with the rest of their holdings. In response, the BRA received a simple but steadfast "No." Matt Phillips then explained that the BRA would be pursuing other options to make FERC go away.

After roughly eleven minutes of explanation, Matt Phillips finally read the text of a resolution that must have seemed like it was written by the finger of God if your name was Mike Patterson. The same would have been true if you were a leaseholder, or a banker who was funding the deal.

Allow me to present the "Immaculate Resolution" in its entirety, and explain each provision along the way.

---

[142] BRA Staff, "Board Actions–Special Meeting," *Brazos River Authority*, May 20, 2008, accessed June 13, 2014. http://wayback.archive-it.org/414/20090705213233/http://www.brazos.org/board_actions/05-20-08_Quarterly_Board_Actions.pdf.

RESOLUTION OF THE BOARD OF DIRECTORS OF
THE BRAZOS RIVER AUTHORITY
October 27, 2008
Agenda Item 13
Possum Kingdom Bid Document

"**BE IT RESOLVED**, that the Board of Directors of the Brazos River Authority hereby directs staff to issue a request for bids for the purchase of Brazos River Authority's property which is subject to (i) a residential lease, save and except that portion of the leased premises that is located within the Federal Energy Regulatory Commission (FERC) project boundary or (ii) a commercial lease where the leased premises is wholly located outside the FERC project boundary; and

The opening paragraph of the "Immaculate Resolution" took the undeveloped land off of the table. The only property that was being offered for sale was the leased lots that needed to be laundered through a middle man or taken over by a landlord.

BE IT FURTHER RESOLVED that the request for bids require that any purchaser must assume and ratify exiting leases and for a period of a least one year after the purchase offer the following options to current residential and commercial lessees:

    1. Purchase the lessee's leased property in cash or through preferred lender financing for 90% of 2008 land only assessed value (as determined by county appraisal district).

This first resale option mandated by the "Immaculate Resolution" not only venerated Mike Patterson's banking cartel, it also required that any competing bidder also establish their own syndicate of "preferred lenders." Craig Walker, Mike Patterson's only competitor five weeks earlier, had stated publicly that he did not intend to incorporate any bank debt into his purchase of the property. This would have left Craig Walker poorly positioned to create his own syndicate of "preferred lenders."

Additionally, the first resale option established a fixed resell price that was tied to the arbitrary 2008 appraisal district values. These had been rolled back to the 2007 values, subsequent to Donna Rhoades' failed attempt to bring the assessments up to par.

> 2. Purchase the lessee's property via seller financing for 100% of 2008 land only assessed value (as determined by county appraisal district).

The second option mandated that any third-party purchaser would then become a lender of last resort for any leaseholder who could not qualify for a conventional loan. Again, the sale price was tied to a fixed, arbitrary value. And again, this provision would have been a discouragement for most traditional real estate investors.

> 3. A new 99 year lease with a rental rate of 6% of 2008 assessed land value with an annual CPI increase. The new 99 year lease must also include an option to purchase at the tax assessed value without any exemptions as of the time of purchase (but not less than the 2008 tax assessed value).

The third option mandated that any third-party purchaser would become a landlord who would charge rent at a specified rate for the next century. The winning landlord would also be required to provide a purchase option to the individual leaseholders that would exist for ninety-nine years.

> 4. For over-65 lessees, the option to sign a new 10 year lease with a rental rate of 6% of 2008 assessed land value with an option to defer all

lease payments until the end of the 10 year term
and also includes an option to purchase at the
tax assessed value without any exemptions as of
the time of purchase (but not less than the 2008
tax assessed value).

The fourth option mandated strikes me as nothing short of predatory.
Those leaseholders who were over the age of sixty-five would be allowed
to keep living on their property for the next ten years without paying
anything whatsoever. However, at the end of that ten-year period, they
would either have to true-up with the third-party purchaser on the deferred
rent or surrender their property—house included.

5. The option to stay on the lessee's current
lease and receive protections previously adopted
by the Brazos River Authority Board, which are:

i. Ratification of existing lease

ii. Eight (8) years of rental protection – purchaser must use
the current Brazos River Authority lease rate methodology
for that time period

iii. Eight (8) years to purchase lease hold property at the
greater of (a) the tax assessed value of the land only at the
time of purchase or (b) the 2008 tax assessed land only
value

iv. Extension of any lease as necessary to allow the full
eight-year (8) period of time to purchase; and

The fifth option stipulated was a catch-all. This option simply provided
an existing leaseholder with eight years to figure out which of the other
four buckets they belonged in.

BE IT FURTHER RESOLVED that the request for
bids require any purchaser to purchase all roads which
are currently maintained by Brazos River Authority and

maintain such roads (or cause to be maintained), provide an access easement to Brazos River Authority, and ensure that the users of the leased property and property retained by Brazos River Authority are able to access and use such roads; and

This provision required that any third-party purchaser also be willing to become a paving company that would maintain the asphalt roads that surrounded the lake. In October 2008, the stock market was crashing and very few real estate investors were ready to repurpose themselves as road maintenance workers.

BE IT FURTHER RESOLVED that the request for bids may include any small, undeveloped strips between leased lots and roads which the Brazos River Authority determines are not otherwise usable or required for Brazos River Authority's current or future operations; and

We will be discussing these "undeveloped strips" in detail later. For the time being; let me simply say that an undeveloped strip would eventually turn into some free land. If you happened to be a major league baseball player by the last name of Wells or a professional golfer by the last name of Jacobsen, an "undeveloped strip" would eventually turn into quite the windfall.

BE IT FURTHER RESOLVED that the request for bids encourage, but not require any purchaser to deed at no cost to the current lessee those divested properties currently leased by non-profit organizations and to set aside funding for municipal incorporation; and

What an incredibly thoughtful thing to do. Who could possibly be opposed to giving the Boy Scout's or the Volunteer Fire Department their land for free? Of course, if you were Mike Patterson, or a competing bidder who was coming over the top, you would be able to deduct these charitable gifts from the profits derived from the transaction.

BE IT FURTHER RESOLVED that the request for bids notify the prospective bidders that the Brazos River Authority is in the process of requesting approval from FERC that all residential leased property located within the FERC project boundary be excluded from the FERC project boundary, and that if at the time a bid is accepted FERC has approved such exclusion, the bid will include such property and its associated leases; and

Simply put, this provision announced to all parties concerned that the BRA was taking steps to ensure that the leaseholders could own their property all the way to the water's edge. FERC was going to be eliminated from the equation one way or another.[143]

BE IT FURTHER RESOLVED that if at the time a bid is accepted FERC has not authorized the Brazos River Authority to exclude from the FERC project boundary those portions of the residential leased property located within the FERC project boundary, only those portions of the property and associated leases that are outside the FERC project boundary will be assigned to the purchaser, and purchaser will become the lessor as to those portions of the property so purchased and covered under such existing leases; and the Brazos River Authority will remain as lessor under such existing leases to the extent such leases are within the FERC project boundary until such time as the leases expire or are otherwise terminated; and

In other words, a third-party purchaser would not be required to deal with FERC. The BRA would remain the landlord for the property on the water's edge. However, the BRA would not be charging the leaseholders rent for the use of this property.

[143] Libby Cluett, "BRA Divestiture Takes Big Step," *Mineral Wells Index*, October 28, 2008, accessed February 1, 2012 (since removed). http://www.mineralwellsindex.com/local/x154989797/BRA-divestiture-takes-big-step/print.

BE IT FURTHER RESOLVED that the Board of Directors of the Brazos River Authority hereby directs staff to evaluate granting a residual interest in residential leased property located within the FERC project boundary whereby at the time the FERC license terminates or such property is excluded from the FERC project boundary, such property shall revert to the then-current owner of the land adjacent to such property; and

This meant, hypothetically, that if the hydroelectric plant that gave rise to FERC's jurisdiction around the lake were ever to be decommissioned, the leaseholders would be given automatic title to the FERC buffer zone between their individual lots and the water's edge at no additional cost. In effect, this provision put the hydroelectric plant on the endangered species list.

BE IT FURTHER RESOLVED that the Board of Directors of the Brazos River Authority hereby directs staff to evaluate options for continuing to provide lessees and/or adjacent landowners the same level of access to the FERC project area that exists today while remaining compliant with all FERC requirements;

This simply meant that until the BRA could make FERC go away, the leaseholders would have to put up with people being able to walk across their property.

BE IT FURTHER RESOLVED that the Board of Directors of the Brazos River Authority hereby directs staff to pursue submitting to FERC an Application to Amend the License to exclude those portions of the residential leased property located within the FERC project boundary from the FERC project boundary, and mitigate this exclusion by placing other Brazos River Authority property within the FERC project boundary; and

And finally, this paragraph in the resolution meant that the newly constituted board of the Brazos River Authority fully intended to ensure that FERC went away. The next plan of attack was to attempt to swap the FERC buffer zone around the water's edge for other property that the BRA was holding. FERC would later reject that offer but this paragraph can be construed as evidence that in late 2008, the hydroelectric plant at Possum Kingdom Lake was still a viable asset.

> **BE IT FURTHER RESOLVED** that the Board of Directors of the Brazos River Authority hereby directs staff to develop with outside counsel Declarations of Restrictions, Covenants and Conditions to protect the scenic value and the environment in and around Possum Kingdom Lake, consistent with the provisions of the Shoreline Management Guide and the requirements of the FERC License, such Declarations to be included in the RFB and filed in the property records of the counties where the land subject to the RFB is located.

> The aforementioned resolution was approved by the Board of Directors of the Brazos River Authority on October 27, 2008, to certify which witness my hand and seal.

> Christopher DeCluitt

> Presiding Officer[144]

In summary, the "Immaculate Resolution" eliminated all traditional real estate developers from the field of potential bidders. If that seems like a bold assertion—keep reading. The "Immaculate Resolution" also venerated Mike Patterson's syndicate of "preferred lenders" and required that any competing bidder employ a syndicate of their own. More importantly, the resolution adopted on October 27, 2008 signaled the BRA's intention

---

[144] BRA Staff, "Agenda Item 13, Possum Kingdom Bid Document," *Brazos River Authority*, October 27, 2008, accessed November 25, 2010. https://web.archive.org/web/20090705212256/http://www.brazos.org/board_actions/10-27-08_Quarterly_Board_Actions.pdf.

of doing whatever was necessary to ensure that the leaseholders would eventually enjoy exclusive access to their property down to the water's edge.

After the resolution was formally read by Matt Phillips, a process that took almost five minutes, the board of the Brazos River Authority was polled. The vote to proceed with the issuance of a Request for Bids was unanimous including the two "yes" votes cast by Director Peter Bennis and Director Mary Ward. Obviously, Mary Ward was not quite ready to start abstaining.

From start to finish, *Agenda Item 13: Possum Kingdom Bid Document* consumed seventeen minutes and forty seconds. During the entire presentation, not one single board member asked a question or made a comment on the public record.

Prior to the official reading of the resolution, Matt Phillips disclosed that the board's current course of action might require the sanctification of the Texas legislature. He also informed those in attendance, and the rest of the public, that there was a bill in the works. And, he informed anyone who cared to listen that the BRA was being left out of that loop.

> With regard to the legislature, and this is something that I wanted to address because Mr. Staley talked about it earlier. It may be, that while the board is pursuing a third party option, it may be that legislation is necessary to validate some of the things that we're thinking about doing. And we would obviously want to partner with the folks at the lake to make sure everybody is ok with it.
>
> I think that that is something that we would need—that we would all need to go there together if such legislation is needed.
>
> Um, if we move forward and do pursue a third party RFB, and it doesn't work out, I think we will all end up down in Austin trying to pursue some sort of legislation.
>
> It is our understanding that there is legislation out there. Uh, BRA has not seen it. We have not been made privy to it. We would obviously, as Mr. Staley indicated, be willing to and wanting to work on it. Because, as the entity that

would have to implement it—we would pretty much need to be at the table for that.

So we would definitely want to be part of it.[145]

As a follow up to the board meeting that was held on October 27, 2008, Libby Cluett of the Mineral Wells Index interviewed Mike Patterson for his comments.

> Lessee Michael Patterson, who submitted an all-inclusive bid to purchase BRA land for a lessee group, told the Index Tuesday, "I think [Monday] was a great day for all PK BRA lessees and the BRA. We, the lessees, got what we asked for. I cannot imagine the BRA being any more accommodating."
>
> "We don't know when [the RFB] will be posted," said BRA Public Information Officer Judi Pierce. "There are things we have to do with FERC first before posting the bid."
>
> She said the board removed the option of selling unencumbered areas – areas not under lease. Currently the BRA is discussing giving about 425 acres, all open land with no leases and contiguous with Possum Kingdom State Park, back to the park, she added.
>
> "Not having to deal with the undeveloped properties will make my effort much simpler," Patterson stated. "Once we know which commercial properties will be included, I will adjust my bid accordingly."
>
> Patterson explained that the BRA took elements of the proposal he presented to the board last month and incorporated these into their resolution.
>
> "I think that is a very good thing," he said. "My proposal had four proposed options for lessees (two sale and two

---

[145] Board Meeting "Agenda Item 13," *Brazos River Authority Board Meeting Minutes*, October 27, 2008, accessed November 10, 2014. (Fast forward 08:20). http://www.brazos.org/Portals/0/board_audio/10272008_BRD10.MP3.

lease) that we did not have before. Those options are now imbedded in the BRA's RFB."[146]

So in other words, the *Patterson Plan* had now become the Brazos River Authority's plan. Not only was Mike Patterson's scheme for reselling the property adopted as the BRA's scheme, but that pesky undeveloped land that a land developer would be interested in was now off of the table. Is it just me, or is this deal starting to look like a tailor-made transaction?

---

[146] Libby Cluett, "BRA Divestiture Takes Big Step," *Mineral Wells Index*, October 28, 2008, accessed February 1, 2012 (since removed). http://www.mineralwellsindex. com/local/x154989797/BRA-divestiture-takes-big-step/print.

Chapter 14

ANYONE BUT CRADDICK

Let's rewind the clock to the final hours of the legislative session in 2007 when House Speaker Tom Craddick was self-imploding and under attack by Jim Keffer and other Republicans. While this attempted palace coup ultimately failed, the seeds were sown for an all-out battle at the beginning of the next legislative session. This first failed attempt to oust Speaker Tom Craddick occurred roughly two weeks after the first failed attempt to force the Brazos River Authority to sell the shoreline of Possum Kingdom Lake to the weekenders.

Over the months that followed the 2007 session, State Representative Jim Keffer convinced himself and many others that he could—and should—become the next Speaker of the House in Texas. Keffer enlisted the services of Bryan Eppstein and began paying tens of thousands of dollars to the locally famous political consultant. He then spent the majority of 2008 campaigning for the speaker's office. The Austin Chronicle filed a report projecting the impending showdown on October 30, 2008:

> It's scarcely a secret that a swathe of House Democrats and Republicans hope that Speaker Tom Craddick's gavel-swinging days are over. But now, in a pretty brazen step, Representative Jim Keffer, R-Eastland, has announced that it's a done deal, and he may well be the new sheriff in town.

He explains that he spent the last year talking to both Democrat and Republican reps about the future, and it sounds like he thinks he has the votes to take the speaker's seat come January.

This comes' after Democratic House Caucus Leader Jim Dunnam has already said that Craddick is out as speaker. Plus, as Burnt Orange Report has noticed, Craddick has had to pour $1.5 million of his own cash into his state house race to see off Democrat Bill Dingus.[147]

Consistent with the Austin Chronicle's article, State Representative Jim Keffer had indeed issued a press release on the previous day entitled *"The Times They Are-a-Changing."* His remarks suggested that he was convinced that he had his hand wrapped securely around the Speaker's gavel.

"Within 24 hours of the polls closing after Tuesday's historic election, I predict there will be a new consensus choice for Texas House Speaker." Keffer said he plans to consolidate his Republican and Democratic support for Texas House Speaker on election night, Tuesday, November 4th. "I will begin updating the press beginning at 8:00 p.m. on election night," said Keffer. Keffer has extensively traveled the state this past year meeting with House members and state house candidates, often times spending the night with them in their homes.

After meeting with House members in their districts, Keffer said he is "100% sure a new Speaker for the Texas House of Representatives will be chosen for next session." According to Keffer, "regardless of how the Republican and Democrat numbers change in the Texas House, there is a majority desire for a new Speaker." "The sentiment

---

[147] Richard Whittaker, "Keffer Targets Craddick," *The Austin Chronicle*, October 30, 2008, accessed August 25, 2011. http://www.austinchronicle.com/blogs/news/2008-10-30/696658/.

for change is not personal, members in the Texas House just want bipartisan leadership which is committed to restoring the rules of conduct and fairness" Keffer stated. "Those who served last session remember all too well the four months of absolute chaos that preceded Craddick's last minute claim of absolute authority."

"The issues and challenges before Texas are all too serious to repeat this chaotic journey again." Keffer said he has offered one important promise to his House colleagues, "I will be a Speaker for the members, not the special interests." Keffer said he also supports a three term limit on the Speaker's post and strongly favors returning to House rules on seniority to insure fairness in committee appointments. "When I came to Austin, there was an orderly process to the House," Keffer said.

"It's time to heed the call and put our State House back together."[148]

Jim Keffer's optimism regarding his chances to become the next Speaker of the Texas House was genuine. None other than the highly regarded *Texas Tribune* recognized Keffer as having been the early frontrunner to challenge Tom Craddick in 2009.

The race happened against an interesting political backdrop. After the elections of November 2008, the House was divided almost evenly among party lines –76 Republican, 74 Democrats. Members were set to come together on the first day of the session – Jan. 13, 2009 – to elect a speaker.

Just weeks after the November election, Craddick had nine opponents for his job – five Democrats, four Republicans. The prominent Republican challenger to first emerge was

---

[148] Ross Ramsey, "The Week in the Rearview Mirror," *The Texas Tribune*, October 27, 2008, accessed May 1, 2012. https://www.texastribune.org/texas-weekly/vol-25/no-41/rearview/.

state Rep. Jim Keffer, R-Eastland, who was formerly Ways
and Means committee chairman under Craddick.[149]

When the polls closed on the Tuesday following his press release,
James "Jim" Keffer was reelected for yet another term. While this came as
a surprise to no one, the statewide results in the House of Representatives
in November 2008 were nothing short of alarming. Out of the 150 house
districts in Texas, 76 were captured by Republicans while 74 were captured
by Democrats. In a state that was supposedly the reddest of all red states,
this result was the absolute antithesis of the achievement of absolute power.

Obviously, a change in the leadership of the Republican Party of Texas
was now in order. How could a state that was so dominated by the right
be sharing legislative power so equally with the left? And, more important,
how could this obvious misrepresentation of the political landscape in
Texas be cured? The answer to these questions came from a small group
that would instantly become known as the "Gang of 11."

On Friday, January 2, 2009, ten republican state representatives
met in the home of Byron Cook in Austin, with an eleventh Republican
joining them on the phone. This "Gang of 11" was comprised of state
representatives Jim Pitts from Waxahachie, Brian McCall from Plano,
Byron Cook from Corsicana, Charlie Geren from Fort Worth, Tommy
Merritt from Longview, Delwin Jones from Lubbock, Edmund Kuempel
from Seguin, Jim Keffer from Eastland, Rob Eissler from The Woodlands,
Burt Solomons from Carrollton, and Joe Straus from San Antonio.

The meeting held in Byron Cook's home was intended to be something
of a secret and more or less off the record; however, news of the meeting was
leaked to the press and there were reporters gathered outside Cook's home
by the time the "Gang of 11" retired from their deliberations that evening.

After several rounds of secret ballots, State Representative Joe Straus
was chosen by the "Gang" as the consensus candidate for Speaker of the
House. This outcome took virtually everyone by surprise. Joe Straus was the
most junior lawmaker in the room among a crowd of Speaker candidates
with legislative tenure. According to the Austin American-Statesman,

---

[149] Staff, "TRIBPEDIA: 2009 House Speaker's Race," *The Texas Tribune*,
Circa 2010, accessed June 13, 2011. http://www.texastribune.org/
tribpedia/2009-house-speakers-race/about/.

Representative Straus had to fax in his official candidacy papers just before the meeting that night.

On the following Saturday morning, the nucleus of the "Gang of 11" met briefly in Austin. After that, they dispersed and began canvassing their fellow House members for their pledges. At the same time, the Democrats were meeting in downtown Austin to discuss the potential selection of Joe Straus and count their commitments to the consensus candidate.

By Saturday night, it was starting to look like Joe Straus might have enough votes to oust Craddick. Sixty-four of the seventy-four Democrats had signed pledges to oppose Craddick "under any circumstances." If you add the "Gang of 11" Republicans to this total, you reach seventy-five votes which equaled exactly one-half of the Texas house. It was now a toss-up.

On the following evening, Tom Craddick scheduled a strategy session at a steakhouse in downtown Austin where about fifty of his supporters were scheduled to meet. Before they could sit down to eat, Joe Straus released a list of eighty-five supporters who had committed to vote for him to be the next Speaker of the House. Tom Craddick then told the group that he would be withdrawing from the race. On the opening day of the eighty-first legislative session of the Texas House of Representatives, January 13, 2009, Joe Straus was unanimously elected.

To say that Representative Joe Straus from San Antonio seemingly came out of nowhere to assume the Speaker's gavel is an incredible understatement. Equally surprising is the fact that James "Jim" Keffer was among his supporters.

While it is impossible to know what deals were made during the weeks between the general election in November 2008 and the beginning of the legislative session in January 2009, what you can be sure of is this: There were some deals made and there were some favors owed. One of those deals might have had something to do with:

"The sale by the Brazos River Authority of certain residential and commercial leased lots and other real property in the immediate vicinity of Possum Kingdom Lake."

But, who knows?

Chapter 15

THE RIGGED DEAL

In a game of high stakes poker, someone has to be the first to act. In *The Tale of the River Card*, the Brazos River Authority opened the action. Seventy-three days after the board of the BRA had voted to sell the entire inhabited shoreline of Possum Kingdom Lake, *Request for Bids No. 09-04-391* rolled off of the printer and onto the real estate market.

This sixteen-page document referenced sixteen other voluminous exhibits and was posted on the BRA's website on January 8, 2009.[150] This was six days before the eighty-first legislative session convened and six days after the "Gang of 11" met to anoint State Representative Joe Straus as the next Speaker of the House.

Even though it had taken seventy-three days to compile the pertinent information, prospective bidders were given only ninety days to digest that mountain of information and construct an informed bid. To make matters worse, the ground rules related to some of the basic terms and conditions were still being negotiated among the players on the inside of the deal. To say the least, the *Request for Bids* was a moving target.

To dumb it down for the masses, the Brazos River Authority posted a *Fact Sheet* that explained the contents of the Request for Bids.

---

[150] BRA Staff, "RFB 09-04-391," *Brazos River Authority*, January 8, 2009, accessed July 4, 2009. https://web.archive.org/web/20090201160953/http://www.brazos.org/rfb.asp.

LAND TO BE INCLUDED IN SALE

- Approximately 900 acres of residential leased property outside the FERC buffer zone or 1,200 acres should FERC approve the sale of the buffer zone

- Approximately 50 acres of commercial leased properties

- 49 miles of roads

- Numerous small strips of land adjacent to above tracts and roads, that are unnecessary for future BRA operations

**acreage amounts are approximate and subject to clarification by future survey

LAND/OTHER INTEREST NOT BEING CONVEYED

- The FERC project area, unless FERC approves the BRA's request to sell the FERC buffer strip, in which case this will be included in the sale

- Commercial leased property located wholly or partially within the FERC project area

- All undeveloped BRA land

- BRA Airport at PK

- Mineral rights

- Groundwater rights

The *Fact Sheet* went on to explain the *Requirements of the Purchaser* which stipulated the "leaseholder protections" that Mike Patterson had baked into his proposal. It also laid out the timeline for the process.

BID TIMELINE

- January 8, 2009: RFB issued

- February 13, 2009: Written questions from potential bidders must be submitted

- February 23, 2009: BRA to respond to written questions from potential bidders; amendments to the RFB are to be posted by BRA

- April 8, 2009: Deadline for submission of bids

- April 27, 2009: BRA Regular Quarterly Board Meeting*

* The BRA Board may review bids in open session at the quarterly meeting in April or at a specially called meeting in the future.[151]

The BRA's Request for Bids also introduced a few new subtleties. The term "preferred lender" was abbreviated to "lender" and the twenty-five-foot FERC buffer zone was expanded to a seventy-five foot setback. Mike Patterson objected to both of these alterations to his plan. In an email dated January 13, 2009, he submitted a request to the BRA to amend its Request for Bids to reflect the arrangement that had been agreed to previously.

---

[151] BRA Staff, "RFB 09-04-391 Fact Sheet," *Brazos River Authority*, January 8, 2009, accessed July 4, 2009 (since removed). http://www.brazos.org/generalPDF/RFB_FactSheetFinal.pdf.

In its resolution, dated October 27, 2008 the Board directed the Authority to develop a Request for Bids. That resolution, when describing the first of the four required lessee options, in pertinent part provided (emphasis added):

> 1. Purchase the lessee's leased property in cash or through *preferred lender financing* for 90% of 2008 land only assessed value (as determined by county appraisal district)

However, Section VI.d.i, Page 8 of the RFB in pertinent part only provides (emphasis added):

> i. Permit the lessee to purchase its leased lot in cash or through *lender financing* for 90% of land only assessed value without any exemptions (as determined by county appraisal district) (the "Assessed Value") for the year 2008, such option to be available for a period of at least one year from Closing.

Comments/Questions:

Will the Authority amend the RFB:

a) to include the term "preferred lender financing" rather than "lender financing"?

b) to define "preferred lenders" as those lenders helping with the purchase loan from the BRA to the Successful Bidder as designated by the Successful Bidder?

In other words, Mike Patterson was asking "Hey, what the hell? I thought we had a deal?"

Three days later, Patterson sent another email to the BRA questioning the 75-foot setback:

Comments/Questions:

It would appear that this is a new 75' setback requirement. Such a required setback from the 1000 foot contour line will allow non-conforming uses to be rebuilt in the event of a fire or other defined casualty, but would not allow properties with minimum valued improvements to be removed and replaced using the same setback as existed for the removed improvements even if the replacement does not extend into the FERC Project Area. This could have a substantial impact on the tear down market for those lesser improved properties. Please help me understand. What is the benefit to the BRA or to the lake area itself to impose such a requirement? I am concerned that this new requirement will have an immediate and very negative impact on the value of all BRA leased lots. Some smaller lots having less depth that perhaps only have a mobile home or other minimal structure could not be removed and replaced with a more valuable structure. Please revisit and reconsider this new requirement. It could have a substantial negative impact on value of the lots and consequently the bid amounts from bidders. Shouldn't the requirement only be for the new improvements to stay out of the applicable FERC Project Area and the 5 foot side setbacks?[sic]

Roughly three weeks after the Brazos River Authority officially put the shoreline of Possum Kingdom Lake up for sale, the board held its regularly scheduled quarterly meeting on January 26, 2009. During *Agenda Item 8: 1st Executive Session*, the board addressed Mike Patterson's concerns about the changes to his deal within the Request for Bids. While he may have had a firm grip on the process, he would only get half of what he had asked for.

Mike Patterson's request to reinstate and re-venerate the concept of his "preferred lenders" was rejected.[152] The board stated that it was "never their intent" to limit the lessees' financing options to "preferred lender financing." Conversely, Mike Patterson's request to withdraw the 75-foot setback was approved.[153] After these two housekeeping items were taken care of, the board of the Brazos River Authority then, astoundingly, voted yet again to hire a firm to market the property.[154]

Not only had the BRA not yet hired a marketing firm, they had not even issued a Request for Proposals for such services. This was remedied with the issuance of *RFP 09-02-402 Real Estate Consulting Services.* Unfortunately for the taxpayers of Texas, this process took time and the necessary time was running out rapidly.

Following some sort of selection process, Integra Realty Resources was chosen to market the property. This was the same company that had been hired a year earlier to appraise all of the lots, and then fired two months later after Christopher DeCluitt took over as the Presiding Officer. Within this agreement, Integra Realty would be paid to perform three distinctive services:

1. Marketing – NTE: $60,000
2. Managing and Evaluation of $45,000
    Bids – NTE:
3. Closing of Sale Pursuant to Accepted $75,000
    Bid – NTE: [155]

---

[152] BRA Staff, "Executive Session 8A–Bid Clarification–Possum Kingdom RFB," *Brazos River Authority*, January 26, 2009, accessed July 4, 2009. http://www.brazos.org/Portals/0/board_actions/01-26-09_Qrtly-Board-Action.pdf.

[153] BRA Staff, "Change in PK RFB Declarations Regarding Setback," *Brazos River Authority*, January 26, 2009, accessed July 4, 2009. http://www.brazos.org/Portals/0/board_actions/01-26-09_Qrtly-Board-Action.pdf.

[154] BRA Staff, "Authorization to Seek Proposals for Real Estate Consultant," *Brazos River Authority*, January 26, 2009, accessed July 4, 2009. http://www.brazos.org/Portals/0/board_actions/01-26-09_Qrtly-Board-Action.pdf.

[155] NTE = Not to Exceed.

On March 19, twenty days before the deadline to submit a bid for the property, the Brazos River Authority sent Integra Realty Resources a signed contract authorizing Integra to start marketing the Authority's most valuable asset. Four days after that, Ben Loughry, the managing partner of Integra Realty, who was also serving as the chairman of the Fort Worth Chamber of Commerce, sent an email to the Brazos River Authority acknowledging receipt of the contract.

Within this email, Ben Loughry informed the Brazos River Authority that his firm had immediately started marketing the BRA's property. He then informed the BRA that they were screwing this deal up royally. Fortunately, for the edification of the rest of us, Ben Loughry put his position in writing:

> March 23, 2009
>
> Mr. John Dickson
>
> Property Administrator
>
> Brazos River Authority
>
> 4600 Cobbs Drive,
>
> P.O.Box 7555
>
> Waco, Texas 76714-7555
>
> RE: Marketing/Development of Evaluation and Selection Process;
>
> RFB No. 09-04-391
>
> Dear John;
>
> This is to acknowledge receipt of the fully executed Professional Services Contract with the Brazos River Authority we received last Thursday, March 19, 2009. On Friday we immediately sent notice of the bid to over 600 Integra Realty Resources Managing Directors and associates across the country informing them of the bid with instructions for visiting the Authority's web site and viewing the request for bid and additional information listed on the site.

We are simultaneously working to identify investors and developers who may have an interest in this type of investment and are sending them the website location information.

As we have previously pointed out, the marketing time line for this assignment is not conducive to achieving the maximum exposure of the investment to the market.

The exact parameters of the minimum bid pricing and resale price cap are still to be finalized, and this, combined with general market risk aversion, does not encourage investor interest. The time restraints now in place limit the pool of investors capable of formulating an informed bid to the handful of investors who have previously shown an interest in the transaction.

The number of investors capable of analyzing this deal, and who have the equity to close the transaction has been greatly reduced by the current economic environment. The potential investors with the required expertise and capital are waiting for the anticipated discounted sale of distressed real estate from the FDIC and TARP restructuring proposals. These competing investments do not carry the burden of a market pricing cap. The announcement this morning by the US Treasury to utilize TARP funds for the sale of toxic assets will make our sale more difficult.

It is for these reasons that we recommend an extension to the marketing period for this property and bid date for at least 90 days. In the interim, a discussion should take place regarding the overall timing of this sale.[156]

Sincerely,

Ben D. Loughry[157]

---

[156] Emphasis added.

[157] Ben D. Loughry, Letter to Brazos River Authority, March 23, 2009, Freedom of Information Response.

In other words, trying to sell 1200 acres of lakefront property while the entire world is experiencing a recession is a really bad idea. Likewise, trying to sell 1200 acres of lakefront property in a fast-track fashion is an even worse idea. Most importantly, Ben Loughry was pointing out that even though this bogus deal was almost at its deadline, the Possum Kingdom Lake Association and their preferred legislators were still negotiating the resell price for the individual properties. This observation was illuminated in the following statement:

The exact parameters of the minimum bid pricing and resale price cap are still to be finalized...

With this letter, Ben Loughry documented the fact that the playing field was limited to those who already knew how the cards were being stacked in the deck.

At this point in the process, only two parties had previously shown an interest in buying the property. Arguably, one of those interested parties was taken out of the equation when the undeveloped land was taken off of the table. That left only Mike Patterson.

Ben Loughry's concerns were warranted. Of the ninety days that the BRA had allocated for potential investors to evaluate the potential investment and bid on the property, seventy days had expired and only twenty days were remaining. As a result, Integra Realty Resources would be scraping the bottom of the barrel to find potential investors in satisfaction of their marketing contract.

Evidently, Ben Loughry did not understand the urgency of the situation. The Palo Pinto Appraisal District was about to issue the new tax assessments for 2009 and Donna Rhoades would once again attempt to bring those assessments up to par value. If the BRA were to extend the deadline another ninety days, the 2009 assessments would most certainly have been brought into the equation.

The negative financial impact to the weekenders of such a delay would have been catastrophic. During the recruitment process to create his cartel of preferred lenders, Mike Patterson documented the difference between the 2008 and 2009 assessed values. This was done on May 7,

2009, and would have occurred early in Ben Loughry's recommended 90-day extension.

PK BRA to Patterson PK Land Partnership, Ltd
Lender Survey

Tentative terms:

Purchase price: $50,000,000

With possible add-ons: $52,400,000

2008 Assessed value: $102,827,863.00

2009 Assessed value: $178,890,270.00

Loan $35-40 million

Interest rate: 10%

Origination fee: 2%

Term: 2 years

Payments: Interest only yearly

Personal guaranty: Michael H. Patterson[158]

The purpose of this document was to convince Mike Patterson's potential preferred lenders that the total property was actually worth at least 75% more than the 2008 assessed values. As the 2008 values would be used to price the land, this demonstrated that the loan-to-value ratios on the resulting mortgages would be extremely favorable. In fact, these loans would actually become premium assets for the participating banks.

---

[158] Mike Patterson, "Lender Survey," *Patterson Equity Partners*, May 7, 2009, accessed July 4, 2010. https://web.archive.org/web/20151126190710/http://www.pklandpartnership.com/downloads/PK%20BRA%2018.pdf.

Mike Patterson attempted to reinforce this assertion by sharing his own 2009 *Notice of Appraised Value* that he had received from the Palo Pinto Appraisal District. In the case of his lakefront property at 2929 Colonel's Row, the assessed value had jumped from $65,560 in 2008, to $318,430 in 2009.[159] This *Notice of Appraised Value* was received on April 28, 2009— twenty days after Patterson's winning bid was submitted.

To further illustrate his representation of the hidden value in the Possum Kingdom land, Mike Patterson also published a "fair market appraisal" that he had obtained for his own lakefront lot. This appraisal, which was performed by Robert E. Ellis on November 12, 2008, valued Patterson's lakefront lot at $350,000.[160]

Mike Patterson published these documents on the internet, clearly demonstrating that the property was extremely undervalued by the appraisal district. If you use the first document entitled *Lender Survey* as a benchmark, Mr. Patterson's bid of $50 million represented 49% of the aggregate assessed value of the property that was sold as of 2008. By comparison, his bid represented only 28% of the aggregate assessed value in 2009 when the bid was actually accepted.

Similarly, if you use the property tax statements that Mike Patterson received in 2008 and 2009 as a benchmark, these documents suggest that his bid of $50 million represented only 8% of the aggregate value. And finally, if you use the fair market appraisal that Patterson had performed on his own property at 2929 Colonel's Row as a benchmark, his bid represented only 7% of the real value of the property when this deal was consummated.

So, in other words, time was of the essence and the properties needed to be sold *now!* Having the chairman of the Fort Worth Chamber of Commerce burden the record by informing the BRA that their plan was ill-conceived was in no way helpful to the cause. Even worse, having

[159] Mike Patterson, "2009 Tax Assessment," *Patterson Equity Partners*, May 7, 2009, accessed July 4, 2010.
https://web.archive.org/web/20151126190748/http://www.pklandpartnership.com/downloads/PK%20BRA%2012.pdf.
[160] Robert E. Ellis, "Summary Appraisal Report for the Property at 2929 Colonel's Row," *Patterson Equity Partners*, May 7, 2009, accessed July 4, 2010. https://web.archive.org/web/20151126190851/http://www.pklandpartnership.com/downloads/PK%20BRA%204.pdf.

Ben Loughry do so in writing, and as a paid consultant for the BRA, was downright detrimental. Loughry's statement that the only investors "capable of formulating an informed bid" were limited to the "handful of investors who have previously shown an interest in the transaction" was a smoking gun by all accounts.

The staff and legal representatives of the Brazos River Authority insist that the members of the board of the BRA were informed of the letter that was written by Ben Loughry on March 23, 2009. However, there is no mention of such disclosure anywhere in the public record. And, try as they did, the staff and legal representatives of the BRA can produce no evidence in response to an Open Records Request that such disclosure ever occurred.

What is known is that Ben Loughry's warnings and recommendations were totally ignored by the Brazos River Authority. Instead, the precisely orchestrated property laundering scheme continued at full speed. The results for the taxpayers of Texas were disastrous.

Consider for a moment that a fee of $60,000 on a real estate transaction that yielded $50 million is a commission of point-twelve percent (.12%). Compare that to the last time you sold a piece of property and gave up a full 6%. In this world of ours you get what you pay for. The following email is the single best example of the results of Integra Realty's marketing efforts.

From: Leon Backes

Sent: Monday, April 06, 2009 11:35 AM

To: Lupe Diaz

Cc: Jay Hawes

Subject: RFB for Bids for Possum Kingdom Lake Property.

I just received a letter from Integra Realty regarding the 1,200 acres at Possum Kingdom Lake. I went to the website and saw it required a closing by April 8th. Is this still the schedule? Since I just received the notice, this seems very quick. There was no contact info at Integra on the letter.

Thank You,

Leon Backes

Provident Realty Advisors, Inc.

W 972-385-xxxx

M 214-673-xxxx

F 972-239-xxxx

lbackes@providentxxxxx.net[161]

As an explanation of this email, the only other party to bid on the entire inhabited shoreline of Possum Kingdom Lake sent an email to the BRA two days, three hours, and twenty-five minutes before the deadline. Leon J. Backes was asking if the deadline was firm given that he had just found out about the sale. Backes also informed the BRA that Integra Realty had not provided any contact information in their mass mailing. Instead, potential bidders were instructed to contact Jose "Lupe" Diaz. If this was a competitive bidding process, I will kiss your ass.

The second of the three elements of the professional services that were to be rendered by Integra Realty relating to the sale of the BRA's property was *Managing and Evaluation of Bids*. This service carried a price tag that was not to exceed $45,000. Here is what you get for that kind of money when you are selling the shoreline of one of the most pristine lakes in the state of Texas.

From: Tommy Pigg [mailto:tpigg@xxx.com]

Sent: Wednesday, April 08, 2009 4:35 PM

To: John Dickson

Cc: Douglas Kincaid; Tommy Pigg

Subject: PK bids

Good afternoon John,

---

[161] Leon J. Backes, Email to Brazos River Authority, April 6, 2009, Freedom of Information Response.

Did we get any bids by the deadline?

Thank you,
Tommy Pigg[162]

The only other correspondence between Integra Realty and the staff of the BRA relating to Integra's marketing of the property involved questions about when the BRA's website would be completed. These all occurred during the last two weeks of the *competitive* bidding process.

At this point, it would be easy to conclude that the highly paid CEO, along with the balance of the staff of the Brazos River Authority, had been derelict in their fiduciary duties regarding the sale of the property at Possum Kingdom Lake. On the other hand, if you give the staff the benefit of the doubt, you might conclude they were simply caving in to the pressure that was being levied by the politicians and the hand-picked board members.

On April 8, 2009, the Brazos River Authority received two bids for the property. At 10:00 AM on the following Monday, April 13, 2009, the staff of the BRA opened the two competing bids to expose the following results.

Bid Tabulation
Purchase of Property at Possum Kingdom Lake
RFB No. 09-04-391
10:00 AM, Monday, April 13, 2009[163]

Patterson PK Land Partnership, Ltd: $50,000,000.00

Leon J Backes: $12,000,000.00

That is a big spread. In fact, that spread is so wide that it fully supports Ben Loughry's assertion of the following:

The time restraints now in place limit the pool of investors capable of formulating an informed bid to the handful of

---

[162] Tommy Pigg, Email to Brazos River Authority, April 8, 2009, Freedom of Information Response.
[163] BRA Staff, "RFB 09-04-391 Bid Tabulation," *Brazos River Authority*, April 13, 2009. https://web.archive.org/web/20090705214552/http://www.brazos.org/rfb/RFB No. 09-04-391Bid-Tabulation.pdf.

investors who have previously shown an interest in the transaction.

It is worth noting that the opening of the bids was not performed during a meeting of the board of the Brazos River Authority. In fact, since the board had approved the issuance of an RFB during a meeting almost six months earlier, there was only one other regular board meeting. This occurred on January 27, 2009. During that meeting, the board had voted to eliminate the use of the term "preferred lender" and had voted to eliminate the introduction of an even wider buffer zone around the lake. Everything else related to the construction, distribution, and execution of the supposedly competitive bidding process had occurred in the background.

Chapter 16

THE FLOP

Back on January 17, 2009, the Possum Kingdom Lake Association had posted a newsletter on their website that provided their membership with an update on the most recent events and the events that were soon to come.[164]

> January, 2009 – Newsletter
>
> POSSUM KINGDOM LAKE ASSOCIATION NEWSLETTER
>
> P. O. BOX 492 Graford, Texas 76449
>
> **Happy New Year! 2009 will be the Year for BRA Divestiture**
>
> Efforts Continues on Divestiture [sic]
>
> The PK Lake Association Board continues to work on divestiture. Efforts to accomplish divestiture are moving forward in two ways, BRA is working on a 3rd party Bid Request and the Lake Association is working on a Bill that

---

[164] Roughly two weeks after *Playing Possum – The Tale of the River Card, Round I* was published; the majority of the PKLA postings that had the word "Newsletter" in the title were deleted from their website. The majority of the other postings remain as of this writing.

will be filed in the Legislature that will require the BRA to sell the leaseholds.

Working Calendar of Events

• **October 27ᵗʰ** - BRA Board approved resolution to post 3ʳᵈ party Bid and allow sale of residential leases and 19 commercial leases and allow BRA staff to write letter to FERC requesting permission to remove the buffer zone in front of residential lease and allow purchase to 1000'.

• **November 19ᵗʰ** - BRA staff and PKLA committee met in Stephenville to talk about aspects of 3ʳᵈ party Bid. The meeting was informative but as BRA moved toward 3ʳᵈ party sale, the Lake Association remained committed to passing a Divestiture Bill in the 81ˢᵗ Legislature.

• **December** - Senator Craig Estes files SB 372. This bill is a Divestiture Bill that looks like the bill used in the 2007 legislative effort.

• **January 8ᵗʰ** - BRA posts Bid Request for 3ʳᵈ party sale on their web-site.

9ᵗʰ - PKLA directors met via phone conference to review Divestiture Bill. Directors unanimously voted to approve the current Bill draft. Directors also unanimously gave Monte Land the authority to negotiate changes to the Divestiture Bill as meetings are held to work on the draft. Monte will be allowed to establish a committee to advice in these negotiations. [sic]

13th - 81st Legislative Session convened and new Speaker Joe Straus was elected in the House.

14th - A Lake Association committee met with Representatives Keffer and Geren along with staff from other Legislative offices to discuss the Divestiture Bill. This Bill remains a work in progress as changes are suggested. Representative Keffer's staff will work with Legal Council to make all language meet legal requirements. The House adjourned until February 1st.

17th - Town Hall meeting to discuss Incorporation drew a large crowd of concerned PK folks. A lawyer that specializes in incorporation spoke to the group about the process and pros and cons.

26th - BRA Board should meet for their quarterly meeting.

• **February 1st** - The Texas House of Representatives will reconvene. Our hope is that Speaker Straus will be ready to assign committees and name Chairmen. Our Divestiture Bill is expected to be sent to the Natural Resource Committee. We need to file the Bill so that it will have a House number. After the Bill has a number it will be sent to committee for hearing and once voted out of committee will travel back to the floor of the House for a vote. The Bill will then go to the Senate and the entire process begins again.

Just as soon as the Divestiture Bill is assigned a number, we will be calling on membership to approach their Legislators again reminding them to support the Divestiture Bill. A copy

of the Bill will be posted on our web-site when
changes are approved by Legal Council. An
e-mail alert will advise membership.

We want to encourage our membership to read
BRA's Request for Bid. Please pay attention to
Exhibit H. The restrictions outlined for the
sale of the lease appear to be more restrictive
for future landowners than what we currently
observe being leaseholders. If you do not have
a computer, members, please call BRA and
request a copy of this document.[165]

This newsletter served to inform the Possum Kingdom Lake
Association's membership that the divestiture of the lakefront property
was being diligently pursued on every front. The board of the PKLA was
dealing directly with the Brazos River Authority as well as the legislators
who would be legitimizing the transaction via legislation.

On the day after the Brazos River Authority put the property up for
sale, the directors of the PKLA met to review the most recent version of
what would soon become House Bill 3031. This piece of legislation would
ultimately be used to determine what the leaseholders would have to pay
for the dirt beneath their homes. Evidently, the directors of the PKLA liked
what they saw. This is most likely because the original version of House
Bill 3031 dropped the mandatory resell price from the 90% of assessed
values called out in the RFB, down to 65% of the assessed values. The
PKLA unanimously voted to accept the current terms and conditions of
the pending legislation. They also designated Monte Land as their official
spokesman.

Empowering Monte Land to negotiate on behalf of the leaseholders
was a curious choice. Based on his testimony in 2007, Monte Land was
obviously not the sharpest tool in the shed. On the other hand, he did

[165] PKLA Staff, "January 2009 Newsletter," *Possum Kingdom Lake Association*, circa
January 2009, accessed July 10, 2011.
https://web.archive.org/web/20101126160001/http://pklakeassn.org/
NEWSLETTER%20JAN%2009.htm.

have the ability to come off as a sympathetic figure in the form of a retired school teacher, rather than a banker, or a lawyer, or a developer.

On January 13, the overthrow of Tom Craddick was completed and Joe Straus was elected as Speaker of the House in Texas. On the following day, a committee from the PKLA met with State Representatives Jim Keffer from Eastland and Charlie Geren from Fort Worth. The purpose of this meeting was to discuss the details of the pending bill. Both Keffer and Geren were part of the "Gang of 11," and it *might* have been time to make good on some of that horse trading. But again, who knows?

On March 10, 2009, House Bill 3031 was filed by State Representative Jim Keffer. The original bill was substantial. It contained fifty-two pages of some of the most precise legal language that you will ever see and Jim Keffer was cited as the sole author. This version of the bill mandated that any third party that submitted a bid to purchase the property from the BRA would pay at least 50% of the aggregate assessed value. That math meant that the minimum bid had to be at least $50 million. Mark that number as the "floor."

The original version of House Bill 3031 also mandated a resell price. Any party that purchased the inhabited shoreline of Possum Kingdom Lake would be required to immediately turn around and sell the individual lots, to the individual leaseholders, at a specified price. If this wasn't the epitome of a laundering scheme then I don't know what is. The original price tag for the laundering process was set at 65% of the 2008 assessed value of the individual lots.

As of 2008, the aggregate assessed value of the property in question was right at $100 million per the county appraisal districts involved. That put the top end of the resell value at $65 million. Mark that number as the "market cap" that Ben Loughry referred to in his letter dated March 23, 2009.

The difference between the floor of $50 million and the market cap of $65 million created a gross margin for the winning bidder of $15 million. While that kind of money is nothing to sneeze at during an historic recession, there was still a better deal to be had for Mike Patterson.

House Bill 3031 also mandated that any party that purchased the inhabited shoreline would also serve as the lender of last resort for those leaseholders whose credit rating disqualified them from being able to borrow money from a bank. HB 3031 went so far as to specify the required down payment for such folks—10%; the required interest rate—6%; and the required amortization—thirty years. In essence, HB 3031 chartered the "Possum Kingdom State Bank."

Article III, Section 52 of the Texas Constitution states the following:

> The Legislature shall have no power to authorize any county, city, town or other political corporation or subdivision of the State to lend its credit or to grant public money or thing of value in aid of, or to any individual, association or corporation whatsoever.

And yet, the original version of House Bill 3031 did exactly that. The wealthy weekenders were granted a "thing of value" in the form of a 35% discount on the assessed value of their individual lots. At the same time, the poor, elderly locals were granted a pre-approved loan.

On March 28, 2009, the directors of the Possum Kingdom Lake Association met again to discuss their progress on the legislative front. The minutes from that meeting conveyed the following information to the dues-paying members. These meeting minutes also explained that a state asset was being negotiated away at a deep discount behind closed doors.

> The majority of the meeting was spent discussing HB 3031. Directors agreed that in talking to membership, their main focus was purchasing their leases. Last week, another meeting in Austin brought to the attention of directors that the BRA would not support a floor of 50% with a [cap of] 65% of 2008 assessed land values. Senator Estes and Representative Keffer pointed out that HB 3031 might not get out of committee if changes were not agreed to. In an effort to move HB 3031 forward, agreement was made on no floor and 90% assessed land value.
>
> Discussion regarding value continues to be problematic. Moving from 65% to 90% of assessed value is viewed as a major concern for many members. HB 3031 has many restrictions removed that are still found in the

Bid Request. Director John Connally made a motion to support HB 3031 with these changes. Tom Harris seconded the motion. The motion passed.

Keeping in mind that changes can be made to HB 3031 at each step of the process, we are hopeful that HB 3031 can be scheduled next week for hearing in the Natural Resource committee.[166]

The critical point here is that there were only eleven days left to submit a bid in response to RFB Number 09-04-39. The fact that the Possum Kingdom Lake Association was still negotiating the terms and conditions of House Bill 3031 made the offering that the BRA had on the table a moving target for any prospective bidder. If you were not an insider, you simply had no shot at this deal.

On the day before the deadline to submit a bid for the property, April 7, 2009, the Natural Resources Committee of the Texas House of Representatives held its first hearing to consider the merits of House Bill 3031. A few months earlier, Speaker Joe Strauss had appointed Democrat Allan Ritter to serve as the chairman of this committee. The "Gang of 11" had needed the support of sixty Democrats to oust Tom Craddick and gaining that support had required some horse trading. Since Allan Ritter had actually filed to run against Tom Craddick for Speaker of the House, a committee chairmanship would not have been an extraordinary concession.[167]

The hearing began with Chairman Ritter opening the testimony.

Ritter: Jim, you ready?
Keffer: I'm ready.

[166] PKLA Staff, "Board of Directors Meeting," *Possum Kingdom Lake Association*, March 28, 2009, accessed July 10, 2011. https://web.archive.org/web/20151126195624/http://pklakeassn.org/minutes%20 3-28-09.htm.
[167] Richard Whittaker, "The Straus 85: Now it's 88," *The Austin Chronicle*, January 4, 2009, accessed June 23, 2012. http://www.austinchronicle.com/daily/ news/2009-01-04/722629.

> **Ritter:** The chair lays out House Bill 3031 and recognizes Jim Keffer to explain this great measure.[168]

Alan Ritter's voice contained more than a mild dose of sarcasm.

Before we hear from Representative Keffer, let me offer a brief explanation of House Bill 3031. For starters, HB 3031 was merely a codified version of the "Immaculate Resolution" with the necessary legal jargon woven in. Secondly, the "Immaculate Resolution" was merely a *"Whereas"* version of the proposal that Mike Patterson had pitched during the private meeting held in Waco on September 8, 2008, among a host of legislators and some representatives of the BRA. This same proposal was pitched publicly by Mike Patterson to the board of the BRA, and the general public, on September 22, 2008.

Whether implicitly, or explicitly, Mike Patterson was effectively the ghost writer of House Bill 3031. Given that Mike Patterson's lobbyist Jay Propes was publicly recognized as the author of Senate Bill 1326 in 2007, my leanings are towards the latter.

Representative Keffer walked up to the podium with substantially more confidence than he had left with two years earlier.

> **Keffer:** Thank you, thank you, Mr. Chairman.
>
> Members, it has been about a six year journey to get here and I do appreciate the opportunity to lay 3031 out to you. And, you are getting a handout now and we do have a substitute.
>
> **Ritter:** The chairman lays out a substitute for House Bill 3031 and recognizes Representative Keffer to explain.
>
> **Keffer:** Thank you, thank you. As I said, we've been working on this for many years. This bill, as it has turned out, has been emotional, contentious, and there are many, many moving parts that we had to deal with.

---

[168] Rep. Jim Keffer, "House Natural Resources Committee," House Audio/Video Archives, *Texas House*, April 7, 2009, accessed November 19, 2010. (Fast forward to 23:28). http://tlchouse.granicus.com/MediaPlayer.php?view_id=25&clip_id=3774.

And really, even today, there's no simple explanation of this bill. But, I want you to know that many, many parties, many people, have put countless hours into this bill and come together so that we are able to present you today with an agreed-to bill, uh, all having to do with Possum Kingdom Lake, located, if you don't know, about 75 miles west of Fort Worth, primarily in Palo Pinto County. It is one of the premier recreational lakes in Texas and is managed by the Brazos River Authority.

The Authority exists to develop, manage, and protect the water resources of the Brazos River Basin to meet the needs of Texas. However, through the evolutional, historical circumstances the Authority – and all this since 1941 when the lake was finished – the Authority has found itself in the land management business.

Today there are almost 1600 residential properties around the lake that the Brazos River Authority currently leases to private citizens. The lessees are from all over the state.

This committee substitute of 3031 serves a dual purpose – to get the BRA on their way out of the land management business and to allow the lessees to buy the land underneath their homes.

Now, you have a handout that was just given to you, a condensed summary of the bill. Uh, quickly, 3031 authorizes the Authority, BRA, to seek bids for the purchase of the residential leased land in one bulk sale. BRA has until the end of 2010 to close a third party transaction.

Then, parallel to that, lessees have the option to close with the third party on the same day that the third party closes with the BRA. Lessees have until the end of 2012 to make a decision.

Number one: to buy in cash or through lender financing for 90% of the 2008 county land-only assessed value. […]

In other words, House Bill 3031 was a property laundering scheme pure and simple. And, if you were fortunate enough to win the right to serve as the straw man on this deal, HB 3031 would prove to be the gift that kept on giving. The committee substitute that Chairman Alan Ritter laid out changed the resell price cap from 65% to 90% of the assessed values and eliminated the minimum bid price.[169]

Representative Keffer then took the members of the Natural Resources Committee through the litany of purchase and lease options that were being provided to the leaseholders under the guise of "leaseholder protections." Jim Keffer then offered the grand finale of the leaseholder protections.

> If the BRA is unable, as they go out for RFB as we speak, if they are unable to close with a third party by the end of 2010, they must offer to sell directly to the lessees, at again, the assessed value – 90% of assessed value.
>
> **Ritter:** Members, any questions for Mr. Keffer?
>
> Well then, we'll start doing witnesses.

Brief testimony related to Chairman Ritter's altered version of HB 3031 ensued, beginning with Monte Land, the president of the Possum Kingdom Lake Association. At the time, Mr. Land and his wife owned a quaint little cottage on Possum Kingdom Lake valued at roughly $400,000.[170]

> **Land:** Thank you Mr. Chairman, members, my name is Monte Land. I am president of the Possum Kingdom Lake Association. I have been president, I think, for the past four or five years.

---

[169] Committee Staff, "Bill Analysis, Comparison of Original and Substitute, C.S.H.B. 3031," *Texas House Natural Resources Committee*, April 7, 2009, accessed July 23, 2010. http://www.capitol.state.tx.us/tlodocs/81R/analysis/html/HB03031H.htm.

[170] The Palo Pinto Appraisal District valued the land and the cottage at $408,600 in 2010.

I am here to, uh, testify briefly in favor of the bill on behalf of the lessees and the members of our association at Possum Kingdom Lake.

Uh, that's pretty much it unless you have questions. I would be glad to answer any.

Ritter: Members, do you have any questions for Mr. Land?

There was nothing but dead silence. Chairman Alan Ritter then patted himself on the back for offering up the committee substitute that eliminated the floor and raised the cap to 90%.

Ritter: I don't have any, but it really seems like y'all have come together and tried to find a really workable solution to this.

Land: As Representative Keffer mentioned, this has been a long road and I will be glad to get down it.

It would not be long before Alan Ritter would announce that he was leaving the Democratic Party and rebranding himself as a Republican.[171] His political conversion gave the Republican Party a super-majority in the Texas House in 2010 at 101 to 49. I would hate to seem accusatory, but I am starting to think that Speaker Strauss' overthrow of Tom Craddick might have had some strings attached. But again, who knows?

Two other individuals testified in favor of HB 3031 that day. The first was James Lattimore, who was also one of the roughly sixteen hundred leaseholders. Mr. Lattimore testified that his lease has been in the family for thirty years, and that he had bought it out of his father's estate. He stated that he had one simple objective: "to buy the land."

The land that James Lattimore referred to was assessed by the Palo Pinto appraisal district in 2002 at exactly $40,000. In 2008, the same parcel was assessed at $70,130. In 2009, the value of the property was up to $80,150. When he purchased the parcel from Mike Patterson in 2010 for

---

[171] On December 14, 2010, an email from the Republican Party of Texas announced that Allan Ritter had switched from the Democratic Party to the Republican Party.

roughly $60,000, the land had been assessed at $173,000. It is not hard to understand why he was in favor of the bill. The cost of owning a lake house at Possum Kingdom was going up rapidly and time was of the essence.

The last of the three witnesses to testify in favor of HB 3031 that day was an attorney from Arlington, Texas by the name of Toby Goodman. Goodman had registered as a representative of the Possum Kingdom Lake Association. He was also a former Texas State Representative who had served District 93 in Arlington from 1991 until 2007. His legislative career ended in the wake of an ethics investigation that alleged he had used campaign contributions to purchase real estate for his own personal use.[172] On February 12, 2008, the Texas Ethics Commission ruled that Goodman had done exactly that and levied a $10,000 civil penalty. Due largely to this scandal, Toby Goodman was defeated in the general election in 2006 by Democratic challenger Paula Pierson.

Coincidentally, Paula Pierson became a co-author of HB 3031 on April 9, 2009, the day after Mike Patterson submitted his winning bid.

Now before you start thinking that this is a great example of bipartisan cooperation to serve the will of the people, consider this: On March 1, 2009, thirty-eight days prior to his testimony, a Tarrant County family law judge overturned the Texas Ethics Committee's ruling and fine against Toby Goodman in a summary judgment. (Judges in Texas are elected).

On April 7, 2009, Toby Goodman simply stood, stated that he was in support of HB 3031, and offered to answer any questions. There were none.

At this point in the proceedings, it might have seemed logical for someone on the committee to move that the uncontested "agreed-to" bill be reported favorably to the full house with the recommendation that it pass. Instead, Chairman Ritter withdrew his substitute version and the mandatory resell price reverted to 65% of the 2008 assessed value. Consideration of HB 3031 was tabled and the bill was left pending in committee. It would seem that even an "agreed-to bill" needs forty-eight

---

[172] "In the Matter of Toby Goodman, Final Order," *Texas Ethics Commission*, February 12, 2008, accessed December 4, 2010.
http://www.ethics.state.tx.us/sworncomp/2006/2608184.pdf.

hours to marinate. The entire proceedings including the discussion of a companion bill, HB 3032, had lasted only 20 minutes.[173]

The difference between being required to sell $100 million worth of property for 90%, rather than 65%, is a tidy $25 million. If you were not in the room that day you might have missed this minor detail. But, of course, Mike Patterson was there. At a little before 3:00 pm on April 8, Patterson submitted a winning bid of $50 million to the BRA. His bid package included the text of the enhanced version of HB 3031 that had been introduced and then withdrawn. In effect, Mike Patterson had made over $1 million per minute on April 7, 2009.

The day after the bid deadline, April 9, 2009, the House Committee on Natural Resources reconvened and once again considered HB 3031. Once again, a substitute of the bill was introduced, although this time by Representative Stephen Frost. Once again, the mandatory resell price was raised to 90% and the minimum floor price was removed. The vote of the House Natural Resources committee was unanimous.[174]

A motion was made that HB 3031, as substituted, be reported favorably to the full house with the recommendation that it pass and be sent to the Committee on Local and Consent Calendars.

To this day, the Brazos River Authority maintains that it was forced by the Texas Legislature to sell the property through a bulk sale to a third party. And yet, it is impossible to ignore that the property was put up for sale before the Eighty-First Legislative Session even began. Likewise, it is impossible to ignore the fact that the winning bid was submitted before the first vote on House Bill 3031 ever occurred.

And, it is extremely difficult to understand why House Bill 3031 was treated so favorably by the Natural Resources Committee in 2009 when Senate Bill 1326 had been annihilated by this same committee in 2007.

---

[173] Committee Staff, "Meeting Minutes, HB 3031," *Texas House Natural Resources Committee*, April 7, 2009, accessed July 23, 2010. http://www.capitol.state.tx.us/tlodocs/81R/minutes/html/C3902009040708001.HTM.

[174] Committee Staff, "Meeting Minutes, HB 3031," *Texas House Natural Resources Committee*, April 9, 2009, accessed July 23, 2010. http://www.capitol.state.tx.us/tlodocs/81R/minutes/html/C3902009040900001.HTM.

Chapter 17

THE TURN

In 2007, the weekenders' first attempt to legislate a land grab for the shoreline of Possum Kingdom Lake met severe opposition at virtually every step of the way. While the board and the staff of the Brazos River Authority testified passionately against Senate Bill 1326, Republican and Democratic legislators alike questioned the propriety and equity of the measure.

Senate Bill 1326 had barely passed through the Senate Committee on Natural Resources. This occurred over the opposition of the chairman of the committee, Senator Kip Averitt. It was also opposed by Senators Robert Duncan, Glenn Hegar, and Carlos Uresti. Senators Averitt, Duncan, and Hegar were Republicans while Senator Uresti was a tenured Democrat.

From there, Senate Bill 1326 had traveled to the House Committee on Natural Resources where it was decisively defeated. Within this committee, the key opposition came from State Representatives Mike O'Day, Dan Gattis, and Brandon Creighton—all Republicans. The key point of contention then was that the weekenders were asking for a 10% discount off the fair market value.

In between these two committee meetings of the Texas legislature, the board and the staff of the Brazos River Authority had held an Emergency Meeting on April 27, 2007, to fend off the forced divestiture. This meeting was punctuated by some of the most colorful quotes that were introduced into the record during this entire tale. Here are a few examples:

Director Wade Gear: They are asking us to gut a state agency and my hand isn't going to be on that knife.

Director Pamela Jo Ellison: It's not whether you're going to get raped or not —it's to what extreme are you going to?

Director Billy Wayne Moore: This establishes a very dangerous precedent and the next state park for sale—I want it!

Director Jean Kilgore: If we vote to do this, we are their alibi.

These events in 2007 beg the obvious question regarding the events of 2009: What changed?

Well, to say the least, a lot of things changed between these two legislative sessions, beginning with the ouster of Tom Craddick and the selection of Joe Straus as the Speaker of the House. The selection of Joe Straus as Speaker resulted in no shortage of new committee chairmen and new committee members. This was especially true of the House Committee on Natural Resources. Of the nine members of this committee that soundly defeated Senate Bill 1326 in 2007, only two were reappointed by Joe Straus in 2009. These were Republicans Brandon Creighton and Jodie Laubenberg.

If the name Jodie Laubenberg sounds familiar, it should. Laubenberg, who had represented the 89th district of Texas since 2003, was also the House sponsor of the now infamous Senate Bill 5 that was introduced on June 11, 2013.[175] This occurred during the first special session called by Governor Rick Perry which ended in the eleven-hour filibuster by State Senator Wendy Davis, propelling her into the national spotlight. Over the course of a few hours, Senator Davis went from having a few hundred followers on Twitter to over one hundred thousand. In response to that response, Senator Davis decided to run for governor of the state of Texas in 2014. (Davis was soundly defeated by Greg Abbott).

When asked once about the issue of denying a woman access to an abortion subsequent to being raped, Representative Jodie Laubenberg

---

[175] Depending on your point of view, the term *famous* might be equally appropriate.

had declared the scenario irrelevant. Her explanation was that when a woman gets raped, she goes to the local hospital where a rape kit is then administered. She further explained that these kits "clean you out," and you will not get pregnant. Thus, the issue of rape is a non-issue.[176]

During the hearing of the House Committee on Natural Resources in 2007, Representative Laubenberg had only asked one question and that was directed to Mr. Lance Byrd:

> **Laubenberg**: When you said you're willing to pay the fair market value, is that with the encumbered, uh, or unencumbered?

Beyond that, Representative Laubenberg had sat silently throughout the entire proceedings while her fellow Republican representatives Mike O'Day, Dan Gattis, and Brandon Creighton carved up Senate Bill 1326 like a Sunday brisket.

In 2009, Jodie Laubenberg chose not to participate at all. She was absent on both April 7 and April 9, leaving Representative Brandon Creighton as the only member of the House Natural Resources Committee who participated in the deliberations in both 2007 and 2009. The other nine members of the committee were new to the argument and seemed more than willing to accept Jim Keffer's assertion that this was an "agreed-to" matter.

Representative Brandon Creighton was arguably the most qualified member of the Natural Resources Committee when it came to evaluating the terms and conditions of a sale of lakefront property. Since the year 2000, Creighton had served as the vice president of acquisitions and general counsel for The Signorelli Company. This firm touts itself as one of the largest, privately held real estate development firms in Texas.[177]

The Signorelli Company credits Brandon Creighton with being instrumental in the establishment of the firm's custom home-building division. Within this division, Signorelli has created multiple upscale communities including two of particular note: the Commons of Lake Houston and Bella Vita on Lake Conroe. Both of these developments offer magnificent lakefront homes.

It seems reasonable to conclude that Representative Creighton possessed a strong understanding of the nuances of lakefront property and this was demonstrated during the House testimony on Senate Bill 1326 in 2007. During this hearing, Creighton had lectured leaseholder Robert Aldrich on the folly of building an expensive home on leased property without the benefit of a purchase option. Even more telling is the fact that Brandon Creighton chose not to be present at the conclusion of the testimony, eliminating the quorum that was required to vote on SB 1326. In effect, Representative Brandon Creighton killed the bill in 2007.

Two years later, Representative Brandon Creighton sat quietly while Representative Jim Keffer explained how the property would first be sold to a third party and then resold to the individual leaseholders "for 90% of the 2008 county land-only assessed value." Given Creighton's expertise in this field, it is impossible for me to believe that he did not possess a keen understanding of the difference between county assessed values and fair market value as determined by an appraisal.

During the testimony regarding House Bill 3031 in the Natural Resources Committee in 2009, Representative Brandon Creighton asked no questions. When the vote was taken after the testimony, Representative Creighton voted aye. And, when Representative Tracy King moved that the bill be placed on the docket of uncontested bills, Creighton offered no objection.

[177] Staff, "Senator Brandon Creighton, J. D. Executive Vice President – Acquisitions and General Counsel," *The Signorelli Company*, n.d., accessed November 26, 2015. https://web.archive.org/web/20150211122804/http://signorellicompany.com/our-leadership. https://web.archive.org/web/20151129205858/http://www.signorellicompany.com/brandon-creighton.

One of the first questions that should be asked when the question of "why" is raised should be directed to Brandon Creighton, who now serves as a state senator:

> Given that you were likely the most knowledgeable person in the room, why did you change your position between 2007 and 2009 on the *"sale by the Brazos River Authority of certain residential and commercial leased lots and other real property in the immediate vicinity of Possum Kingdom Lake?"*

While Representative Creighton was the first legislator to drop his opposition to the forced sale and support it with his vote, he would not be the last. Nor would the reversal of certain legislators' positions be the only thing that changed in 2009.

On April 14, 2009, the Administration & Audit Committee of the BRA's board met to determine who should be awarded the next contract to provide professional auditing services to the authority. After a vote to adjourn, but while the microphone was still open, the CEO of the Brazos River Authority, Mr. Phil Ford, shared the following information with those who were still listening.

> Let me give you thirty seconds of just a quick thing, of what's going to happen – because, out of necessity – of what's happening tomorrow with some of you and sixteen of your colleagues being passed through the Senate.
>
> Uh, I guess it's the uh, whatever committee that is that picks y'all – the Appointments Committee.
>
> But anyway, that will happen on the 15th and on the 22nd it will be approved by the entire Senate, and so that means the new board members will be here for the 27th.
>
> The 27th is going to turn into a two day affair. Because, we need to be fair to those people, we are going to try to give them about a three-hour, four-hour charm-school between 9 o'clock in the morning and about 12:30.

At 12:30 we'll break for lunch, come out of lunch after 30 minutes, and then we'll start off with the retirement committee, which will run about an hour and a half, and then we will get into the normal board meeting around 3 o'clock.

At 3 o'clock, we will do the consent agenda, and then we will go into the first issue about voting on, accepting, or the discussion on what the board desires to do with the divestiture RFB. Then we will adjourn, have dinner, and come back the next morning and run the rest of the meeting.[178]

To the casual observer, CEO Phil Ford's comments might have seemed like routine housekeeping. But to someone who has long since recognized Phil Ford's propensity for leaving clues at the end of an unrelated agenda item, his words read like a status report on the forced divestiture process. Phil Ford had referred to this process in April 2007 as a "hostage negotiation" with "someone holding a gun."

Phil Ford was making it clear that the forced divestiture process was well orchestrated and nearly complete. He was also making it clear that all of the "t's" would be crossed and that all of the "i's" would be dotted. And, most importantly, he was signaling that Governor Rick Perry had few more divestiture-friendly appointments up his sleeve. On the day after Mike Patterson submitted his winning bid to launder the property to the weekenders, Governor Rick Perry completed his overhaul of the board of the Brazos River Authority.[179]

Mark Carrabba was replaced by Kari Belt of Gatesville. According to Governor Perry's press release, Ms. Belt was a Vacation Bible School co-director and a graduate of Texas A&M University.

---

[178] Administration & Audit Committee, "Discussion," *Brazos River Authority Board Meeting Minutes*, April 14, 2009, accessed November 10, 2014. (Fast forward to 17:00). http://www.brazos.org/Portals/0/board_audio/4-14-2009-AA7.mp3.

[179] Gov. Rick Perry, "Gov. Perry Appoints Seven to Brazos River Authority Board of Directors," *Office of the Governor*, April 9, 2009. http://wayback.archive-it.org/414/20100820085630/http://governor.state.tx.us/news/appointment/12233.

Wade Gear, the people's champion, was replaced by James F. "Jim" Landtroop of Plainview. According to Governor Perry's press release, Mr. Landtroop was the coach of the Plainview Christian Academy Men's Varsity Basketball team, an elder at Plainview Bible Church, a member of the National Rifle Association, and a graduate of Texas A&M University.

Patricia Bailon, the widow of Roberto Bailon, was replaced by Sara Lowrey Mackie of Salado. According to Governor Perry's press release, Ms. Mackie was the executive director of the Institute for the Humanities at Salado, and a graduate of the University of Texas at Austin.

Zachary Brady, the board member who was never confirmed, was replaced by G. Dave Scott of Richmond. According to Governor Perry's press release, Mr. Scott was the executive vice president of the Port City Stockyards. He was also a life member of the Fort Bend County Fair Association. Even more impressive was the fact that he was a board member of the Houston Livestock Show and Rodeo where he had served as a past chairman of the Range Bull and Heifer Committee. Mr. Scott attended the University of Houston and Sam Houston State University. It is not clear from the press release if Mr. Scott ever graduated from either of those universities.

Scott Smith, who served on the board of the BRA for fourteen months before Governor Perry appointed him to the State Pension Review Board, was replaced by Robert E. "Bob" Tesch of Georgetown. According to Governor Perry's press release, Mr. Tesch was the president and owner of a commercial real estate firm, Tesch and Associates Incorporated. Bob Tesch was a graduate of the University of Texas at Austin.

In addition to appointing a Vacation Bible School director, a basketball coach, a humanities director, and a commercial real estate professional, Governor Perry also reappointed Nancy Porter of Sugar Land. Ms. Porter was the director of communications for the Fort Bend Independent School District, a volunteer for Young Life, and a graduate of the University of Houston.

Similarly, John D. Steinmetz of Lubbock was also reappointed. Less than two years later, Governor Perry would appoint John Steinmetz to the Board of Regents of Texas Tech University. Steinmetz would eventually resign from the board of the BRA after it was learned that he had falsely claimed to possess a graduate degree from Texas Tech on his appointment application.

Over the course of one year and one week, Governor Rick Perry had made seventeen new appointments to the 21-member board of directors of the Brazos River Authority. He had also reappointed four others. Would you be surprised to learn that the vote to accept Mike Patterson's bid would be unanimous?

On April 21, 2009, the Texas Senate Journal recorded the following vote.

SENATE JOURNAL
EIGHTY-FIRST LEGISLATURE — REGULAR SESSION
AUSTIN, TEXAS
PROCEEDINGS
FORTY-FIRST DAY
(Tuesday, April 21, 2009)
NOMINEES CONFIRMED

The following nominees, as reported by the Committee on Nominations, were confirmed by the following vote: Yeas 30, Nays 0.

Members, Board of Directors, Brazos River Authority:

Richard L. Ball, Palo Pinto County; Grady Barr, Taylor County; F. LeRoy Bell, Taylor County; Kari Belt, Coryell County; Peter G. Bennis, Johnson County; John A. Brieden III, Washington County; James F. "Jim" Landtroop, Jr., Hale County; Sara Lowrey Mackie, Bell County; Nancy Kay Whitehead Porter, Fort Bend County; G. Dave Scott, Fort Bend County; Jon E. Sloan, Williamson County; John D. Steinmetz, Lubbock County; Robert E. "Bob" Tesch, Williamson County; Mary Ward, Hood County; Salvatore A. Zaccagnino, Burleson County.[180]

---

[180] "Senate Journal," Eighty-First Legislature, Regular Session, Texas Senate, April 21, 2009, p. 1294. http://www.journals.senate.state.tx.us/sjrnl/81R/pd-f/81RSJ04-21-F.pdf.

For five of the twenty-one members of the Brazos River Authority, the first item of business that they would ever consider, and then vote on, was the sale of the shoreline of Possum Kingdom Lake. This of course would occur after they had been subjected to a three hour charm school. Based on the official record, there is no way to document whether or not those new board members were informed during their charm school of Ben Loughry's March 23, 2009 warning not to go through with the current RFB process.

The second question to be asked when we get to the "why" stage of this exercise will need to be directed to former Governor Rick Perry:

> Why in the world, given the importance of water in the state of Texas, would you appoint such ridiculously unqualified people to the board of one of the most important water authorities in the state over such a short period of time?

On April 27, 2009, the Brazos River Authority began a two-day meeting that included *Agenda Item 2: 1ˢᵗ Executive Session: Reconvene; Action Taken.*

During this closed executive session that lasted three hours, the Board considered the merits of Mike Patterson's $50 million bid to buy the entire inhabited shoreline of Possum Kingdom Lake. When the Board reconvened in open session on April 27, a resolution was presented by Matt Phillips to accept Mike Patterson's winning bid. When the Board was polled, the vote was unanimous with two abstentions. The first to abstain was the President and Chief Executive Officer for Pinnacle Bank, Mr. Peter Bennis. As noted earlier, Pinnacle Bank was one of Mike Patterson's preferred lenders. The second to abstain was Mary Ward—a regional president of the bank for which Mike Patterson served as a director.

The second day of the two-day meeting ended on April 28, 2009 with *Agenda Item 23: Legislative Updates and Adjourn.* During this agenda item, Matt Phillips explained the details of House Bill 3032 which was tightly coupled with House Bill 3031. Sadly, many of the board members expressed significant disdain and some mild outrage when they were informed that the Texas legislature was directing them to sale over 800 acres of land around Possum Kingdom Lake to the owners of the Set Ranch for fair market value. Based upon their questions and their comments, it was obvious that the new board members had no idea what they had approved on the previous day regarding House Bill 3031.

At the end of *Agenda Item 23*, Phil Ford interrupted the call for adjournment with the following comment:

> Our next big challenge, quite frankly, is trying to pull together all this stuff on the bid to make sure that we can meet the timelines. Uh, I was talking to, uh, Director [Mary] Ward this morning who – that's what she does for business – and she's – she too is concerned about the timelines and meeting all the criteria that you have to do, to do the closing. So we'll be getting back to you quickly on where we stand with that. Thank ya'll for coming.[181]

By "that's what she does for business," Phil Ford was reminding those in attendance that Mary Ward was a banker with Southwest Securities, FSB who ultimately reported to Mike Patterson. And while Ms. Ward had just abstained from the vote to accept Mike Patterson's bid, Phil Ford was pointing out that she was by no means abstaining from any discussion about what Mr. Patterson was involved in. This was in direct contradiction to a statement that she had made to the general public roughly seven months earlier:

> I feel that in order to avoid any appearance of impropriety that I would, uh, abstain from any discussion or voting on any proposal that Mr. Patterson is involved in.[182]

---

[181] Board Meeting, "Agenda Items 20 & 23," *Brazos River Authority Board Meeting Minutes,* April 28, 2009, accessed November 10, 2014. (Fast forward to 41:20). http://www.brazos.org/Portals/0/board_audio/4-27&28-2009-BRD24.mp3.

[182] Special Board Meeting "Agenda Item 1," *Brazos River Authority Board Meeting Minutes,* September 22, 2008, accessed November 10, 2014. (Fast forward to 01:35:39). http://www.brazos.org/Portals/0/board_audio/09222008_SP-BRD2.MP3.

When Mike Patterson had submitted his bid to purchase the property on April 8, 2009, he had been required to sign his name to the following statement.

Bid Form for
Purchase of Property at Possum Kingdom Lake
RFB No. 09-04-391

> By signing this Bid, the undersigned hereby affirms that he or she has not given, offered to give, nor intends to give at any time hereafter any economic opportunity, future employment, gift, loan, gratuity, special discounts, trip, favor or service to a public servant in connection with this Bid. Failure to sign this Bid, or signing it with false statement, shall void the submitted Bid or any resulting purchase agreement, and the Bidder shall not be considered for future Bids.

The gravity of this affirmative statement is immeasurable. If the winning bidder enticed even one of the twenty-one board members to act on his or her behalf, through something as simple as a promise of continued employment during the Great Recession, then the purchase agreement would be voided and the property in question would arguably have to be returned to the state of Texas.

Similarly, if the winning bidder promised to secure a promotion for one of the twenty-one board members the same would be true. Here's another spoiler alert: Mary Ward was about to change job titles.

Chapter 18

THE BACKDOOR FLUSH

By the time that House Bill 3031 reached a committee of the Texas Senate, the Brazos River Authority had already awarded the right to purchase the shoreline of Possum Kingdom Lake to Mike Patterson. At this point, a casual observer might have concluded that Patterson was holding an unbeatable hand.

The truth of the matter, however, is that Mike Patterson was still playing an extreme long shot. If this had been an honest game of Texas Hold'em, Patterson would have been facing less than a 5% chance of pulling this off—4.2% to be exact. He still needed two specific cards to be dealt in order to take down the pot. In poker, this is known as coming through the back door. In the lore of Texas real estate, this will become known as the "Texas Miracle."

The next card that Patterson needed was the elimination of opposition in the Texas Senate. In 2007, Senate Bill 1326, the predecessor to House Bill 3031, had been appropriately routed to the Senate Committee on Natural Resources. This committee was comprised of eleven members and was chaired by Senator Kip Averitt. The other ten members of this committee were Senators Craig Estes, Kim Brimer, Bob Deull, Robert Duncan, Kevin Eltife, Glenn Hegar, Juan Hinojosa, Mike Jackson, Kel Seliger, and Carlos Uresti.

On April 23, 2007, the Senate Committee on Natural Resources considered Senate Bill 1326 and the vote was far from unanimous. As the eleven senators were polled that day, Senator Duncan had replied, "Not yet," while Senator Uresti had replied "Present" and Senator Hegar had replied "I'm here." The final tally was eight ayes, one nay, and two present not voting.[183]

In the absence of a unanimous vote, Senate Bill 1326 was then subjected to a vote of the entire body of the Senate. This required each of the thirty-one Texas senators to take a public position on the matter. When SB 1326 went to the floor of the Senate on May 4, 2007, the resulting vote was twenty-three ayes and five nays.[184] The five senators who voted against Senate Bill 1326 were Kip Averitt, Robert Nichols, Steve Ogden, Dan Patrick, and Glenn Hegar.

With the exception of Senator Kim Brimer, who had lost his seat to an upstart legislator by the name of Wendy Davis, the membership of the Senate Natural Resources Committee in 2009 had remained unchanged from 2007. Senator Kip Averitt was still the chairman and he had spearheaded the effort to kill the forced divestiture bill in the previous session. There was no reason to expect that his opposition to selling the property for less than fair market value had waned.

Senator Averitt's opposition would be a deal killer. In order to steer House Bill 3031 through the process as an uncontested piece of legislation, a unanimous vote from the Committee on Natural Resources would be required. To say the least, Mike Patterson needed an ace in the hole. That ace would prove to be the lieutenant governor of Texas: David Dewhurst.

The lieutenant governor of Texas serves as the president of the Senate. The lieutenant governor's duties include presiding over the Senate, appointing chairs of committees and committee members, assigning and referring bills to specific committees, making procedural rulings, and recognizing members during debate. The lieutenant governor may also serve as a tie-breaker should a vote on the Senate floor end in a tie. This is an elected position that is voted on statewide.

---

[183] Sen. Kip Averitt, "Senate Natural Resources Committee," Senate Audio/Video Archives, *Texas Senate*, April 23, 2007, accessed July 10, 2013. (Fast forward to 03:48). http://tlcsenate.granicus.com/MediaPlayer.php?view_id=16&clip_id=2810.
[184] "Senate Journal," Eighty-First Legislature, Regular Session, Texas Senate, May 4, 2007, p. 1715. http://www.journals.senate.state.tx.us/sjrnl/80r/pdf/80RSJ05-04-F.PDF.

In 2002, the voters in Texas elected David Dewhurst to serve as their lieutenant governor. This was the same year that Rick Perry was first elected to serve a full term as governor and the same year that Greg Abbott was elected to the office of attorney general. These men served together as the three highest elected officials in the state of Texas for a record twelve years. During that period of time, Rick Perry, Greg Abbott, and David Dewhurst became the most powerful triumvirate in the history of Texas politics.

While changing the mind of Senator Kip Averitt promised to be an impossible task, eliminating Averitt's opposition required nothing more than the stroke of a pen. Lieutenant Governor David Dewhurst simply routed HB 3031 to a different Senate committee that was comprised of only five members. This committee was appropriately named Agriculture and Rural Affairs and was chaired by none other than the sponsor of House Bill 3031, Senator Craig Estes.

By routing House Bill 3031 to the Agriculture and Rural Affairs committee, Lt. Governor Dewhurst positioned the bill as a "local matter" that warranted minimal scrutiny. Consequently, the odds of securing a unanimous vote from that committee were enhanced appreciably. Lieutenant Governor David Dewhurst had served up the first necessary card.

On May 11, 2009, Senator Estes chaired a fifty-eight minute meeting of the Agriculture and Rural Affairs committee to consider the lofty bills that Lt. Governor David Dewhurst had steered his way. A cynic might have concluded that no one really cared about these matters. At the outset of the hearing, only Chairman Craig Estes was in attendance. Estes called the hearing to order with four authoritative pounds of the gavel. He then stated the following:

> The senate committee on Agriculture and Rural Affairs
> will come to order and we will dispense with calling the
> roll until we get some more people here.
>
> But, we will hear some bills.[185]

---

[185] Sen. Craig Estes, "Senate Agriculture and Rural Affairs Committee," Senate Audio/Video Archives, *Texas Senate*, May 11, 2009, accessed November 19, 2010. http://tlcsenate.granicus.com/MediaPlayer.php?view_id=14&clip_id=2419.

And so he did. With no other members present, Senator Estes sat alone at the center of the dais and opened testimony on the bills that were before his committee.

The first matter brought before Senator Estes that day was House Bill 1965. This bill dealt with the overpopulation of whitetail deer in Texas and the manner in which a deer carcass could be transported or disposed of. HB 1965 had been unanimously passed by the Committee on Culture, Recreation, and Tourism in the Texas House.

I pointed out earlier that a wise politician in Texas does not craft questionable special-interest legislation in the middle of a session. Instead, the prudent course of action is to do so in between sessions and then walk your bill through the process like a champion steer at the local stock show. I meant that.

Six other bills were laid out during the first thirty-five minutes of the hearing that day. Each of those six bills had already unanimously passed through the Agriculture & Livestock Committee in the House. The topic of these six bills ranged from the breeding of horses to the marketing of shrimp.[186] For all practical purposes, the Senate Committee on Agriculture and Rural Affairs was actually the "Nobody Gives a Damn" committee.[187] This was a brilliant move on the part of Lt. Governor Dewhurst.

After roughly twenty minutes of testimony, Senator Estes was joined by two other members of his committee, Senators Carlos Uresti and Mike Jackson. By virtue of the fact that three of the five members were now present, Chairman Estes announced that a quorum had been established. Four minutes later, Estes announced that Senator Glenn Hegar was on his way to the hearing. Chairman Estes then stated that they would continue to lay out bills and then vote on the bills upon Hegar's arrival.

Following the bills that had originated in the House Committee on Agriculture & Livestock, the Senate committee on Agriculture & Rural

---

[186] Raenetta Nance, Clerk, "Meeting Minutes, HB 3031," *Texas Senate Committee on Agriculture and Rural Affairs*, May 11, 2009, accessed July 23, 2010.http://www.capitol.state.tx.us/tlodocs/81R/minutes/html/C5052009051115001.HTM.
[187] Senate Staff, "Bills by Committee, Agriculture and Rural Affairs," *Texas Legislature*, June 1, 2009, accessed July 23, 2010. http://www.capitol.state.tx.us/Reports/Report.aspx?ID=committee&LegSess=81R&Code=C505#out.

Affairs turned its attention to the sale of some real estate in a rural area known as Possum Kingdom Lake.

Senator Carlos Uresti assumed the chair.

The committee then took up a companion bill to House Bill 3031. This was House Bill 3032. I have not mentioned much about HB 3032 yet out of a desire to limit the confusion. This bill actually enjoyed a modicum of legitimacy and that is probably why Senator Estes introduced it first.

> **Uresti:** The chair lays out House Bill 3032 by Representative Keffer and recognizes the senate sponsor, Senator Estes, to explain the bill.
>
> **Estes:** Uh, thank you chairman. These two bills, members, are some things that I have been working on for literally years. And, it has to do with Possum Kingdom, and both of these bills that we are going to be talking about are *local* bills and these things have been worked out with all of the parties concerned.
>
> But let me just tell you about this bill.
>
> It involves the Set Ranch, located in Palo Pinto and Stephen Counties, which has been a working cattle ranch since the original Texas land grants of 1854. And, it continues today as a working cattle ranch, wildlife and land management, and soil and water conservation program.
>
> During the acquisition of this property for the construction of Morris Sheppard Dam at Possum Kingdom Lake, the Brazos River Authority acquired more than 4300 acres of the Set Ranch for the reservoir. This bill would require the sale of a certain portion – and that's 880 acres of that land – back to the Set Ranch at its *fair market value*. The land that's identified includes only land which has no public access and is completely surrounded by the Set Ranch land from which it was acquired in the 1940's.
>
> And, uh, the Brazos River Authority is OK with this, and the Set Ranch folks are OK with it. So, I'm OK with it. And we have some witnesses.

Uresti: OK.

The chair will open up public testimony on House Bill 3032.

I have a card from Carolyn Land for the bill who does not wish to testify – Texas citizen.

Maria Custard – as a resource witness – with Custard-Pitts Land & Cattle Company – Are there any questions of Maria Custard?

Marla Custard, I beg your pardon.

Estes: Thank you for being here (as he nodded towards Marla Custard).

Uresti: Jack Fickessen – with Custard-Pitts Land & Cattle – is a resource witness for the bill – any questions of Mr. Fickessen?

Matt Phillips, resource only, Government and Customer Relations Manager with the Brazos River Authority – Any questions of him?

Is there anyone else that wishes to testify on, for, or against House Bill 3032? The chair sees none and we will close public testimony and leave that bill pending as well.[188]

The testimony regarding the sale of 880 acres by the Brazos River Authority to the owners of the Set Ranch lasted for one minute and seventeen seconds. After Senator Uresti asked if there was anyone else who wished to testify on the measure, the video camera panned the room. There were seven gentlemen dressed in coats and ties standing along the back wall. There were also two women sitting on the back row. Sitting on rows three and four were Mike Patterson and Monte Land.

---

[188] Sen. Carlos Uresti, "Senate Agriculture and Rural Affairs Committee," Senate Audio/Video Archives, *Texas Senate*, May 11, 2009, accessed November 19, 2010. (Fast forward to 35:36).
http://tlcsenate.granicus.com/MediaPlayer.php?view_id=14&clip_id=2419.

To be certain, there was no one present who opposed House Bill 3032. And since Senator Estes had stressed that the acreage would be sold at "fair market value," why would you?

The hearing continued. The last card that Mike Patterson needed was to have Senators Carlos Uresti (D) and Glenn Hegar (R) reverse their position on the forced divestiture of the property at Possum Kingdom Lake.

> **Estes:** Thank you very much, Chairman. And the last bill that we have on our list to call up is House Bill 3031.
>
> **Uresti:** The chair lays out House Bill 3031 by Representative Keffer and recognizes the Senate sponsor, Senator Estes, to explain the bill.

The floor was then turned over to Senator Estes, who looked down at his notes while reading his opening remarks.

> **Estes:** Thank you, Chairman. Again, this is a bill that I worked on very hard last session and it didn't *quite* make it across the finish line. And I really appreciate Chairman Keffer getting this bill over to us. There again, this is an agreed-to bill by all parties and, uh...
>
> I believe that between the times that Chairman Keffer laid this out over in the House and it came over to us, a deal has been struck to do what we are trying to do in this bill, and so in a sense, this is enabling legislation.
>
> Possum Kingdom Lake is located seventy miles west of Fort Worth, primarily in Palo Pinto County. It is one of the premier recreational lakes in Texas. It is managed by the Brazos River Authority.
>
> The Authority exists to develop and manage and protect the water resources of the Brazos River Basin to meet the needs of Texas. However, due to the evolution of historical circumstances since 1941, this Authority has found itself in the land management business. There are almost 1600

residential properties around the lake that the Brazos River Authority currently leases to private citizens. And, these lessees are from all over the state.

So this bill serves a dual purpose. It gets the Brazos River Authority out of the way – uh – out of the land management business, and allows the lessees to buy the dirt underneath their homes. And, uh, it has been a long time coming. And, uh, as I said, the ink has already been put to the deal so hopefully we will agree with it.

Uresti: Good.

Please note that Senator Estes did not refer to Possum Kingdom Lake as a crappy old mud-hole out in the middle of nowhere. Instead, he characterized Possum Kingdom Lake as one of the premier recreational lakes in Texas. He was correct in this assessment—the land was extremely valuable.

At this point, Senator Carlos Uresti began to read from a script to ask a well-crafted question of Senator Estes. If you had been in the room that day, it is possible that your intelligence would have been insulted. And, you would have realized that Mike Patterson was about to see the final card that he needed turned face-up.

Uresti: I have a question of you, sir. Is it the intention of this bill to, among other things, be consistent with and effectuate the divestiture agreement of sale and purchase by and between the Brazos River Authority and any third party purchaser according to RFB Number 09-04-391, and all of its amendments?

Estes: I appreciate you asking that and the answer is definitely, "Yes!"

Uresti: Good, I was just curious.

Estes: And we wanted that to be put in the record. I appreciate that.

Uresti: Thank you, any other questions? Senator Jackson?

Senator Mike Jackson: Senator Estes, I was here when you worked on this bill [in 2007] and we've heard testimony long and hard. There was a lot of disagreement I guess on it. I just have one question. It looks like somebody has done a lot of work because you've got a fifty-one page bill here.

But one of the issues that came up last session – and I didn't hear the answer, maybe you do have the answer – I think there is literally millions of dollars' worth of property that people have some very expensive lake homes on that they are leasing. And now we will be offering that property for sale. But the age old question is "follow the money."

Who gets the money?

Estes: Well, the BRA does.

Jackson: Is that a good deal?

Senator Jackson and Senator Estes then engaged in a dialogue on the merits of the Brazos River Authority going through the sunset process. Senator Estes cut that discussion off with a presumptive close.

Estes: Anyway, it's been a long time coming and it's wonderful that we've got everybody that's agreed to this and I appreciate your support.

Senator Jackson responded by leaning back in his chair and laughing. If it was not already obvious that Jackson had no idea as to what was contained within HB 3031, it soon would be.

Uresti: The chair opens up public testimony on House Bill 3031.

I have a card from Mike Patterson, for the bill. Mr. Patterson, did you want to testify? OK, come forward please and identify who you're with.

Michael Harold Patterson made his way to the podium. He sat down, adjusted his glasses, and put his final spin on the deal.

> **Patterson:** My name is Mike Patterson. I'll keep it very brief.
>
> I was the successful third party bidder who will be obligated to resell to the lessees according to the RFB, you know, all their lots, according to some very specific terms and conditions, and things that the BRA or the state could not do on their own, for example, seller financing and some ninety-nine year leases.
>
> I'm here today to say, "thank you," number one. And Senator Estes you downplay your role in making this thing happen. You and Representative Keffer opened a lot of doors and helped solve a very complex problem to the satisfaction of the great majority of those interested stakeholders out there.
>
> And I'm just here to say, "thank you," and to answer any questions that you might have.
>
> **Uresti:** Any questions?
>
> **Estes:** Thank you for working through this issue. It's been a long time. How long have you been working on this?
>
> **Patterson:** Um, a year.
>
> **Estes:** Thank you very much, Mike. I appreciate it. I hope it works out.
>
> **Patterson:** Thank you, sir.
>
> **Uresti:** The Chair recognizes Monte Land.
>
> **Estes:** If I may, Chairman, the chair recognizes that Senator Hegar is here. We're on our last bill and we are ready to vote on all of these, and I need input from y'all if there is anything that you are not ready to vote on.
>
> **Land:** Mr. Chairman, members of the committee. My name is Monte Land.

I am president of Possum Kingdom Lake Association representing most of the people that live at the lake who are the lessees. My wife and I are also thirty-four year owners of a lease at Possum Kingdom Lake and have lived at Possum Kingdom permanently now for seven years.

And, as has already been mentioned by Mr. Chairman here, this is something that's been in the making for a long time. The people out there have been working on this thing for at least six to seven years. And, uh, the people at the lake support this bill, and we hope that you will also support it.

Estes: Well, I would just like to say "thank you" for all the help that you and your association have been. It's been a pleasure working with you.

Uresti: Senator Jackson?

What would happen over the next sixty seconds would wind up costing the taxpayers of Texas several hundred millions of dollars.

Jackson: Under this worked out deal, who is in charge of appraising the property values for the land?

The honest answer to this question would have been, "Absolutely, no one."

Unlike House Bill 3032, which directed the Brazos River Authority to sell roughly 880 acres of property to the Set Ranch, subject to a fair market appraisal, House Bill 3031 included no such provision. Instead, HB 3031 created a laundering process that required a straw man to resell the property to the individual leaseholders at a preset, formulaic price that had nothing to do with fair market value.

This would have been an excellent opportunity for Senator Uresti or Senator Hegar, who was now present and listening to the testimony, to set the record straight. Both of these senators had opposed the forced divestiture in 2007 and now Uresti was actively supporting HB 3031's parade walk through the stock show while Hegar was passively allowing it to happen.

In response to Senator Jackson's question about appraisals, Monte Land's entire face turned into a giant grin that looked like a possum eating Elmer's glue.

> **Jackson:** Come on. You've been working on this for six years. You have got to know that.
>
> **Land:** Yes sir, the appraisals—the way the land is to be sold—based on the bill in the third party sale—it's going to be based on the appraisals of the land through the county appraisal district.

Monte Land chose his words very carefully. Rather that pointing out that the bill would be using the "assessed" values produced by the over-litigated appraisal district, he stated that "appraisals" would be used. This was categorically false. In response to Monte Land's statement, Senator Mike Jackson then turned to Senator Craig Estes who was not in the frame of the camera. Senator Jackson asked Senator Estes a simple, yet direct question.

> **Jackson:** And it says fair market value?

Senator Estes' answer cannot be heard on the video archives. However, his response obviously satisfied Senator Jackson. You can decide yourself whether Senator Jackson was slightly misled, or flat out lied to, by viewing the video archive:

> http://tlcsenate.granicus.com/MediaPlayer. php?view_id=14&clip_id=2419.

If you fast-forward to 37:59 you can avoid having to listen to the plight of the white-tailed deer in state of Texas at the time.

Senator Jackson continued his line of questioning almost immediately after asking Senator Estes if House Bill 3031 required the property to be sold for fair market value.

Jackson: Ok, one other question. Obviously, I think I saw somewhere there are 1600 properties, or something, around the lake there.

After this bill passes, is there going to be further residential and commercial development around the lake that will have to be dealt with, as obviously our population grows?

Land: Yes sir.

Estes: If I may add, not all of the property around the lake is under BRA control. There is lots of private land too. There is just a smattering of BRA land.

Jackson: But, I guess the BRA will still be involved in land sales though, as a result of this, until all of the properties are, uh...

Estes: No they won't; because, the third party, Mr. Patterson, is going to be the one that is going to do the selling thing. It's like a bulk sale to him, and then he is going to resell it to the homeowners.

Land: As I understand it, it is basically just the current lessees – the current residential – that are leasing right now. Any new development, you would have to ask the BRA about that.

Jackson: Ok. Thank you, sir.

Senator Carlos Uresti then read off a list of cards that had been submitted by witnesses who did not wish to testify. Senator Jackson then attempted one last time to figure out exactly what was being considered by the Agriculture and Rural Affairs Committee.

Jackson: Did you say that there is a resource witness from the Brazos River Authority? I would like to call him forward.

Uresti: Mr. Phillips?

Matt Phillips, the BRA's Manager of Government and Customer Relations, then walked to the witness table and took his seat in front of the microphone. To say that Matt looked uncomfortable would have been an understatement.

> **Phillips:** Mr. Chairman, members, Matt Phillips, Brazos River Authority.

I will say it one last time. Matt Phillips is a true professional. While he was squirming in his chair and pulling on his collar, Matt never once perjured himself. He did, however, neglect to clarify that the property would not be sold for fair market value. The reason for this was simple: Senator Mike Jackson failed to ask him.

> **Jackson:** Ok. Did you hear my questions earlier about the property that is under BRA control that is not being leased currently? And what will happen to that property in the future?
>
> **Phillips:** The bill does not address that property. Obviously, some of that property is included in House Bill 3032, which you heard previously. Not all of it, however. We will continue to hold some undeveloped property.
>
> **Jackson:** Ok, and what—is that just your—you'll just hold it?
>
> **Phillips:** Well, the board would obviously have to decide if they wish to sell that property in a different manner. But we would have the ability to do so, yes.
>
> The property in question is *some* of our property. In total, we have about fourteen-thousand acres. Eighty-five hundred of that is within what is called the FERC project boundary, which we cannot sell, because it is Federal Energy Regulatory Commission-controlled. Fifty-five hundred of that is outside of the FERC project area, and of that, what is included in this bill, is roughly twelve hundred acres.

Jackson: So you've got thirty-two hundred acres, roughly, sitting out there that you can just sell it if you want to, like it's your property.

Phillips: Yes, sir. I would say this. We will not be leasing that property. We have not written new leases for some time, as a policy of the board. We have not leased any un-leased property.

Jackson: And why wouldn't you?

Phillips: Um, probably—partly—because of the reason that we are sitting here today.

Jackson: Well, I guess when y'all go through sunset you'll figure all of that out, right?

Estes: I like your attitude, Senator, that's great.

Well, let me just say, Matt, you and your organization, and General Ford, have been great to work with on this. It's been a long, hard road for everybody. And, I really appreciate y'all figuring it out for us.

I am trying extremely hard to keep the profanity to a minimum, but this was a prick move on the part of Senator Estes. Just as Attorney General Greg Abbott had placed the responsibility for determining whether the property was being sold for fair market value squarely on the shoulders of the board of the BRA, Senator Estes was now trying to pretend that the staff of the BRA was responsible for making Mike Patterson's "Texas Miracle" come true. The only thing that the staff of the Brazos River Authority had figured out was that they were state employees who answered to the governor's appointees. Suggesting that the staff of the BRA had stitched this deal together was pure chicken shit.

Uresti: Is there anyone else that wishes to testify on, for, or against House Bill 3031? The chair hears none, public testimony is closed and we will leave that bill pending.

Estes: All right, thank you.

> Members we are finished hearing all of the bills. We have two bills that have committee substitutes, and the rest of them are just bills with no committee substitutes.
>
> The chair is ready to vote these out. Is there any bill that a member has a problem with voting out today?

Estes looked to his right at Senator Carlos Uresti and then back to his left at Senators Mike Jackson and Glenn Hegar. Seeing no opposition on their faces, he stated with a tone of relief, "Alright."

Senator Estes then took the four members of his "Nobody Gives a Damn" committee through a litany of votes on each of the bills that had been presented. In each case, the vote was unanimous. It was also recommended that each bill be sent to the Local and Uncontested Calendar Committee of the Senate. This meant that they would be voted on en masse by the Texas Senate along with all of the other bills that no one gave a damn about.

Mike Patterson's deal was done. And, it had only required him to testify in front of the Texas Legislature for a total of forty-five seconds. The only thing that he was required to do was simply say, "Thank you."

For those of you who complain about gridlock and yearn for bipartisan compromise, here is your chance to celebrate. Of the four senators in the room that day, three of them were Republicans and one of them was a Democrat—Carlos Uresti. Two of the four had opposed selling the property at Possum Kingdom Lake at a discount two years earlier. Now, the Democratic senator, Carlos Uresti, was reading from a script to actively advance the passage of the bill while the Republican senator, Glenn Hegar, was passively supporting the measure through his silence.

When we get to the "why" phase of this tale, we are also going to need to ask Senator Carlos Uresti and Senator Glenn Hegar why they changed their respective positions on selling the property for fair market value. Senator Hegar was arguably the most important swing vote in 2009. This would be entirely inconsequential were it not for one fact: In 2014, State Senator Glenn Hegar took one more step up the ladder of the Republican hierarchy and became the state's comptroller. In essence, Glenn Hegar is now the Chief Financial Officer of the state of Texas.

Four days after the Senate Committee on Agriculture and Rural Affairs weighed the merits of House Bill 3031, the Texas Senate passed the bill along with the others that had been placed on the Local and Consent Calendar. Twelve days after that, on May 27, 2009, Governor Rick Perry signed House Bill 3031 into law. This law became effective immediately and Mike Patterson's deal was almost complete.

There were only a few more things left to do. The next action item on the list was for Mike Patterson to actually come up with the money to bankroll his deal. After that, Patterson would need to convince Monte Land and the Possum Kingdom Lake Association that it was time to declare victory and cash out. And, most importantly, the players involved would need to find a way to make the Federal Energy Regulatory Commission go away. As long as FERC held jurisdiction over the shoreline, the weekenders at Possum Kingdom Lake would not be able to own the dirt beneath their homes all the way down to the water's edge.

Chapter 19

WELL, FERC ME!

I would like to invite anyone who is still of the opinion that the shoreline of Possum Kingdom Lake was sold for a price that even approached fair market value to a friendly game of poker.

I would also like to extend that same invitation to anyone who still believes that the property in question was sold through a competitive bidding process. Or that this was simply a *local* issue. Or, that the highest elected officials in the state of Texas were not actively involved in orchestrating this outcome. Or, that the taxpayers of Texas did not get totally screwed.

Believe it or not, there are people out there who still contend that this was a legitimate transaction. Those folks also maintain that what happened to the hydroelectric power plant at Possum Kingdom Lake was merely a series of incredibly unfortunate coincidences.

Throughout this entire tale, the wildcard in the deck has been the Federal Energy Regulatory Commission, more commonly known as FERC. Because the federal government provided over half of the funds required to build the dam, FERC held jurisdiction over both the dam and the shoreline.

This relationship was memorialized in a Texas Historical Marker that was erected in 1983.

Marker #: 5363006269

Built in response to disastrous Brazos River flooding, Morris Sheppard Dam and Possum Kingdom Reservoir were early attempts at water conservation and flood control in Texas. The U.S. Government funded $4,500,000 of the three-year, $8,500,000 project through the Works Progress Administration, a Depression era recovery agency. Named for U.S. Senator Morris Sheppard and completed in 1941, the dam is 2,740 feet long and 190 feet high. Nine spillway gates allow for the passage of flood waters and drift material. Power generating facilities consist of two 11,250-killowatt units which serve much of the surrounding area. The creation of Possum Kingdom Lake from the impounded waters of Morris Sheppard Dam sent bridges, roads and an entire town underwater. Recovery was initially slow, but quickly picked up after World War II with the establishment of major fishing lodges, camping areas and other recreational facilities. The growth and success of the area is a tribute to the spirit of the surrounding communities which continue to benefit from the project's original purposes of water conservation and supply, and hydroelectric power generation.[189]

The Federal Power Commission issued the original license for the project on May 25, 1938. The renamed Federal Energy Regulatory Commission granted the BRA a new license for the project in 1989 with a thirty-year term. That renewed license had an expiration date of August 31, 2019.[190] This, of course, meant that FERC would retain jurisdiction over the dam and the shoreline for at least ten years after the Brazos River Authority sold the property in 2009.

---

[189] "Morris Sheppard Dam and Possum Kingdom Lake–A Project of the Brazos River Authority," *Mineral Wells Convention & Visitors Bureau*, accessed January 5, 2014. http://www.visitmineralwells.org/content.cfm?B=1&L=108.

[190] Secretary Kimberly D. Bose, "Order Granting Approval under Section 22 of the Federal Power Act and License Article 5," *Federal Energy Regulatory Commission*, September 18, 2008, accessed October 1, 2013.http://www.ferc.gov/whats-new/comm-meet/2008/091808/H-2.pdf.

From the day that the dam and the hydroelectric plant went into operation in 1941, the Brazos River Authority has been selling its electricity to the Brazos Electric Power Cooperative. As Possum Kingdom Lake was out in the middle of nowhere, the BEPC was the only game in town. Consequently, the relationship between the BRA and the BEPC was as old as the lake itself.

Both the original and the renewed FERC licenses required that a control strip be maintained along the entire 310 miles of the shoreline. The purpose of the control strip, which was more commonly referred to as the *buffer zone,* was to ensure the protection of "the scenic, aesthetic, public recreation, and other environmental values of the reservoir shoreline."[191]

The buffer zone was approximately twenty-five feet deep. In effect, the buffer zone was also federal property. This meant that any U.S. citizen had the right to walk along the water's edge right through someone else's backyard. It also meant that the leaseholders were not allowed to build structures or fences along the shoreline. As you might imagine, this lack of control did not sit well with the weekenders and many of them built whatever they cared to on the buffer zone.

As you might also imagine, dams require maintenance. This is especially true if the dam contains a power plant that generates electricity. In 2001, the Brazos River Authority issued $8,925,000 in bonds to replace the spillway gates. In 2005, the BRA issued another $12,875,000 in bonds to complete those replacements. The 2005 bond issue was also intended to make some repairs to the power generation facilities. One of the resulting projects was so successful that it actually won an award. This particular project was completed in August 2007 at a cost of $1.1 million.[192]

And yet, for all of this time, money, and effort, the Brazos River Authority was unable to keep the power units running. Unit Number 1 was taken offline due to concerns about corrosion in the penstocks in May

---

[191] Director Joseph D. Morgan, "Order Denying Request to Change Project Boundary," *Federal Energy Regulatory Commission*, June 25, 2009, accessed October 1, 2013.
http://elibrary.ferc.gov/idmws/common/OpenNat.asp?fileID=12056953.

[192] "AWARD OF MERIT: Repairs to the Morris Sheppard Dam and Powerhouse at Possum Kingdom Lake," *International Concrete Repair Institute*, 2008, accessed June 4, 2013.
http://www.icri.org/awards/2008/morrisshepparddam.asp.

2007. Unit Number 2 was taken offline in August 2007 due to electrical malfunctions.

The BRA chronicled the challenges surrounding the operation of the electrical generation facilities in its Annual Operating Plan for Fiscal Year 2009. This report also illuminated the fact that the BRA was still trying to do the next right thing.

> In September 2003, a Memorandum of Understanding and a Letter of Agreement was signed between the Authority and Brazos Electric Power Cooperative (BEPC) to address rehabilitation needs of the hydropower facility and to adjust wholesale power purchase rates in order to generate a positive financial operating margin. Through the negotiation process, it was determined that a lease type arrangement with BEPC would be more advantageous for both parties. Therefore, on November 1, 2007, a Facility Use Agreement, as well as a Facility Cost Agreement, was signed by both BEPC and the Authority. Upon receiving federal approval of these agreements, BEPC can begin their evaluation and repair process.[193]

On December 6, 2007, the BRA submitted a request to FERC seeking permission to outsource the entire operation of the hydroelectric plant to the Brazos Electric Power Cooperative. Within the contemplated *Facility Use Agreement*, the BEPC would become responsible for the operation and maintenance of the power generation facilities which included:

> The powerhouse (integrated in the dam) containing two 11.25-MW generators; an intake tower; two 12-foot-diameter; 140-foot-long penstocks directing water flow from the intake tower to the

---

[193] BRA Staff, "Annual Operating Plan–FY2009," Page 4-12, *Brazos River Authority*, September 1, 2008, accessed June 9, 2011. https://web.archive.org/web/20151127171353/https://dgyancy.files.wordpress.com/2011/02/fy09_upper_basin.pdf. https://web.archive.org/web/20090107041603/http://www.brazos.org/FA_pdf/FY09_Budget_TOC.pdf.

powerhouse; a 6.9 kilovolt (kV) transmission line; and a tailrace channel.[194]

This would have been an outstanding solution for the taxpayers of Texas and the BRA sold it hard to FERC. The BRA's principal argument was that the Facility Use Agreement would:

> ensure that the financial resources necessary to make the required repairs at the project in the near future will be available, along with the resources necessary to remedy any problems that may arise in the future. This in turn will ensure that the project is properly maintained consistent with Commission standards and provide [the Cooperative] with the assurance that it will be able to consistently rely on the project as a source of power to meet the needs of its member cooperatives in the future. The financial burden for repairing, maintaining, and operating the hydroelectric facility would be handed over to a company whose core competency was the generation and distribution of electricity.[195]

This was a quintessential win-win. Moreover, a renewable energy source would be preserved for the benefit of another generation of Texans. Perhaps most important, the Brazos River Authority would enjoy a recurring revenue stream of $475,000 per year over the course of twenty-nine years (the first year would be free of charge).[196] If the BEPC exercised its ten-year

---

[194] John Whittaker, "Application for Approval of a Facility Use Agreement Involving Project Party," *Federal Energy Regulatory Commission*, December 6, 2007, accessed October 1, 2013. http://elibrary.ferc.gov/idmws/common/opennat.asp?fileID=12291037.

[195] Secretary Kimberly D. Bose, "Order Granting Approval under Section 22 of the Federal Power Act and License Article 5," Page 5, *Federal Energy Regulatory Commission*, September 18, 2008, accessed October 1, 2013. http://www.ferc.gov/whats-new/comm-meet/2008/091808/H-2.pdf.

[196] John Whittaker, "Facility Use Agreement, Article XIII," Page 11, *Federal Energy Regulatory Commission*, December 6, 2007, accessed October 1, 2013. http://elibrary.ferc.gov/idmws/common/opennat.asp?fileID=12291037.

option at the end of the agreement, the total take would be $18.5 million over the life of the contract.

By contrast, this was a horrifying solution for the leaseholders. The Facility Use Agreement with the BEPC was a thirty-year deal with a ten year option. If this agreement were to be consummated, most of the leaseholders could expect to die before they, or even their heirs, had the ability to own the last twenty-five feet of their lake lots along the water's edge. This was not an acceptable outcome.

The business decisions related to the repairs for the dam, and the outsourcing of the BRA's power generation operations, were made while the board of the BRA was still constituted by duty-bound Texans. These decisions were also made before Rick Perry's April Fools' Day massacre.

It took over nine months for FERC to analyze and approve the BRA's request to allow the Brazos Electric Power Cooperative to assume the responsibility for operating the power plant. Unfortunately, by the time that FERC had rendered its ruling on September 18, 2008, the "Texas Miracle" was in full motion. Ten days earlier, Mike Patterson had attended a private meeting in Waco where he met with several legislators, lobbyists, and representatives of the BRA. The purpose of this meeting was to discuss the property laundering scheme that would be used to force the divestiture of the shoreline of Possum Kingdom Lake.[197]

Twelve days prior to Mike Patterson's private meeting in Waco, the Brazos River Authority had proffered yet another request to FERC. This occurred on August 27, 2008. FERC summarized the request that was received from the BRA in the following fashion:

> Brazos states that it anticipates that the Texas State legislature will, in its next session, consider legislation requiring Brazos to sell its leased property; including lands within the project boundary, around Possum Kingdom Lake, to the cottage and commercial lessees.

---

[197] Libby Cluett, "One Man's Plan," *Mineral Wells Index*, September 22, 2008, accessed July 10, 2010.
https://web.archive.org/web/20080927030255/http://www.mineralwellsindex.com/local/local_story_266091033.html.

Brazos states that it is willing to comply with state-required divestiture, and is exploring options for the voluntary sale of the lands at issue. It also recognizes, however, that its license requires it to possess project lands in fee or retain the right to use those lands in perpetuity, and that the sale of project lands would require [FERC] Commission approval.

Brazos poses three questions. First, would the Commission approve an application to transfer fee ownership of 330 acres of project land in the buffer strip to cottage site owners? Second, would the Commission approve an application to transfer fee ownership of 550 acres of project lands to commercial lessees? Third, what actions should Brazos take if the Commission answers the first two questions in the negative, and the Texas legislature nonetheless enacts legislation requiring Brazos to transfer the property in question?

The official answer to these three questions from FERC was rendered on the same day that FERC approved the outsourcing arrangement between the BRA and BEPC—September 18, 2008. The summation of that response reads as follows:

The Commission cannot, as Brazos requests, suggest a course of action for Brazos should the Texas legislature require it to transfer the cottage site and commercial lands, notwithstanding the requirements of Brazos' license. However, we note that the Supreme Court has held that, in passing the FPA,[198] Congress enacted a federal scheme for the complete and orderly development of the nation's water power resources that preempts conflicting state regulation. Any state attempt to require a licensee to divest itself of lands that we have determined are needed for project purposes would accordingly be preempted.

---

[198] Federal Power Act, June 10, 1920.

> The Commission puts Brazos on notice that the transfer of project lands without prior Commission approval would be a violation of the license of the Morris Shepherd Dam Project and could subject Brazos to enforcement action, including civil and criminal penalties.
>
> By the Commission.
>
> Kimberly D. Bose,
>
> Secretary.[199]

Did someone in the federal government seriously have the nerve to put an agency of the state of Texas on notice—and then have the audacity to threaten civil and criminal penalties? Those were fighting words in the state of Texas, and it was not likely that they were taken kindly.

As you will likely recall, the former attorney general of Texas (and current governor), Greg Abbott, characterized his typical workday as follows: "I go into the office, I sue Barack Obama, and then I go home."

How do you suppose that Governor Rick Perry, Lt. Governor David Dewhurst, and Attorney General Greg Abbott reacted to this affront to their authority? Kimberly Bose might as well have said something shameful about one of the "Three Amigos'" mothers. From this point forward, the hydroelectric plant at Possum Kingdom Lake was doomed.

While the language in this response was certainly unwelcome, the timing of the response was even more problematic. Four days after this official position was received from FERC, Mike Patterson was scheduled to pitch his property laundering scheme to the BRA and to the public. At roughly forty-five minutes into Mike Patterson's presentation on September 22, 2008, Christopher DeCluitt stated his position on the FERC boundary.

> We can't sell the FERC land because of our license. But, should FERC ever go away, I would be in favor of a remainder right.

---

[199] Secretary Kimberly D. Bose, "Order on Petition for Declaratory Order," *Federal Energy Regulatory Commission*, September 18, 2008, accessed October 1, 2013. http://www.ferc.gov/whats-new/comm-meet/2008/091808/H-4.pdf.

To which Mike Patterson quickly replied,

> Thank you! That's exactly, exactly – if you would do that for us...

Five weeks after the receipt of FERC's response, on October 27, 2008, the board of the BRA met to vote on putting the property up for sale. The result of that meeting was the "Immaculate Resolution." As you may have noticed, over half of that resolution dealt with the disposition of the FERC buffer zone. From the perspective of the leaseholders, one of the key paragraphs in this resolution read as follows:

> **BE IT FURTHER RESOLVED** that the Board of Directors of the Brazos River Authority hereby directs staff to evaluate granting a residual interest in residential leased property located within the FERC project boundary whereby at the time the FERC license terminates or such property is excluded from the FERC project boundary, such property shall revert to the then-current owner of the land adjacent to such property;[200]

In other words, if the license that FERC had issued to the BRA should ever cease to exist, the buffer zone between each leaseholder's lot and the water's edge would automatically be given to each respective leaseholder.

Note that the "Immaculate Resolution" did not state that the leaseholders would be given the opportunity to purchase the buffer zone between their property and the water's edge at some future date. Instead, the resolution used the phrase "granting a residual interest." To me, this sounds incredibly similar to "granting a thing of value."

Christopher DeCluitt, and several other representatives from the Brazos River Authority, stated multiple times in public, and on the record, that they were prohibited by law from selling the FERC buffer zone. If

---

[200] BRA Staff, "Agenda Item 13, Possum Kingdom Bid Document," *Brazos River Authority*, October 27, 2008, accessed November 25, 2010. https://web.archive.org/web/20090705212256/http://www.brazos.org/board_actions/10-27-08 Quarterly Board Actions.pdf.

the BRA could not sell it, then the only way that the leaseholders could eventually own it would be if it were given to them for free.

House Bill 3031 did exactly that: it granted a residual interest in the buffer zone to each individual leaseholder. Since the Texas Legislature is prohibited by the Texas Constitution from granting a thing of value to an individual or group of individuals, I would submit to you that House Bill 3031 was in direct violation of the Texas Constitution.

Fifty-seven days *after* the BRA put the property up for sale via RFB No. 09-04-391, the Authority once again requested that the Federal Energy Regulatory Commission remove the buffer zone in front of each leased lot from FERC jurisdiction. This occurred on March 6, 2009. This was also thirty-three days before the deadline to submit a bid for the property. It is worth noting that this request also occurred thirteen days before the BRA actually hired a firm to market the property that it was selling. One might conclude that the BRA was more interested in getting rid of FERC than they were with realizing the maximum return on the property for the taxpayers of Texas.

This second request of FERC involved a land swap. The Brazos River Authority offered to exchange the 310 acres of FERC land in front of the leaseholders' lots for 930 acres of park land that was close to the lake. Once again, the Federal Energy Regulatory Commission responded with a steadfast "No" on June 25, 2009. The official statement from FERC was succinct and to the point:

> Brazos River Authority's application, filed March 6, 2009, for Commission authorization to change the project boundary for the Morris Sheppard Dam Hydroelectric Project No. 1490, is denied.[201]

Well, FERC me.

At this point, the Brazos River Authority had already voted to accept Mike Patterson's bid for the property and Governor Rick Perry had already signed House Bill 3031 into law. Now it appeared that the leaseholders

---

[201] Director Joseph D. Morgan, "Order Denying Request to Change Project Boundary," *Federal Energy Regulatory Commission*, June 25, 2009, accessed October 1, 2013. http://elibrary.ferc.gov/idmws/common/OpenNat.asp?fileID=12056953.

were not going to be able to take title to the last twenty-five feet between their lake houses and the water's edge for quite some time.

Perhaps this would have been a prime opportunity for former Attorney General Greg Abbott to go to into the office and sue the federal government. Or, perhaps it was not. As Greg Abbott can attest, suing the federal government can be a lengthy and expensive process with mixed results.

To complicate matters further, the Facilities Use Agreement that the BRA had executed with BEPC in 2007 was a thirty-year agreement.[202] If FERC was refusing to relinquish the shoreline, the weekenders were staring at the very real possibility that they would be buying a lake-view lot from Mike Patterson, rather than a lakefront lot. Having come this far, this was an absolutely unacceptable outcome.

Ah, but as former Attorney General Greg Abbott will also tell you, there is always a loophole. What was needed now was a good old-fashioned case of FERC-flu. The hydroelectric plant at Possum Kingdom Lake was about to get very sick.

The Facility Use Agreement between the BRA and the BEPC was indeed a contract.[203] In order for this contract to take effect, both the BRA and the BEPC were required to gain the approval of their respective regulators. The BRA was regulated by FERC, while the BEPC was regulated by a state agency in Texas known as the Rural Utility Service (RUS).

To bridge the gap between the old agreement and the contemplated Facility Use Agreement, the BRA and the BEPC had also entered into a second, interim agreement. This interim agreement, entitled the *Facility Cost Agreement*, specified that the Brazos Electric Power Cooperative would be responsible for the costs of operating the power plant until both parties

---

[202] Federal Energy Regulatory Commission, "Notice of Amendment of License and Soliciting Comments, Motions to Intervene, and Protests," *Federal Register*, February 26, 2008, accessed June 1, 2011. https://www.federalregister.gov/articles/2008/02/26/E8-3549/brazos-river-authority-notice-of-amendment-of-license-and-soliciting-comments-motions-to-intervene.

[203] Justice Rex D. Davis, "Memorandum Opinion, Brazos River Authority v. Brazos Electric Power Cooperative, Inc.," Page 5, *Tenth Court of Appeals*, June 23, 2010, accessed October 5, 2013. https://cases.justia.com/texas/tenth-court-of-appeals/10-09-00403-cv.pdf?ts=1370478226.

had secured their respective regulatory approvals. This interim agreement also had an expiration date of April 30, 2009.[204]

The Brazos River Authority held up its end of the bargain and requested its needed approval from FERC. However, this was before Governor Rick Perry replaced seventeen of the twenty-one board members over the course of one year and one week. Once the new board members realized the mistake that had been made, they embraced a stalling maneuver and simply ran the clock out on the Brazos Electric Power Cooperative.

On the other hand, the BEPC had failed to secure its necessary approval from the RUS. This approval would have triggered the Facility Use Agreement and the BEPC would most likely still be there today. According to the BEPC, the reason for this was simple. The Brazos River Authority had refused to allow the independent engineering firm selected by the Rural Utility Service access to the property. As a result, this firm was unable to inspect the hydroelectric generation facilities as required by the RUS.[205]

On April 30, 2009, three days after the BRA had voted to accept Mike Patterson's bid, the interim Facilities Cost Agreement between the BRA and the BEPC expired. As a result, the long term Facilities Use Agreement could not be triggered.

On July 9, 2009, the BEPC filed suit against the BRA claiming breach of contract. The BEPC also claimed that it had lost several million dollars as a result of the BRA's stonewalling. The newly constituted board of the Brazos River Authority could not have cared less. Two and a half weeks later, on July 28, 2009, the BRA voted to authorize general manager Phil Ford to "take any and all actions deemed appropriate to manage, coordinate, and negotiate any and all litigation" related to the Brazos

---

[204] Justice Rex D. Davis, "Memorandum Opinion, Brazos River Authority v. Brazos Electric Power Cooperative, Inc.," Page 3, *Tenth Court of Appeals*, June 23, 2010, accessed October 5, 2013. https://cases.justia.com/texas/tenth-court-of-appeals/10-09-00403-cv.pdf?ts=1370478226.http://statecasefiles.justia.com/documents/texas/tenth-court-of-appeals/10-09-00403-cv.pdf?ts=1370478226

[205] Sawnie A. McEntire, Davis S. Gamble, "Original Petition, Brazos Electric Power Cooperative, Inc. v. Brazos River Authority," Page 6, *414th District Court*, July 9, 2009, accessed October 5, 2013. https://web.archive.org/web/20151127234118/ https://dgyancy.files.wordpress.com/2011/02/plantiffs-original-bepc-v-bra0001.pdf.

Electric Power Cooperative. Immediately thereafter, the board of the BRA voted to "investigate and initiate" the process for decommissioning the hydroelectric plant and surrendering its FERC license. During this same meeting, the board also voted to ratify the contract and consummate the sale of the shoreline to Mike Patterson.[206]

In response to the lawsuit that was filed by the Brazos Electric Power Cooperative, the Brazos River Authority simply claimed "governmental immunity" from the lawsuit. The BEPC took the matter all the way to the Texas Supreme Court, and on June 24, 2011, the BEPC's final appeal was denied. The Texas Supreme Court affirmed that the BEPC could not sue the BRA. Four weeks later, on July 20, 2011, the Brazos River Authority formally applied to the Federal Energy Regulatory Commission to surrender its license to operate a hydroelectric plant at Possum Kingdom Lake.

Five months later, on December 23, 2011, FERC officially issued an order accepting the surrender of the BRA's license.[207] Following a two and one-half year process to decommission the plant that cost several million dollars, the residual interest that House Bill 3031 had granted to each leaseholder was automatically triggered. The leaseholders immediately owned their lots all the way down to the water's edge. This residual windfall included the one-half acre tract of former FERC property that bordered the $6 million estate located at 1171 Panorama Way.

The official closure of the hydroelectric plant at Morris Sheppard Dam occurred on March 12, 2014.[208] And with that, the "Texas Miracle" was complete.

If you are wondering how the weekenders benefited from the elimination of FERC, consider this. With FERC in the equation, the shoreline property that was originally sold by the BRA was 900 acres which

---

[206] Board Meeting "Agenda Item 25," *Brazos River Authority Board Meeting Minutes*, July 27, 2009, accessed November 10, 2014.
http://www.brazos.org/Portals/0/board_audio/7-27-2009-BRD25.mp3.
[207] Director Edward A. Abrams, "Order Accepting Surrender of License," *Federal Energy Regulatory Commission*, December 23, 2011, accessed October 1, 2013.http://elibrary.ferc.gov/idmws/common/opennat.asp?fileID=12848538.
[208] Regional Engineer Wayne B. King, "Project Surrender," *Federal Energy Regulatory Commission*, March 12, 2014, accessed October 1, 2015.http://elibrary.ferc.gov/idmws/common/OpenNat.asp?fileID=13495481.

was spread over the 310 miles of shoreline. Once FERC was eliminated, the property that was transferred ballooned to 1200 acres. On average, each leaseholder's lot expanded by 33%. If you live in a typical bedroom community in Texas, this additional land grant for each weekender was larger than the lot that your house sits on.

Chapter 20

LAUNDER. RINSE. REPEAT.

While it is true that the vast majority of the players involved in the sale of the shoreline at Possum Kingdom Lake made out like bandits, there was also a large contingency that got left out in the cold.

At the time of the original bulk sale in 2009, there were eighty-nine leaseholders who were not able to participate in the laundering scheme due to the FERC license. This group was comprised of forty-two residential lots that were entirely located within the FERC buffer zone and forty-seven commercial tracts that were located completely or partially within the buffer zone. The aggregate size of these properties was approximately 496 acres.

Four years after the "Texas Miracle," State Senator Craig Estes and State Representative Jim Keffer went back to the legislature to right this wrong. On February 27, 2013, Senator Estes filed Senate Bill 918 which essentially replicated the property laundering scheme of 2009. This bill extended the same repurchase options to the remaining leaseholders.

Senator Estes summarized his legislative intent as follows:

> Now that FERC is in the process of decommissioning the hydroelectric power plant, these leased lands that were previously excluded will be available for sale. This bill seeks to apply the same legislatively authorized divestiture

process to the remaining 89 commercial and residential authority properties as was created under H.B. 3031.[209]

Understand this clearly. FERC was never in the process of decommissioning the hydroelectric power plant at Possum Kingdom Lake—the Brazos River Authority was in sole control of that. The Federal Energy and Regulatory Commission never did anything more than respond to the BRA's requests and proposals. Please also understand that the BRA was also required to foot the bill for mothballing the plant which ran into the millions of dollars.

Senate Bill 918 was first heard in the Senate Committee on Agriculture, Rural Affairs & Homeland Security on March 11, 2013. It passed unanimously with minimal discussion. After Senator Estes asked that the bill be placed on the Local and Uncontested Calendar, Senator Glenn Hegar engaged Senator Estes in the following dialogue:

> **Hegar:** I do have a question Senator Estes. These bills kind of remind me of an old issue involving a colleague sitting between us, uh, "Bexar Met." I think we've had to deal with that issue about—I don't know—every session that I've been up here except this session.
>
> And so my question is, it seems like Possum Kingdom is your Bexar Met. And, uh, you got any plans for legislation next session or do you think this is going to wrap her up?

Senator Hegar was referring to a scandal-ridden water utility by the name of Bexar Metropolitan Water District located in the San Antonio area. His remark drew some awkward laughter that grew as the conversation continued.

---

[209] Senate Research Center, "Bill Analysis, Author's/Sponsor's Statement of Intent, SB 918," *Texas Senate Agriculture, Rural Affairs & Homeland Security Committee*, July 26, 2013, accessed October 23, 2014.http://www.capitol.state.tx.us/tlodocs/83R/analysis/html/SB00918F.htm.

Estes: We hope that we can wrap everything up this session. I will say there is one more issue out there but we are waiting on agreement from the two parties that are negotiating. And if there is no agreement it is unlikely that there will be another bill.

Hegar: I was going to say, can we recall that committee substitute and put that language in there so we don't have to deal with this next session?

The awkward laughter grew more genuine.

Estes: Senator—as you well know—sometimes the fruit has to ripen before it falls to the ground.

Hegar: I just want it to ripen before I quit this legislative process. Thank you, Senator.[210]

With that comment, the entire room broke out in unanimous laughter. State Senator Glenn Hegar was the decisive swing vote in 2009 when he reversed his opposition to the forced sale and voted in favor of House Bill 3031. If Senator Glenn Hegar ever tries to tell you that he was not fully aware of the contents of HB 3031, remind him of this conversation.

Senate Bill 918 was then routed to the House Committee on Natural Resources where it was heard on May 7, 2013. Representative Jim Keffer spent a total of two minutes and fifteen seconds explaining that the bill simply completed the transaction that was sanctified by House Bill 3031 in 2009. There were no questions asked and the bill was left pending in committee.[211]

One week later, on May 14, Senate Bill 918 was again considered in a formal meeting of the Natural Resources committee and passed

---

[210] Sen. Glenn Hegar, "Senate Agriculture, Rural Affairs & Homeland Security Committee," Senate Audio/Video Archives, *Texas Senate*, March 11, 2013, accessed November 19, 2015. (Fast forward to 23:00).http://tlcsenate.granicus.com/MediaPlayer.php?view_id=9&clip_id=753.

[211] Rep. Jim Keffer, "House Natural Resources Committee," House Audio/Video Archives, *Texas House*, May 7, 2013, accessed November 19, 2015. (Fast forward to 34:15).http://tlchouse.granicus.com/MediaPlayer.php?view_id=28&clip_id=6744.

unanimously. It was then sent to the Local and Uncontested Calendar committee of the House where it sailed through once again. On May 27, 2013, SB 918 was signed in both the House and the Senate and sent to Governor Rick Perry. Governor Perry signed Senate Bill 918 on June 14, 2013 and the law became effective immediately.

As a result of this passage, the final 496 acres of lakefront property was now eligible to be laundered to the respective leaseholders as soon as the closure of the hydroelectric plant at Possum Kingdom Lake was completed. FERC issued its final order officially declaring the hydroelectric plant closed on March 12, 2014.[212]

Two months later, on May 19, the Brazos River Authority issued Request for Bids 12-07-816 which put the final 496 acres up for sale to the highest bidder. As was the case in 2009, the RFB incorporated a three month window to formulate and submit a bid. This set Monday, July 21, 2014, as the deadline to do so.

As was also the case in 2009, Michael Harold Patterson was ahead of the curve. Five months prior to the issuance of the second RFB, Patterson sent the following email to himself and carbon copied multiple potential investors:

> From: Michael Patterson
>
> Sent: Wednesday, December 04, 2013 7:03 PM
>
> To: Michael Patterson [et. al.]
>
> Subject: Casino Beach project and 2nd BRA bulk purchase at PK Lake
>
> Friends and Prior Investment Clients,
>
> As many of you are aware, because of your participation, in 2010 we were successful in syndicating equity for a Possum Kingdom Lake Brazos River Authority bulk leasehold purchase that generated $30 Million in profits and returned investors their money plus a 100% profit

---

[212] Regional Engineer Wayne B. King, "Project Surrender," *Federal Energy Regulatory Commission*, March 12, 2014, accessed October 1, 2015.http://elibrary.ferc.gov/idmws/common/OpenNat.asp?fileID=13495481.

after a year and one day! That was fun and profitable for everyone involved :-) [sic]

After 3 plus years of tire kicking and fine tuning we are excited to now announce an invitation for you to consider investing in another equity syndication. We are ready to syndicate our Casino Beach at Lake Worth project and possibly a 2nd bulk purchase of leasehold properties from the Brazos River Authority (BRA) at Possum Kingdom (PK) Lake... a "bundled investment opportunity".

Disappointingly, the Brazos River Authority received only one bid for the right to purchase and immediately resell the remaining 496 acres of shoreline property on Monday, July 21, 2014. Color me shocked, but that sole bidder's name was Michael Harold Patterson. Patterson's bid was for $6.5 million while the BRA's documentation indicated that the aggregate assessed value of the remaining property was in the range of $14 million.

The taxpayers of the state of Texas were about to get screwed again. If the board members of the Brazos River Authority rubber stamped this transaction as it had in 2009, Patterson stood to enjoy another multi-million dollar windfall while another state asset would be sold for pennies on the dollar. Having spent four years trying to unravel the "Texas Miracle," my appetite for watching that "miracle" repeat itself was nonexistent.

The board of the BRA was scheduled to meet three months later on October 27. The first item on the agenda would be to vote on whether or not to accept Patterson's sole bid. After considerable thought, I decided to attempt to appeal to their sensibilities on behalf of the rest of us. On the Sunday evening before the meeting, I sent the following letter to the BRA via email:

The intent of this letter, in essence, was to illuminate some of the key events that transpired between 2007 and 2009. It was also intended to remind the board members that they were the final arbiters of what was equitable and in the best interests of the state of Texas. Given that the majority of the *temporary* board members who had only served long enough to approve the deal in 2009 had come and gone, it occurred to me that a reasonable appeal had a shot at being successful.

I placed an asterisk behind the name of each board member who had voted to sell the property in 2009 hoping to catch their attention.

> October 27, 2014
>
> Brazos River Authority Board of Directors:
>
> Dave Scott, Presiding Officer; Richmond, Texas*
>
> Christopher S. Adams Jr., Assistant Presiding Officer; Georgetown, Texas*
>
> Richard Ball, Secretary; Mineral Wells, Texas*
>
> F. LeRoy Bell; Tuscola, Texas*
>
> Kari Belt; Gatesville, Texas*
>
> Peter Bennis; Fort Worth, Texas**
>
> Cynthia Olson Bourland; Round Rock, Texas
>
> Michel Todd Brashears; Wolfforth, Texas
>
> Paul Christensen; Crawford, Texas
>
> Robert M. Christian; Jewett, Texas*
>
> Chet Creel; Olney, Texas
>
> Carolyn H. Johnson; Freeport, Texas*
>
> Jean Killgore; College Station, Texas*
>
> William Masterson; Guthrie, Texas
>
> Henry Munson; Angleton, Texas
>
> W.J. "Bill" Rankin; Brenham, Texas
>
> Sara Mackie Shull; Salado, Texas
>
> Jeffrey Scott Tallas; Sugar Land, Texas
>
> Robert Tesch; Georgetown, Texas
>
> Raleigh R. White IV; Temple, Texas
>
> Salvatore A. Zaccagnino; Caldwell, Texas*
>
> c/o Phil Ford, BRA General Manager
>
> c/o Judi Pierce, BRA Public Information Officer

c/o Matt Phillips, BRA Manager of Government & Customer Relations

CC: Mike Patterson, Sole Bidder

4600 Cobbs Drive

Waco, Texas 76710

RE: RFB No. 14-07-816

Dear Sirs and Madams,

On April 27, 2007, the board of the Brazos River Authority held an Emergency Meeting to discuss the merits and implications of Senate Bill 1326. This bill had been filed by State Senator Craig Estes and carried the following caption:

Relating to the sale by the Brazos River Authority of certain residential and commercial lots in the immediate vicinity of Possum Kingdom Lake to leaseholders of those lots.

The pertinent parts of this Emergency Meeting occurred during Agenda Items 5-6: *Response to Proposed Language for Committee Substitute to Senate Bill 1326 Pursuant to Legislative Inquiries.* The statements that were made that day, by members of the board of the Brazos River Authority, clearly indicate that the tenets of Senate Bill 1326 were not in the best interests of the taxpayers of Texas. Here are three examples:

Director Wade Gear: *"They are asking us to gut a state agency and my hand won't be on that knife."*

Director P.J. Ellison: *"It's not whether you're going to get raped or not, it's to what extreme are you going to."*

Director Jean Kilgore: *"If we agree to this, we are their alibi."*

Consistent with this tone, the General Manager of the Brazos River Authority, Mr. Phil Ford, referred to Senate Bill 1326 as a *"hostage negotiation"* where *"someone is holding a gun."* As a result of this discourse, and the ensuing debate within the Texas Legislature, Senate Bill 1326 failed to pass.

During the recess between the 80th and the 81st sessions of the Texas legislature, State Senator Kip Averitt submitted a Request for Opinion to Attorney General Greg Abbott. This request asked for a determination as to how the property at Possum Kingdom Lake should be valued in the event that the Texas Legislature once again attempted to force the Brazos River Authority to sell its shoreline.

In his response, Attorney General Greg Abbott placed the burden of determining the fair market value of the property in question squarely and solely on the shoulders of the board members of the Brazos River Authority:

By its terms, section 49.226(a) authorizes a district's board of directors to determine the fair market value of land or an interest in land to be exchanged.

As a consequence of this ruling, when the twenty-one board members of the Brazos River Authority votes on the disposition of the single bid that was received in response to RFB No. 14-07-816, they alone—individually and collectively—will bear the sole responsibility for this outcome.

******

In 2009, State Representative Jim Keffer authored House Bill 3031 which was sponsored by State Senator Craig Estes. This bill carried the following caption:

Relating to the sale by the Brazos River Authority of certain residential and commercial leased lots and other real property in the immediate vicinity of Possum Kingdom Lake.

House Bill 3031 passed unanimously.

On March 23, 2009, Mr. Ben D. Loughry, a principal of Integra Realty, sent a letter to the Brazos River Authority with an admonishment that stated the following:

The exact parameters of the minimum bid pricing and resale price cap are still to be finalized, and this, combined with general market risk aversion, does not encourage investor interest. The time restraints now in place limit the pool of investors capable of formulating an informed bid to the handful of investors who have previously shown an interest in the transaction.

That admonishment proved to be correct. Sixteen days later, on April 8, 2009, Mike Patterson, the principal of PK Land Partnership, submitted a bid of $50 million to purchase the inhabited shoreline of Possum Kingdom Lake pursuant to Request For Bids No. 09-04-391. Likewise, Mr. Leon J. Backes submitted a bid of $12.5 million for the same property. There were no other bids received.

On April 27, 2009, the board of the Brazos River Authority met to, among other things, consider the merits of Mr. Patterson's bid. This occurred during Agenda Item 2: *1st Executive Session: Reconvene; Action Taken.*

Ignoring the counsel of Integra Realty, eighteen members of the board of the Brazos River Authority voted "yes" while two members abstained. The abstentions were levied by Mr. Peter Bennis, one of many bankers who were underwriting Mr. Patterson's bid, and Ms. Mary Ward, who served as an executive of a bank that Mr. Patterson governed as a board member.

Mr. Patterson's bid in 2009 of $50 million for 1200 acres equated to an approximate valuation of $41,667 per acre of lake front property. By contrast, the lake front property that Mike Patterson owned at the time of his bid, located at 2929 Colonels Row, was valued at $813,953 per acre according to his own independent fair market appraisal.

This half-acre lot and home is now on the market with an asking price of $1.1 million. If this valuation is used as a proxy for the entire 1200 acres that was sold in 2009, the total value of the land that was sold approximates $976,743,600. That is roughly $1billion dollars.

This referenced document can be found at the following URL:

http://www.pklandpartnership.com/downloads/PK%20BRA%204.pdf

On Wednesday, December 4, 2013, Mr. Patterson sent an email to *Friends and Prior Investment Clients* with the subject line of *Casino Beach Project and 2nd BRA Bulk Purchase at PK Lake.* The opening paragraph of that email stated the following:

As many of you are aware, because of your participation, in 2010 we were successful in syndicating equity for a Possum Kingdom Lake Brazos River Authority bulk leasehold purchase that generated $30 million in profits and returned investors their money plus a 100% profit after a year and one day! That was fun and profitable for everyone involved :-).

If Mr. Patterson, and the syndicate that he refers to, did indeed realize a profit of $30 million in only 366 days, this would strongly suggest that the original 1200 acres of property was sold for substantially less than fair market value. Mr. Patterson's records, which he published to the internet, strongly support this conclusion.

On May 3, 2008, Mr. Patterson received a notice from the Palo Pinto County Appraisal District informing him that the assessed value of his land at 2929 Colonel's Row had been set at $318,430. This valuation for .43 acres yields a value per acre of $740,535. If this valuation is used as a proxy for the entire 1200 acres of residential property that was sold in 2009, the total value of the land that was sold approximates $888,641,860. This valuation suggests that

Mr. Patterson's bid of $50 million was less than 6% of the fair market value of the shoreline.

This referenced document can be found at the following URL:

http://www.pklandpartnership.com/downloads/PK%20BRA%205.pdf

On April 28, 2009, Mr. Patterson once again received a notice from the Palo Pinto County Appraisal District informing him that the assessed value of the land at 2929 Colonel's Row had been set at $318,430. Obviously, the original attempt by the Palo Pinto County Appraisal District to increase Mr. Patterson's assessment to something that approached fair market value had not taken hold.

This referenced document can be found at the following URL:

http://www.pklandpartnership.com/downloads/PK%20BRA%2012.pdf

As of 2014, the assessed value of the land at 2929 Colonel's Row is $230,930 for .43 acres. This equates to a per acre valuation of $537,047. If this valuation is used as a proxy for the entire 1200 acres of residential property that was sold in 2009, the total value of the land that was sold approximates $644,455,814. This valuation would suggest that Mr. Patterson's bid of $50 million was less than 8% of the fair market value of the shoreline.

******

In response to the BRA's most recent Request for Proposal, RFB No. 14-07-816, Mr. Patterson has now submitted a bid of $6.5 million for the remaining 496 acres of property. This equates to $13,105 dollars per acre.

An analysis of twenty of the residential lots that are involved in this sale indicates that the average assessed value for this land is currently $124,000 per acre. The aggregate assessed value for the thirteen acres that comprise these twenty lots is approximately $1,472,000.

Similarly, an analysis of seventeen of the commercial lots included in this sale indicates that the average assessed value for this land is currently $19,415 per acre. The aggregate assessed value for the 291 acres that comprise these seventeen lots is approximately $6,500,000. This amount is equivalent to the bid the Mr. Patterson has submitted for the entire 496 acres that you will be considering on October 27, 2014.

By any objective measure, the single bid that has been received by the Brazos River Authority pursuant to RFB No. 14-07-816 fails to approximate, or even remotely approach, fair market value. Consequently, the board of the Brazos River Authority should decidedly vote to reject this offer.

Only ten of the twenty-one board members who voted to sanctify the terms of House Bill 3031 in 2009 are still serving on the board of the Brazos River Authority today. The balance of the board has been appointed after the fact.

Please consider this. If you vote "yes" to accept the sole bid that was submitted by Mike Patterson for the remaining 496 acres of the BRA's leased property, you will be perpetuating a fraud that is not of your making, or of your design. And, you *will* be their alibi.

I would strongly encourage each of you to consider your vote well. I would further encourage you to vote "no" in regards to the acceptance of Mr. Patterson's offer to purchase 496 acres for $6.5 million.

Best Regards,

John Marshall

On Monday morning, October 27, 2014, the board of the Brazos River Authority opened its meeting at 8:00 AM. The first order of business was to hear comments from members of the public. The first member of the public to walk to the microphone was none other than Michael Harold Patterson who had submitted the only bid for the property. His comments were brief.

> Good morning Mr. Chairman and board. My name is Mike Patterson and we were the bidder on the divestiture package that y'all will be considering today and I'm just here to answer any questions that you have. Thank you.

The presiding officer of the BRA simply replied "Thank you, Mike." and then called the name of the next member of the public who wished to speak. There were several and the public comments lasted for sixteen minutes. Each of the other speakers expressed their dismay at how their properties had been left in limbo and that they hoped that the board would accept the only bid that had been submitted.

The board of the Brazos River Authority then entered into executive session for the better part of two hours to weigh the merits of the only bid on the table. Per the guidance of Attorney General Greg Abbott, the question to be answered was this: Did the $6.5 million bid represent fair market value?

To properly answer that question, the board of the BRA would have to revisit the definition of fair market value. This definition is most commonly recited as follows:

> Fair market value (FMV) is an estimate of the market value of a property, based on what a knowledgeable, willing, and unpressured buyer would probably pay to a knowledgeable, willing, and unpressured seller in the market. An estimate of fair market value may be founded either on precedent or extrapolation.

The conversation that was held behind those closed doors was probably a non-starter. The Brazos River Authority had maintained since 2007 that it was not a "willing or unpressured seller." Rather, the BRA was being forced to sell its property by certain office holders within the Texas Legislature. Beyond that, the available benchmarks that might be used to extrapolate a fair market price strongly suggested that the original sale in 2009, and the proposed subsequent sale in 2014, did not even remotely approach fair market value.

The board reconvened in open session at 10:18 AM and a resolution to reject the sole bid that had been received from Michael Patterson was read into the record. When the board was polled, there were sixteen votes to reject, one vote to accept, and one abstention that was cast by Mr. Peter Bennis.

And, with that, the "Texas Miracle" was finally brought to a halt—at least for the time being....

Chapter 21

THE CRIMINAL COMPLAINT

Since the initial publication of *Playing Possum—The Tale of the River Card, Round I*, I have been asked multiple times why no one has gone to jail over this. The simple answer to that question is that very few people were aware of it given that we were all preoccupied by a crashing economy at the time.

That changed after *Round I* was published.

Lake Granbury is the first lake downstream from Possum Kingdom and relies on the water that flows through the Brazos River to remain healthy. Since the time that the turbines at Possum Kingdom Lake were taken offline in 2007, Lake Granbury had started to recede.[213] To compound the damage, a devastating drought in Texas began in the fall of 2010 and it seemed to target the area that included Possum Kingdom Lake and Lake Granbury. As a result, Lake Granbury began to be bled bone dry.

This combination of an act of God and the acts of man reached near-catastrophic proportions by November 2011. The combination of these events was so severe that it caused the BRA to submit an Emergency Motion to FERC to construct a controlled outlet conduit to bypass the

---

[213] Buddy Rochelle, Letter to Federal Energy Regulatory Commission, June 30, 2009, accessed December 3, 2012. http://elibrary.ferc.gov/idmws/common/OpenNat. asp?fileID=12094508.

mothballed generators at Possum Kingdom Lake to allow water to flow downstream.[214]

To be certain, Lake Granbury was the first community to feel the impact of the decisions that were being made in regard to Possum Kingdom Lake. Unfortunately for the folks in Granbury, there was a significant disparity between these two communities that can best be described as Rich Lake-Poor Lake.

While the weekenders at Possum Kingdom were unusually wealthy and wielded unmatched political clout, the residents at Lake Granbury were Average Joes by comparison.[215] The Rich Lake was able to get House Bill 3031 passed through the Texas legislature unanimously, while the Poor Lake's efforts to deal with the Brazos River Authority proved to be a continuous and costly exercise in frustration.

On the Monday morning that the Brazos River Authority voted to reject Mike Patterson's bid for the remaining 496 acres of shoreline property, October 27, 2014, a group of concerned citizens from Granbury had planned a trip to the meeting to ask the BRA "what the hell is going on?" Unfortunately, that day's meeting started at 8:00 AM rather than at the usual time of 9:00 AM. Consequently, the contingency from Granbury showed up an hour late and missed the opportunity to offer their public comments.

They were, however, able to observe the vote to reject Mike Patterson's bid after the executive session. They were also aware of the letter that had been sent to the board of the BRA recommending a rejection of the offer. And then, they started to question whether or not they had been taking the proper tack.

The folks from Lake Granbury had long since wondered if they were on equal political footing with the folks from Possum Kingdom. For almost three years, the people in Granbury had been challenging the

---

[214] John Whittaker, "Emergency Motion of Brazos River Authority for Expeditious Authorization to Install a Controlled Outlet Conduit Necessary to Meet Critical Water Supply Needs," *Federal Energy Regulatory Commission*, November 10, 2011, accessed October 1, 2013. http://elibrary.ferc.gov/idmws/common/OpenNat. asp?fileID=12816288.

[215] That is a shout out to Joe Williams who spearheads Save Lake Granbury. http://www. empowertexans.com/citizen-profiles/joe-williams-holding-officials-accountable/.

Brazos River Authority's policies regarding these two lakes as well as the BRA's request to sell even more water out of the basin.

The actions of the board of the Brazos River Authority on October 27, 2014, convinced the folks from Granbury that they should take a more aggressive posture. Over the weeks and months that followed, they began to research the "Texas Miracle" at Possum Kingdom Lake and soon realized that they had been victimized by the transaction. They also came to the realization that they had been spending tens of thousands of dollars in legal fees, in an attempt to protect their own local interests, to no avail.

More importantly, the folks from Granbury came to the realization that all of the citizens of Texas had been defrauded by the "Texas Miracle" and that those responsible needed to be held accountable. During the holiday season of 2014, this small group commissioned a "white paper" to research the potential criminal aspects of the deal. That research quickly identified a similar transaction that served as a model for a formal criminal complaint.

In December 2011, Jerald "Jerry" Cobbs was indicted in Travis County, Texas on a charge of *"Securing the Execution of a Document by Deception,"* a first-degree felony punishable by a range of five to ninety-nine years in prison. This indictment resulted from an extensive investigation that was conducted by the Public Integrity Unit within the Travis County District Attorney's office.[216]

Jerry Cobbs was the former Chief Commercialization Officer for the Cancer Prevention and Research Institute of Texas. CPRIT, as it is more commonly known, is an agency of the state of Texas that was approved by the voters and established in 2007. In its original charter, CPRIT was authorized to distribute up to $3 billion in grants for cancer research and prevention.

In June 2011, Jerry Cobbs placed an $11 million grant to Peloton Therapeutics on the agenda of the Oversight Committee of CPRIT. Based on the presumption that the Peloton grant had endured the appropriate vetting process, other officials at CPRIT approved the award. As it turned

---

[216] James Drew, "Ex-official Indicted over $11 million Texas Cancer-fund Grant," *Dallas Morning News*, December 6, 2013, accessed January 5, 2014. http://www.dallasnews.com/news/politics/headlines/20131206-ex-official-indicted-over-11-million-texas-cancer-fund-grant.ece.

out, the grant to Peloton had not, in fact, undergone the requisite business or scientific reviews as required by state law. Specific to the charge, the two officials who were deceived were Bill Gimson, the former CPRIT executive director, and Kristen Doyle, CPRIT's general counsel.[217]

If we refer back to the final hearing of House Bill 3031 in the Senate Committee on Agriculture and Rural Affairs, we are reminded that State Senator Mike Jackson attempted to determine whether the property in question would be sold for fair market value. We are also reminded that Senator Jackson left that meeting with the understanding that this would be the case—based on his questioning of Senator Craig Estes. We are further reminded that this understanding was falsely supported by Mr. Monte Land who testified on behalf of the Possum Kingdom Lake Association.

As a result of this testimony, and the swing votes of Senators Glenn Hegar and Carlos Uresti, House Bill 3031 received a unanimous vote in the Agriculture and Rural Affairs committee. This vote enabled Senator Craig Estes to have the bill placed on the Local and Consent Calendar. That motion produced a favorable report from the committee in the form of a document in the Senate Journal.[218]

Once House Bill 3031 reached the floor of the Senate on the Local and Consent Calendar, it was deemed to have been approved by all members of the Senate with the exception of Senator Lucio, who was absent. This unanimous vote was the product of a presumption that House Bill 3031 had been thoroughly vetted by an appropriate committee. This vote on the floor of the Texas Senate produced yet another document in the Senate Journal.[219]

---

[217] James Drew, "Former CPRIT Official Pleads Not Guilty to State Felony Charge," *Dallas Morning News*, March 16, 2015, accessed March 16, 2015. http://watchdogblog.dallasnews.com/tag/cprit/.

[218] "Senate Journal," Eighty-First Legislature, Regular Session, Texas Senate, May 12, 2009, p. 2307.http://www.journals.senate.state.tx.us/sjrnl/81r/pdf/81RSJ05-12-F.PDF.

[219] "Senate Journal," Eighty-First Legislature, Regular Session, Texas Senate, May 15, 2009, p. 2407.http://www.journals.senate.state.tx.us/sjrnl/81r/pdf/81RSJ05-15-F.PDF.

On May 19, 2009, House Bill 3031 was signed in the House of Representatives by Speaker Joe Strauss in the presence of the members.[220] This was in the form of a document. Also on May 19, 2009, the President of the Senate, Lt. Governor David Dewhurst, announced that he had signed House Bill 3031 in the presence of the Senate.[221] This, too, was in the form of a document. And finally, on May 27, 2009, House Bill 3031 was signed by Governor Rick Perry and became effective immediately.[222] This new law came in the form of a document.

State Senator Craig Estes' testimony on May 11, 2009, led to an avalanche of documents that converted House Bill 3031 into a state law that became effective immediately. Moreover, House Bill 3031 compelled the board of the Brazos River Authority to accept the $50 million bid that was on the table in the form of a board resolution. In turn, the Brazos River Authority then executed the final document that was necessary to sell property worth hundreds of millions of dollars to Michael Harold Patterson—a contract for sale.

The analysis that was commissioned by the folks in Granbury led to a thirteen-page criminal complaint that was submitted to the Public Integrity Unit in Austin. The pertinent points of that complaint read as follows.

COMPLAINT

TO THE DISTRICT ATTORNEY OF SAID COUNTY:

TO THE COUNTY ATTORNEY OF SAID COUNTY:

---

[220] "House Journal," Eighty-First Legislature, Regular Session, Texas House, May 19, 2009, p. 3970.http://www.journals.house.state.tx.us/hjrnl/81r/pdf/81RDAY73C-FINAL.PDF.

[221] "Senate Journal," Eighty-First Legislature, Regular Session, Texas Senate, May 19, 2009, p. 2534. http://www.journals.senate.state.tx.us/sjrnl/81r/pdf/81RSJ05-19-F.PDF.

[222] "House Journal," Eighty-First Legislature, Regular Session, Texas House, May 28, 2009, p. 5217. http://www.journals.house.state.tx.us/hjrnl/81r/pdf/81RDAY-82FINAL.PDF.

NOW COMES the undersigned complainants pursuant to article 2.04 and article 2.05 of the Texas Code of Criminal Procedure. Individually and collectively, we hereby make the following complaint:

We have good reason to believe, and we do believe, that:

Senator Craig Estes,

representing the 30th Senatorial District of Texas, and

Mr. Monte Land,

the current and then President of the Possum Kingdom Lake Association,

on the eleventh day of May, 2009, A.D., in the County of Travis and State of Texas, committed one or more offenses in violation of Title 7 of the Texas Penal Code, *Offenses Against Property*, Chapter 32, *Fraud*, Section 32.46, *Securing Execution Of a Document By Deception*.

Specific to this Complaint, the undersigned have reason to believe, and we do believe, that on the aforesaid date, in the city of Austin, the aforesaid Senator Craig Estes and Mr. Monte Land engaged in deceptive actions during a public hearing to secure a unanimous vote and, in turn, the execution of a document that enabled House Bill 3031 to avoid public examination, debate, and a subsequent vote in the Senatorial chamber of the Texas Legislature.

On May 11, 2009, Senator Craig Estes, who served as the chairman of the Agriculture and Rural Affairs Committee of the Texas Senate, laid out House Bill 3031 before his committee. HB 3031 authorized the Brazos River Authority (hereinafter "BRA") to sell approximately 900 acres of shoreline property to a single entity who would then, in turn, resell the individual properties to the individual leaseholders who were occupying those properties.

During the witness testimony of Mr. Monte Land, who was in favor of HB 3031, Senator Mike Jackson attempted to determine how the individual subject properties would be valued. The following exchanges occurred between Senator Jackson, Senator Estes, and Monte Land:

Sen. Jackson: Under this worked out deal, who is in charge of appraising the property values for the land?

Mr. Land: [laughter]

Sen. Jackson: Come on. You've been working on this for six years. You have got to know that.

Mr. Land: Yes sir, the appraisals – the way the land is to be sold – based on the bill in the third party sale – it's going to be based on the appraisals of the land through the county appraisal district.

Sen. Jackson: And it says fair market value?

Sen. Estes: [inaudible]

Mr. Land: [inaudible]

Sen. Jackson: Ok, one other question. Obviously, I think I saw somewhere there are 1600 properties, or something, around the lake there.

An inspection of the video archive of the public hearing that was held on May 11, 2009, clearly demonstrates that Senator Mike Jackson was seeking to determine whether or not the subject property would be sold for fair market value. Moreover, this examination clearly demonstrates that Senator Mike Jackson was left with the false understanding that the property would, in fact, be sold for fair market value.

The term "fair market value" appears nowhere within the fifty-one pages of House Bill 3031. Rather, HB 3031 directed the BRA to sell the property to a single entity who would then resell the property to the individual leaseholders at Possum Kingdom Lake at a formulaic price in lieu of individual fair market appraisals. As Senator Craig Estes was the sponsor of HB 3031, he was acutely aware of these facts. Likewise, as Monte Land was a key negotiator of House Bill 3031, he was also acutely aware of these facts.

Additionally, the right to purchase the subject property had already been awarded to Michael Harold Patterson for $50,000,000 per a Request for Bids that had been issued and closed by the Brazos River Authority. Both RFB 09-04-391 and House Bill 3031 mandated that Michael Harold Patterson would, in turn, resell the individual properties to the individual leaseholders at Possum Kingdom Lake for 90% of the individual assessed values per the applicable county appraisal district. These assessed values were in no way a product of fair market appraisals. Senator Craig Estes and Mr. Monte Land were also acutely aware of these facts.

By choosing not to correct Senator Mike Jackson's false understanding, Senator Craig Estes and Mr. Monte Land secured Senator Jackson's affirmative vote on House Bill 3031. This produced a unanimous vote of the committee which, in turn, produced a motion from the committee that HB 3031 be placed on the Local & Uncontested Calendar. As House Bill 3031 had already passed through the House of Representatives, this deception ensured that House Bill 3031 would pass through the Texas Legislature without examination.

Applicable Law

Title 7 of the Texas Penal Code, *Offenses Against Property*, Chapter 32, *Fraud*, Section 32.46, *Securing Execution Of Document By Deception*, provides that:

(a) A person commits an offense if, with intent to defraud or harm any person, he, by deception:

(1) causes another to sign or execute any document affecting property or service or the pecuniary interest of any person;

(b) An offense under Subsection (a)(1) is a:

(7) felony of the first degree if the value of the property, service, or pecuniary interest is $200,000 or more.

(d) In this section:

(1) "Deception" has the meaning assigned by Section 31.01.

Title 7 of the Texas Penal Code, *Offenses Against Property*, Chapter 31, *Theft*, Section 31.01, *Definitions*, provides that:

(1) "Deception" means:

(B) failing to correct a false impression of law or fact that is likely to affect the judgment of another in the transaction, that the actor previously created or confirmed by words or conduct, and that the actor does not now believe to be true;

Previously Created False Impression of Fact; Failure to Correct

Immediately prior to the testimony on House Bill 3031, Senator Craig Estes had laid out a companion bill to HB 3031. This was House Bill 3032.

Uresti: The chair lays out House Bill 3032 by Representative Keffer and recognizes the senate sponsor, Senator Estes, to explain the bill.

Estes: Uh, thank you chairman. These two bills, members, are some things that I have been working on for literally years. And, it has to do with Possum Kingdom, and both of these bills that we are going to be talking about are *local* bills and these things have been worked out with all of the parties concerned.

But let me just tell you about this bill.

It involves the Set Ranch, located in Palo Pinto and Stephen Counties, which has been a working cattle ranch since the original Texas land grants of 1854. And, it continues today as a working cattle ranch, wildlife and land management, and soil and water conservation program.

During the acquisition of this property for the construction of Morris Sheppard dam at Possum Kingdom Lake, the Brazos River Authority acquired more than 4300 acres of the Set Ranch for the reservoir, and this bill would require the sale of a certain portion, and that's 880 acres of that land, back to the Set Ranch at its *fair market value.* The land that's identified includes only land which has no public access and is completely surrounded by the Set Ranch land from which it was acquired in the 1940's.

And, uh, the Brazos River Authority is ok with this, and the Set Ranch folks are OK with it. So, I'm OK with it. And we have some witnesses.

Uresti: OK.

House Bill 3032 differed from House Bill 3031 in that HB 3032 did, in fact, incorporate the use of a fair market appraisal to determine the fair market value of the subject property. The testimony on HB 3032, prior to the testimony on HB 3031, created a reasonable presumption that both bills required a determination of fair market value. Senator Mike Jackson attempted to substantiate this presumption during the testimony of Mr. Monte Land by asking a simple question, "And it says fair market value?"

Senator Craig Estes and Mr. Monte Land failed to correct the obvious presumption of Senator Mike Jackson that the property related to House Bill 3031 would be sold for fair market value. In so doing, Senator Estes and Mr. Land were able to secure an affirmative vote from Senator Jackson on HB 3031.

The undersigned complainants have good reason to believe, and we do believe, that the deceptive actions complained of herein violated Title 7 of the Texas Penal Code, *Offenses Against Property*, Chapter 32, *Fraud*, Section 32.46, *Securing Execution Of a Document By Deception*. We further have good reason to believe, and we do believe that the deception complained of herein resulted in substantial and irreparable financial harm to the State of Texas.

The criminal complaint that was filed by the folks from Granbury went on to recite the chronological course of events from 2007 through 2009 regarding the sale of the shoreline at Possum Kingdom Lake. The complaints then closed with the following statement:

Conclusions

The subject property at Possum Kingdom Lake was sold for a material fraction of the property's fair market value.

RFB 09-04-391 did not constitute a competitive bidding process. Rather, RFB 09-04-391 constructed a property laundering scheme that enabled the individual leaseholders at Possum Kingdom Lake to purchase their individual lake lots at a formulaic price in lieu of individual fair market appraisals.

The deceptive actions of Senator Craig Estes and Mr. Monte Land resulted in a unanimous vote of the Agriculture and Rural Affairs Committee on May 11, 2009. In turn, the unanimous vote of this committee placed House Bill 3031 on the Local and Uncontested Calendar. In effect, the deceptive actions of Senator Estes and Mr. Land transformed House Bill 3031 into state law.

The criminal complaint closed with two requests of the Public Integrity Unit in Austin. The first request was to have the PIU perform a surgical investigation of State Senator Craig Estes' testimony on May 11, 2009. The second request was for a far reaching investigation into the entire transaction.

Request for Investigation

The undersigned hereby respectfully request that the Public Integrity Unit of the Travis County District Attorney's office investigate this specific complaint relative to Title 7 of the Texas Penal Code, *Offenses Against Property*, Chapter 32, *Fraud*, Section 32.46, *Securing Execution Of Document By Deception*.

Additionally, the undersigned respectfully request that the Public Integrity Unit of the Travis County District Attorney's office investigate the underlying transaction that led to sale of the shoreline of Possum Kingdom Lake for $50,000,000 to determine if this was a non-competitive, or rigged, bidding process.

In short, the criminal complaint filed by the citizens of Granbury argued that State Senator Craig Estes' deceptive testimony on May 11, 2009, converted House Bill 3031 into state law. In turn, this state law compelled the Brazos River Authority to execute a contract to sale the subject property at a fraction of the property's market value. The primary questions here are: When does a Texas Senator's passionate support of one of his pet projects cross the line? And, when does a simple shading of the truth cross over into aggravated perjury and criminal conduct?

The citizens of Granbury also asked that the entire course of events that culminated in the land sale at Possum Kingdom Lake be investigated. After almost five years, it finally seemed possible that the "Texas Miracle" might actually be examined by the property authorities. Unfortunately for the citizens of Texas, the identity of the proper authority to investigate public corruption was highly uncertain at that point in time.

Eighteen months earlier, Governor Rick Perry had vetoed the funding for the Public Integrity Unit in Travis County. This lack of funding greatly curtailed the Unit's number of employees as well as its ability to conduct investigations. Additionally, the Public Integrity Unit's jurisdiction was limited to public corruption that occurred within the city of Austin or Travis County. Given that the Brazos River Authority is headquartered in McLennan County, a thorough investigation of the "Texas Miracle" was arguably out of scope. This jurisdictional restriction, coupled with the statute of limitations, and compounded by an acute shortage of resources at the Public Integrity Unit, rendered the probability of a comprehensive investigation uncertain.

To further complicate matters, State Representative Phil King introduced House Bill 1690 a few weeks after the folks from Granbury filed their criminal complaint.[223] The purpose of this bill, which was sponsored by State Senator Joan Huffman, was to strip the Travis County District Attorney's office of the authority to investigate public corruption. Instead this authority would be transferred to the Texas Rangers.[224]

In what I am sure is a pure coincidence, State Representative Phil King was one of the first two Texas legislators to formally intercede on behalf of the weekenders at Possum Kingdom Lake. The other was State Senator Craig Estes. Immediately prior to the introduction of the Staubach Report in 2006, these two legislators sent individual letters to the board of the

---

[223] Committee Staff, "House Bill 1690," *Texas House General Investigating & Ethics Committee*, June 18, 2015, accessed June 18, 2015.http://www.capitol.state.tx.us/BillLookup/History.aspx?LegSess=84R&Bill=HB1690.
[224] Bobby Blanchard, "Senate Backs Bill That Would Relocate Integrity Unit," *The Texas Tribune*, April 8, 2015, accessed April 8, 2015.http://www.texastribune.org/2015/04/08/public-integrity-unit-headed-texas-rangers/.

Brazos River Authority stating that their constituents would be financially harmed by the findings of the report and its implementation.

Representative Phil King's letter to the BRA, which copied Attorney General Greg Abbott and was dated May 18, 2006, asked the BRA to defer its deliberations regarding the recommendations of the Staubach Report. To say the least, this letter lit the fuse for the fireworks that would follow for the next three years.[225]

---

[225] John Marshall, "Playing Possum – The Tale of the River Card, Round I, page 57" *iUniverse*, April 29, 2014.

Chapter 22

ONE LAST MIRACLE

Four months after the Brazos River Authority voted to reject Mike Patterson's sole bid of $6.5 million for the final 496 acres of property, a virtually identical Request for Bids was issued once again. This was a second attempt by the BRA to comply with the mandates of Senate Bill 918 which was pushed through by Senator Craig Estes and Representative Jim Keffer during the legislative session of 2013. RFB Number 15-05-864 was issued on February 24, 2015.[226]

For reasons that are not entirely clear, significantly more interest was demonstrated by the real estate market for this repeat offering. The number of questions that were submitted to the BRA regarding the nature of the sale rose substantially as did the number of firms who ultimately chose to submit a bid. In the two previous sales of lakefront property, the Brazos River Authority had received a total of three bids. By contrast, the third offering of property—which was virtually identical to the second—produced twice that number. Six different firms submitted bids.

On June 3, 2015, the staff of the Brazos River Authority opened the six bids. To say the least, the results were curious and would have raised the eyebrows of even the most junior forensic accountant.

---

[226] BRA Staff, "RFB 15-05-864," *Brazos River Authority*, February 18, 2015, accessed July 4, 2015. https://web.archive.org/web/20151128012229/http://www.brazos.org/portals/0/rfb/RFB_No._15-05-864.pdf.

MABE PK II, LLC, Dallas:	$7,651,000
SFG Capital Partners, Waco:	$7,776,000
JRangers 19 Properties, LLC, Dallas:	$8,125,000
PK2 Group, LLC, Bloomington, Indiana:	$8,150,000
Westdale Capital Investors, Dallas:	$8,850,000
Patterson PK2 Land Partnership, LTD, Arlington[227]	$10,150,000

Each of the six bids was at least $1 million higher than the sole bid that had been received eight months earlier for the same offering. And, miraculously, Michael Harold Patterson had managed to maintain his position as the highest bidder. In so doing, Patterson had increased his bid by sixty-four percent. This was a mere $3.65 million.

This outcome raises a few questions. For instance, was Mike Patterson's math wrong when he formulated his sole bid of $6.5 million in October 2014? Or, was his math wrong in 2015 when he increased his offer to $10.15 million? Similarly, why did none of the other five competing bidders in 2015 submit a bid for the same offering in 2014?

Perhaps the increased interest from the real estate community was the result of an increase in the marketing efforts employed by the Brazos River Authority. While this is certainly a possibility, it is not likely. After the board of the BRA voted to reject Mike Patterson's bid back on October 27, 2014, the board also took a vote to hire a marketing firm to try again. This vote resulted in a tie with nine "yes" votes and nine "no" votes. A tie vote is a failed vote and the result was that the staff of the BRA had no authority to hire a firm such as Integra Realty to market the property. The only way that the BRA could have stepped up its marketing efforts would have been to contact real estate investors directly. Perhaps they did so.

The Attorney General of Texas is responsible for investigating bid rigging within the state of Texas. To further this cause, the Attorney General's website publishes a document entitled "*Do You Suspect Collusion?*"

---

[227] BRA Staff, "RFB 15-05-864, Bid Tabulation," *Brazos River Authority*, June 3, 2015, accessed July 4, 2015.https://web.archive.org/web/20151128013244/http://www.brazos.org/portals/0/rfb/RFB No. 15-05-864Bid Tabulation.pdf.

that carries a subtitle of *"Checklist for Possible Collusion."*[228] Some of the points enumerated in this item strike a chord and warrant repeating.

CONDITIONS FAVORABLE TO COLLUSION

Certain market conditions increase the likelihood of collusion. Pay close attention to bids and bidding patterns under the following market conditions:

- A small number of vendors dominate the market. The fewer the vendors, the easier it is to get everyone on the same page.

- Tight specifications mandate no easy substitution of product. Fewer products make it easier for the vendors to coordinate.

- The bids are for a standardized product. Fewer variables in terms of design, quality, or service, make it easier to reach a common pricing scheme.

- Competitors regularly socialize with each other through personal connections or trade associations.

Senate Bill 918 was seventy-nine pages in length and stipulated very specific terms and conditions on how the winning bidder would immediately resell the property to the individual lessees. As evidenced by the receipt of only one bid in 2014 for the 496 acres in question, the field of potential bidders was narrow indeed. The expansion of this field to six participants in 2015 begs the question as to whether or not any of these "competing" bidders had any social or business connections. An examination of that question is in order. Before we do that, however,

---

[228] "Do You Suspect Collusion?" *The office of the Attorney General of Texas,* circa 2015.https://web.archive.org/web/20151128013738/https://www.texasattorneygeneral.gov/files/cpd/collusionfactsheet.pdf.

I should probably provide a brief explanation of what bid rigging and collusion actually are.

Bid rigging is a form of fraud in which a commercial contract is promised to one party even though, for the sake of appearances, several other parties also present bids. This form of collusion is illegal in most countries. In the United States, bid rigging is a felony criminal offense under Section 1 of the Sherman Antitrust Act.

One of the most common forms of bid rigging is "complementary bidding" which is also known as "cover bidding" or "courtesy bidding." Complementary bidding occurs when some of the bidders agree to submit bids that are intended not to be successful, so that another conspirator can win the contract. For example, the cover bids might contain prices that are noncompetitive in relation to the price submitted by the conspirator who is designated to win the contract. Alternatively, the cover bids might contain conditions that the conspirators know will be unacceptable to the agency calling for the bids.

Collusion is an agreement between two or more parties, sometimes illegal and therefore secretive, to limit open competition by deceiving, misleading, or defrauding others of their legal rights. Collusion may also involve the attainment of an objective that is forbidden by law, which is typically accomplished by defrauding the public and gaining an unfair market advantage. Collusion is generally an agreement among firms or individuals to divide a market and set prices while misrepresenting the independence of the relationships among the colluding parties.

Let's take a look at the relationships among the six parties who, in May 2015, submitted bids for the final 496 acres of BRA property.

The second highest bid came from Westdale Capital Investors of Dallas. This bid was in the amount of $8,850,000 and was $1.3 million shy of what Michael Harold Patterson offered. Westdale Capital Investors is a subsidiary of Westdale Real Estate Investment and Management and the firm describes itself in the following manner:

> Westdale is an opportunistic investor with more than 20 years of success as a real estate sponsor. Founded in 1991, Westdale and its 1200 member team control approximately 200 commercial and multifamily properties located in 30

cities, representing a total capitalization in excess of $2.5 billion.[229]

Westdale was founded in 1991 by Joseph G. Beard. Mr. Beard is a former college football star who lettered four times at SMU and earned honors as a consensus selection for All-Southwest Conference. He was also an honorable mention for All-American.[230] One of Mr. Beard's teammates during his playing days was a fullback by the name of Craig James, who shared the Pony Express backfield with future NFL Hall-of-Famer Eric Dickerson. The Pony Express was the cornerstone of what can arguably be referred to as "the best team that money could buy." This assessment is evidenced by the position of former Texas Governor Bill Clements, who once explained "We had a payroll to meet."

The relationship between Joe Beard and Craig James continued beyond their playing days. Together, the two former SMU stars formed a real estate investment firm by the name of Emerging Land Markets. Among other things, this firm invested in property in Palo Pinto County, the home of Possum Kingdom Lake.[231]

In 2011, Craig James decided to launch a political career and ran for the seat being vacated by retiring U.S. Senator Kay Bailey Hutchison. To focus on his new career path, Craig James sold his half of Emerging Land Markets to his business partner, Joe Beard, for $3 million. Joe Beard then signed on as Craig James' campaign treasurer for a senatorial race that

---

[229] "Executive Summary," *Westdale Real Estate Investment and Management*, October 14, 2014, accessed November 27, 1015. https://web.archive.org/web/20141014165743/http://www.westdale.com/pages/executive-summary.aspx.

[230] "Executive Team," *Westdale Real Estate Investment and Management*, October 14, 2014, accessed November 27, 1015. https://web.archive.org/web/20151128014415/http://www.westdale.com/Pages/executive-team.aspx.

[231] Robert T. Garrett, "Senate Candidate Craig James Worth Millions, But Disclosure Offers Few Details," *Dallas Morning News*, April 20, 2012, accessed May 1, 2015. http://www.dallasnews.com/news/politics/headlines/20120420-senate-candidate-craig-james-worth-millions-but-disclosure-offers-few-details.ece.

would pit him against Lt. Governor David Dewhurst and a fellow by the name of Ted Cruz.[232]

This would simply be a convenient literary tieback to one of our opening chapters if Craig James and Mike Patterson were not also closely associated. In response to the wildfires that ravaged the Possum Kingdom Lake area in 2011 and 2012, Mike Patterson, Craig James, and their mutual friend Lance Byrd began to collaborate on a relief charity to address the problem. Their collective response was noble and has since grown into an annual Country & Western benefit concert held at the Rocker B Ranch in Graford. The Rocker B Ranch is owned by Lance Byrd, who is also a principal in the company that produces the event—EncoreLive.

Nonetheless, the mere fact that the two highest bidders in 2015—Michael Patterson and Joe Beard—shared a close mutual friend in the form of Craig James in no way substantiates collusion. Likewise, the mere fact that all three of these gentlemen went to SMU simply serves as fodder for the conspiracy theorists. Moreover, these connections in no way offer any evidence that the two highest bidders discussed their bids before they were submitted.

The third highest bidder out of six was PK2 Group, LLC. According to the Brazos River Authority's bid tabulation, PK2 Group was based in Bloomington, Indiana. It seems odd to me that a real estate firm from Indiana would be interested in laundering property for the state of Texas, but evidently they were. PK2 Group submitted a bid for $8,150,000. Why this group chose not to submit a bid for the same 496 acres in question six months earlier is unknown. What is known, however, is that this entity was established on May 11, 2015—nine days before the deadline to submit a bid for the second offering. It is also known that this entity was chartered in the state of Texas and not in the state of Indiana.

PK2 Group, LLC was established by three managing members. These were D. G. Elmore, Gregg C. Davis, and Todd Taranto. Two of these managing members, Todd Taranto and D. G. Elmore, do indeed reside in the state of Indiana. The third managing member, Gregg C. Davis, is a real estate attorney who practices law in Dallas.

---

[232] Hopefully, I don't have to tell you how that contest turned out.

Gregg C. Davis received his undergraduate business degree from SMU in 1978.[233] D. G. Elmore received his undergraduate business degree from SMU in 1980.[234] By sheer coincidence, Michael Harold Patterson received his undergraduate business degree from SMU in 1977. If you visit page 295 of the SMU yearbook for 1976, you will find a fraternity picture of Phi Gamma Delta. Within that photo, you will find a fellow by the name of Mike Patterson and another by the name of Gregg Davis.[235] As likely as it may seem that these two fellows might have known each other, Mike Patterson claims otherwise:

> I was a member of Phi Gamma Delta 73-77, but don't remember a Gregg Davis.[236]

Todd Taranto, the outlier who actually signed the bid for PK2 Group, received his undergraduate degree from West Point.[237] If someone limited their rudimentary research to this one individual, he or she would have likely been satisfied and moved on. And, they would have probably failed to notice that the cashier's check submitted by PK2 Group, LLC as a deposit was actually remitted by Decision Tree Resources, Inc.—a totally separate entity.

The bid that came in fourth place out of six was submitted by JRangers19 Properties, LLC. This real estate investment firm was established on May 14, 2015—six days before the deadline to submit a bid. The founder of this company is a gentleman from Dallas by the name of Colin Watson who

[233] "Gregg C. Davis," *Thompson & Knight*, June 22, 2014, accessed November 27, 2015. https://web.archive.org/web/20140622231650/http://www.tklaw.com/Gregg-Davis.
[234] "D. G. Elmore," *LinkedIn*, n.d., accessed November 27, 2015. https://www.linkedin.com/pub/d-g-elmore/5/35/844.
[235] "Southern Methodist University, Rotunda Yearbook, Class of 1976," *E-YEARBOOK.COM*, n.d., accessed November 27, 2015.http://www.e-yearbook.com/yearbooks/Southern Methodist University Rotunda Yearbook/1976/Page 295.html.
[236] Mike Patterson, Email to John Marshall, November 25, 2015.
[237] "Todd Taranto," *Elmore Companies, Inc.*, August 3, 2013, accessed November 27, 2015.https://web.archive.org/web/20130803175547/http://elmorecompanies.com/investment-professionals.

specializes in Energy Financing for Bank of Texas.[238] The address for this newly created real estate firm is a home in Dallas.

The bid that came in fifth place was submitted by SFG Capital Partners, based in Waco, Texas. As Waco is also the headquarters of the Brazos River Authority, it is entirely possible that the staff of the BRA proactively invited SFG Capital to review the offering and submit a bid. If this is correct, then it would have also been entirely appropriate. SFG Capital is an established company and the losing bid submitted by this firm was $7,776,000.

The lowest of the six bids was submitted by MaBe PK II based in Dallas. This firm was established on May 7, 2015—thirteen days before the submission deadline. The principal of MaBe PK II is Stephen A. Lowder. Mr. Lowder was also one of the largest investors in Michael Harold Patterson's original partnership back in 2009. Stephen Lowder also registered as a witness during the legislative hearings that produced House Bill 3031. It might be safe to assume that Mike Patterson and Stephen Lowder are familiar with one another. It might even be possible that they socialize together on occasion. But, who knows?

The document entitled *"Do You Suspect Collusion?"* published by the Texas Attorney General's office also includes the following warning:

SUSPICIOUS BIDDING OR PRICING PATTERNS

Certain bidding or pricing patterns appear inconsistent with operation of the free market and warrant further investigation:

- The same vendor has been the low/high bidder on successive occasions over a period of time without any apparent market advantage/disadvantage to account for the bid.

Well, Michael Harold Patterson came in first place three out of three times so I guess we can check this box off as well. At the risk of sounding like a conspiracy theorist, the probability of collusion is greater than zero.

---

[238] "Colin Watson," *LinkedIn*, n.d., accessed November 27, 2015. https://www.linkedin.com/pub/colin-watson/1a/689/757.

I suspect collusion and I think that this matter *might* warrant further investigation.

The proper authority to investigate collusion and bid rigging in the state of Texas is the Attorney General. As of this writing, that gentleman's name is Ken Paxton. Ironically, Attorney General Ken Paxton is currently under three felony indictments for securities fraud.

Please "Don't mess with Texas"—we have enough messes of our own!

Chapter 23

FOLLOW THE MONEY

A long tale about public and private corruption in the state of Texas would not be complete without a chapter entitled "Follow the Money."

During his questioning on May 11, 2009, State Senator Mike Jackson made some astute observations. He then asked an equally astute question of Senator Craig Estes:

> Senator Estes, I was here when you worked on this bill [in 2007] and we've heard testimony long and hard. There was a lot of disagreement I guess on it. I just have one question. It looks like somebody has done a lot of work because you've got a fifty-one page bill here.
>
> But one of the issues that came up last session—and I didn't hear the answer, maybe you do have the answer—I think there is literally millions of dollars' worth of property that people have some very expensive lake homes on that they are leasing. And now we will be offering that property for sale. But the age old question is: "*follow the money*."
>
> Who gets the money?[239]

---

[239] Sen. Mike Jackson, "Senate Agriculture and Rural Affairs Committee," Senate Audio/Video Archives, *Texas Senate*, May 11, 2009, accessed November 19, 2010. (Fast forward to 40:30).
http://tlcsenate.granicus.com/MediaPlayer.php?view_id=14&clip_id=2419.

The nuances of Senator Jackson's question were more profound than he could have possibly imagined. And, as important as it is to understand who got the money, it is equally important to understand where the money came from in the first place.

To say the least, Michael Harold Patterson was not the typical tycoon who bought property from the state of Texas in $50 million increments. In 2007, Patterson reported taxable income in the amount of $425,886. In 2008, Patterson reported taxable income of $609,394. While there is no shortage of Texans who would be envious of those earnings, this is not the kind of financial success that would indicate that Mike Patterson was wielding a stockpile of cash in 2009 while the rest of us were "staring into the abyss."

Likewise, the personal financial statement that Mike Patterson circulated to his potential investors and lenders raised more questions than it answered. His homestead in Arlington, Texas was valued at $1.25 million while the note on the property indicated that he still owed almost half of that to the bank ($602,600). His weekend home at Possum Kingdom Lake was valued at $820K while the note indicated that he still owed Affiliated Bank in Arlington more than half of that amount ($447,000). Similarly, Patterson claimed to have cash on hand of $804,120 and yet had an outstanding personal line of credit with the First National Bank of Graham for $768K.[240]

Nonetheless, Mike Patterson's personal financial statement represented that he had a net worth of $12.7 million. His other assets included things like five automobiles worth $150K, three boats worth $125K, four Harley Davidson motorcycles worth $80K, and a life insurance policy with a cash value of $35,119. I will leave it to the financial experts to assess the efficacy and veracity of the rest of Mike Patterson's personal financial statement. It was rather apparent that Mike Patterson would be forced to use other people's money to get his deal done. This would include the earnest money needed to fund his original bid to the Brazos River Authority.

---

[240] Mike Patterson, "Michael H. Patterson Financial Statement as of 2/2/2010," *Patterson Equity Partners*, February 3, 2010, accessed November 27, 2015.https://web.archive.org/web/20151128035935/http://www.pklandpartnership.com/private/mhp%202-2-2010%20finan%20statement.pdf.

Rightly or wrongly, money flows to where it is treated best. While Mike Patterson may not have possessed the financial wherewithal to put a deal of this nature together, he was holding something far more valuable: the winning bid at Possum Kingdom Lake. Metaphorically, Patterson held in his hand a $30 million scratch-off from the Texas Lottery. Moreover, he was also holding a freshly printed law, courtesy of House Bill 3031, that made the whole thing legal.

The only thing that Mike Patterson had to do to get $50 million to start flowing his way was to share the wealth. Patterson's plan called for $40 million in loans from small Texas banks. In the wake of the financial crises of 2008, a syndicated loan of this nature would have carried the reek of a new toxic asset. On the other hand, if the principals of those small banks were participating in the action, they *might* be persuaded to convince their loan committees to ignore the deal's hairy warts.

The Equity Tranche

To make his deal come to life, Mike Patterson surrendered two-thirds of his action to a handful of friends and a few bank principals who were on the inside. For the life of me, I will never understand why any of those bankers allowed their names to be associated with a cathouse deal of this nature—but they did.

Mike Patterson rounded up forty stake horses to invest in a company that would buy 900 acres of public land from the state of Texas.[241] In total, Patterson accepted $2,486,083 in capital from his investors in 2009 and carved off a 33.67% stake for himself in the amount of $1,214,917. This brought the total capital of his Texas hedge fund to $3,701,000. And with that, they bought hundreds of millions of dollars' worth of property.

As I mentioned in *Playing Possum—The Tale of the River Card, Round I*, this is a story about a bunch of good old boys from Arlington, Texas making their play and making it big. In the spirit of a true Texan, Mike Patterson doled out 39.47% of the action to his amigos from back home. This stake totaled $1,479,833.

---

[241] Mike Patterson, "U.S. Return of Partnership Income–2009," *Patterson Equity Partners*, April 19, 2010, accessed November 27, 2015.http://www.pklandpartnership. com/private/PPKLP%202009%20Tax%20Return.pdf.

If you refer back to Chapter 2 of *Playing Possum*; you might recall that Mike Patterson called out five "friends in need" when he was recognizing his "Unsung Heroes."

> Friends – Friends in need are friends indeed!!! Thank you guys for hanging with me!

- Eric Nelson,

- Chris Ringel,

- Jim Maibach,

- Greg McCarthy*, and

- Bennett Carter*

These five gentlemen along with four others, all from Arlington, received a 3.33% stake in the deal for $125K each. If it is true that the investors realized an aggregate profit of $30 million in 366 days, a stake of that size would have returned approximately $9 million—or eight times their money. The names of the four other lucky hombres were:

- Garry Graham*

- Nathan Watson

- Anthony "Tony" Loth, and

- Murphy Markham

The three gentlemen whose names above are followed by an asterisk are also principals of Affiliated Bank, which is based in Arlington, Texas. Garry Graham is the CEO and Chairman of the Board of Affiliated Bank while Bennett Carter is an Executive Vice President and the Chief Lending Officer. Eric Nelson is simply a member of Affiliated Bank's board of directors.[242] Affiliated Bank loaned Mike Patterson $2 million of the $2.5 million in earnest money required by the Brazos River Authority when the winning bid was accepted. If that strikes you as a conflict of interest, then you are probably not from a state that is "Wide Open for Business."

Jim Maibach served alongside Mike Patterson on the board of directors of Southwest Securities Federal Savings Bank when this deal was consummated. As a friendly reminder, a woman by the name of Mary Ward was working for this bank as a regional president when Mike Patterson submitted his winning bid. Simultaneously, she was also serving on the board of the Brazos River Authority. By the time that Mike Patterson had lined up his investors and his banking syndicate to close his deal, Mary Ward's job title at SWS had changed to President – Government Relations. If that strikes you as a *quid pro quo* then you are probably a conspiracy theorist.

Chris Ringel was a business partner with Mike Patterson on a different deal by the name of Lake Country River Ranch.[243] Greg McCarthy was an attorney who practiced in a law firm with Mike Patterson's son, Travis Patterson.[244] McCarthy was also a budding author who wrote a legal thriller about a medical malpractice case in Texas.[245] Don't laugh. Mary Ward and Chris Adams, who served on the board of the Brazos River Authority together, also collaborated on a novel entitled *Dallas: Lone Assassin or Pawn*. (You can't make this stuff up).

[242] Mike Patterson, "Preferred Lenders–Affiliated Bank FSB," *Patterson Equity Partners*, October 8, 2010, accessed July 23, 2011. https://web.archive.org/web/20101008234649/http://pklandpartnership.com/Affiliated.aspx.

[243] "Lake Country River Ranch LLC," *CorporationWiki*, n.d., accessed November 27, 2015.http://www.corporationwiki.com/Texas/Arlington/lake-country-river-ranch-llc/34730108.aspx.

[244] Greg McCarthy, "Our Attorneys," *Patterson Law Group*, November 28, 2015, accessed November 28, 2015.https://web.archive.org/web/20151128152419/http://ghaslate.com/pattersonlaw/our-attorneys/.

[245] "About Greg McCarthy," *GregMcCarthyBooks.Com*, November 28, 2015, accessed November 28, 2015.https://web.archive.org/web/20151128152707/http://gregmccarthybooks.com/about.htm.

Nathan Watson, Tony Loth, and Murphy Markham seem to be homeboys from back in the hood. Obviously, Michael Harold Patterson was keeping it real.

Within his thank you note entitled "Unsung Heroes" examined in the first installment, Mike Patterson also gave a tip of his hat to a group that was actually close to Possum Kingdom Lake.

> - The "Wichita Falls" support group. Led by
> Earl Denny and Tommy McCullough (Tommy
> is a lessee and President of Fidelity Bank in
> Wichita Falls). You got the ball rolling for us.

Although Earl Denny and Tommy McCullough did not actually invest in Patterson's equity tranche, five other individuals from Wichita Falls did. The largest of these was Randolph Wachsman, who put up $50K for a stake of 1.33%. The other four individuals were Warren Ayres, George Gault, Jack Holmes, and John Shalk, who each put up $25K for a .67% stake. Before you snicker at those paltry sums, consider that a 4% stake in a $30 million outcome is $1.2 million.

Warren Ayers served on the Board of Directors of Fidelity Bank in Wichita Falls while George Gault served on the board of First Financial Bank. Randolph Wachsman was not directly associated with either Fidelity or First Financial; but, he was a business partner with Tommy McCullough and Warren Ayres in a company by the name of Wichita Falls Growth Fund, LLC.[246]

Fort Worth was also well represented with eight investors subscribing to the offering. The largest and most colorful of these was Roy English, who invested $125K for one of the last 3.33% stakes. For those of you who aren't from around here, Roy English served as the County Judge of Tarrant County from 1987 to 1990. He is also a relative of Michael Harold Patterson.

The second largest investor from Fort Worth was a woman by the name of Nancy Bryant. Nancy put $75K into the pot for a stake of 2%. Nancy's

---

[246] "Wichita Falls Growth Fund, LLC, Directors," *Wysk*, n.d., accessed November 28, 2015. http://www.wysk.com/index/texas/wichita-falls/6emdtp7/wichita-falls-growth-fund-llc/officers.

husband, Vernon Bryant, is the Chairman and CEO of Southwest Bank in Fort Worth. According to Patterson, Southwest Bank had offered to put $8M of Bryant's bank's money into the debt tranche of the transaction.

Two other notable investors from Fort Worth were Brent Clum and Louis G. Baldwin. Both Clum and Baldwin worked for XTO Energy, serving as EVP and CFO respectively. Each of these gentlemen put up $25K and received a stake of .67%, which would have produced a $200K return. Both of these gentlemen also owned weekend homes at Possum Kingdom Lake.

Brent Clum was a newcomer to the Possum Kingdom Community. In 2007, he purchased a home on a half-acre lot from his superior Louis G. Baldwin.[247] In 2009 when this deal transpired, the assessed value on Baldwin's property was $83,090. Four years later Clum purchased the lot next door, bringing his total acreage up to a full acre on Hideaway Lane. In 2009, this second lot was assessed at $73,180. So, according to Mike Patterson, Clum was able to put up $25K, get his money back in 366 days, get both pieces of property basically for free, and make a profit to boot.

Louis G. Baldwin entered the Possum Kingdom Community in 2001 when he bought the lake house that he eventually sold to Brent Clum. At the same time that he brought Clum into the fold, Baldwin purchased four other lots on Hamilton Drive. These lots totaled 4.1 acres and had an assessed value in 2009 of $554K. Consequently, Baldwin's investment in Patterson's deal was not enough to cover the total purchase cost of his property. As a result, Baldwin only purchased two of the lots from Patterson during the "contemporaneous close" and purchased the other two lots in 2011. We will discuss the notion of a contemporaneous close shortly.

Another $25K investor from Fort Worth was Rebecca Lucas. Ms. Lucas was identified by Mike Patterson as someone who always provided "unwavering support." She was also the domestic partner of Tarrant

---

[247] Palo Pinto Appraisal District, "Property ID: R000022476," *Southwest Data Solutions*, n.d., accessed November 28, 2015. http://www.isouthwestdata.com/client/webProperty.aspx?dbkey=palopintocad&stype=name&sdata=clum&time=20157121623057&id=R000022476.

County District Attorney Joe Shannon. If you read *Round I,* then you would probably agree that we have worn out that topic.

The most ironic $25K investor from Fort Worth was a fellow by the name of Shawn Hessing. Mr. Hessing became the Chief Financial Officer of Oak Hill Capital Partners in 2011. In that same year, Oak Hill Capital began a takeover of Southwest Securities Group, the parent company of the bank on whose board Mike Patterson and Jim Maibach served.[248] Read into that what you will, but be advised that Shawn Hessing also owned a half-acre lot at Possum Kingdom Lake and had a vested interest in the outcome of the transaction.

We could go on and on about the investors in Michael Patterson's deal, but I think you get the point. I will leave you with two last fun facts concerning the investors. The first is that the former mayor of Graham invested $25K in the deal. That gentleman's name was Wayne Christian, who had a modest lakefront lot of .38 acres.

The second fun fact is that no one from Southwest Securities, other than Mike Patterson and Jim Maibach, had anything to do with the funding of this deal. Southwest Securities passed on the debt tranche and none of the principals of Southwest Securities participated in the equity tranche. While Mike Patterson may have been able to convince Mary Ward to politic his deal, he was unable to get his own bank to put up a penny. This should have been a red flag to everyone else. There was way too much money to be made and nobody cared if Southwest Securities wanted to take a pass at the pig trough.

Having explored the equity side of this deal, which was nominal, let's turn our attention to the money put up by the bankers who actually made this deal happen.

The Debt Tranche

At the heart of Mike Patterson's deal was the concept of the "Preferred Lenders." Any bank that provided a significant portion of the $50 million that Patterson needed to purchase the property from the Brazos River

---

[248] "Hilltop Holdings and Oak Hill Capital Partners Each to Invest $50 Million," *Oak Hill Capital Partners,* July 20, 2011, accessed November 28, 2015. https://web.archive.org/web/20110720142220/http://www.oakhillcapital.com/oak_hill_news/2011/20110321.html.

Authority would earn the designation of a Preferred Lender. In exchange, Patterson would offer a 10% discount on the laundering price to anyone who chose to finance their laundry using a Preferred Lender. This part of the deal was a thing of pure genius and it worked.

The banks that signed up to serve in this capacity were advertised on the website that Patterson pushed out to the weekenders. This list of banks was also notably devoid of any banks that most of us have ever heard of. Nonetheless, these tiny community banks came through with the money that Patterson needed—and for good reasons.

On June 3, 2008, Mike Patterson sent an email to his banking connections in an attempt to generate interest in his laundering concept. Within that email, Patterson pointed out that the aggregate value of the property in question, along with the houses that had been built on the properties, could exceed $1 billion.[249] His banking buddies took the bait.

According to Patterson's website, and his disclosures to the Brazos River Authority and to his investors, the following banks agreed to provide $40.5 million to fund his laundering scheme:

- Affiliated Bank, FSB (Arlington)

- Fidelity Bank (Wichita Falls)

- First Financial Bank (Mineral Wells)

- First National Bank (Graham)

- First State Bank (Graham)

- Graham Savings and Loan, FA (Graham)

- The Highlands Bank of Dallas (Dallas)

---

[249] Mike Patterson, "Patterson to Lender Clients Request for Consideration," *Patterson Equity Partners*, June 3, 2008, accessed July 23, 2011. https://web.archive.org/web/20151128180538/http://www.pklandpartnership.com/downloads/6-3-2008%20Patterson%20to%20Lender%20Clients%20Request%20for%20Consideration.pdf.

- Northstar Bank of Texas (Denton)

- OmniAmerican Bank (Fort Worth)

- Pinnacle Bank (Azle/Keene)

- PrimeWest Mortgage, a division of FirstBank
  & Trust (Lubbock, Red Oak, Wichita Falls)

- Southwest Bank (Arlington)[250]

With this coalition, Mike Patterson secured the debt and equity capital that he needed and virtually none of it was his own money. After that, the only thing he had to do was to get the right politicians to support his scheme and then convince anyone who was watching that his scheme was legitimate. Obviously, he was successful on all fronts.

The Contributions

Generally speaking, a campaign contribution in Texas is above reproach as there are no limits on what an individual contributor can provide to an individual candidate. Likewise, the suggestion that a campaign contribution is the result of, or the anticipation of, a political favor is ludicrous in a state that is "Wide Open for Business."

We Texans are pure of heart and none of us would ever resort to buying off politicians unless it was absolutely necessary. On the other hand, there is nothing wrong with simply greasing the skids on occasion. The following are some political contributions that were made by Mike Patterson following the annihilation of Senate Bill 1326 in 2007. Some key events are blended in to illuminate the timing.

---

[250] Mike Patterson, "Preferred Lender Invitation," *Patterson Equity Partners*, October 18, 2009, accessed November 28, 2015.
https://web.archive.org/web/20090718045024/http://www.pklandpartnership.com/Lenders.aspx.
Mike Patterson, "Roster of Preferred Lenders," *Patterson Equity Partners*, July 25, 2010, accessed November 28, 2015.https://web.archive.org/web/20100725001212/http://www.pklandpartnership.com/lenders.aspx.

08/31/2007: Sen. Kim Brimer	$500
08/31/2007: Rep. Paula Pierson	$1,000
10/21/2007: Sen. Chris Harris	$1,000
10/29/2007: Sen. Chris Harris	$500
02/09/2008: Rep. Bill Zedler	$250
04/15/2008: Sen. Kim Brimer	$1,000
04/19/2008: Rep. Paula Pierson	$1,000
08/18/2008: Sen. Kim Brimer	$5,000

On September 8, 2008, Senator Kip Averitt hosted a meeting in Waco to allow Mike Patterson to present his plan for laundering the lakefront property to several politicians and staffers of the BRA. This meeting was attended by Senator Chris Harris, Representative Charlie Geren, Representative Jim Keffer, Keffer's chief of staff Trent Thomas, and Senator Craig Estes' chief of staff, Lewis Simmons. Carmen Cernosek, who served as the Natural Resources Director for Lieutenant Governor David Dewhurst, was also present.

09/15/2008 : Rep. Charlie Geren	$2,000
09/18/2008 : Rep. Paula Pierson	$100

On September 22, 2008, Mike Patterson presented his plan for laundering the lakefront property to the Brazos River Authority and the general public.

09/24/2008: Rep. Dan Branch	$2,000
09/25/2008: Rep. Jim Keffer	$2,000
10/07/2008: Lt. Gov. David Dewhurst	$500
10/15/2008: Rep. Bill Zedler	$500
10/23/2008: Sen. Kim Brimer	$5,000
10/24/2008: Sen. Kip Averitt	$5,000
10/27/2008: Sen. Craig Estes	$5,000
10/28/2008: Sen. Chris Harris	$5,000

Please note that the denominations increased.

On October 27, 2008, the board of the Brazos River Authority approved a resolution that directed the staff to issue a Request for Bids for the property at Possum Kingdom Lake. It was asserted during public testimony that, "some, if not all, of the conditions" contained in *The Patterson Plan* had been incorporated into the resolution.

10/28/2008: Sen. Chris Harris	$5,000
11/21/2008: Sen. Mike Jackson	$1,000

Yes, that is the same Senator Mike Jackson who asked if the property would be sold for fair market value.

On January 8, 2009, Request for Bids No. 09-04-391 was issued. Three months later, on March 9, 2009, House Bill 3031 was filed. On April 8, 2009, Mike Patterson submitted his winning bid in the amount of $50 million. On the following day, April 9, 2009, House Bill 3031 passed out of the house committee. On April 27, 2009, the BRA voted to accept Mike Patterson's bid. On May 11, 2009, House Bill 3031 passed out of the senate committee. On May 27, 2009, House Bill 3031 was signed by Governor Rick Perry and became effective immediately.

It should be noted that the members of the Texas Legislature are not allowed to accept political contributions while the legislature is in session. The eighty-first session of the Texas Legislature adjourned *sine die* on June 1, 2009.

06/30/2009: Rep. Paula Pierson	$5,000

On July 27, 2009, the board of the Brazos River Authority authorized the BRA's general manager to sign a 235 page contract for sale with Mike Patterson.[251]

This contract provided a seventeen month window for closing the transaction and carried a deadline of December 31, 2010. By virtue of this time frame, Mike Patterson and his small group of investors were afforded the ability to avoid a short-term capital gains tax on the laundering process.

[251] BRA Staff, "Executive Session 25 A," *Brazos River Authority*, July 27, 2009, accessed July 4, 2011.http://www.brazos.org/Portals/0/board_actions/07-27-09-Quarterly-Board-Actions.pdf.

This is noteworthy considering that the vast majority of the property was never actually titled in the name of Mike Patterson or his equity partnership.

Patterson and his team accelerated their efforts once the contract was signed. The Patterson PK Land Partnership website, launched six months before the property was put up for sale, was enhanced to provide information to the individual leaseholders. These enhancements included instructions on how to consummate the laundering process, which was predicated on the notion of a "contemporaneous close."

The simplest explanation of a contemporaneous close is this: Any weekender who wanted to avail themselves of the laundering process that was venerated by House Bill 3031 needed only to inform Mike Patterson of their desire to do so. By simply signing a resale agreement and committing to finance their individual transactions through one of Mike Patterson's "Preferred Lenders," each leaseholder was given the opportunity to purchase the land beneath their weekend home at a price that would never be seen again. While Mike Patterson's Texas hedge fund would enjoy a handsome initial profit of roughly $30 million, each leaseholder would enjoy a handsome discount as well.

And then, the final thank-you notes were written:

09/18/2009: Rep. Chris Turner	$1,000
09/28/2009: Rep. Charlie Geren	$500
09/28/2009: Sen. Craig Estes	$2,500
11/03/2009: Zachary Brady	$1,000
11/04/2009: Sen. Kip Averitt	$20,000
01/23/2010: Sen. Carlos Uresti	$5,000
02/24/2010: Gov. Rick Perry	$5,000
03/23/2010: Lt. Gov. David Dewhurst	$10,000
03/24/2010: Rep. Delwin Jones	$1,000
03/31/2010: Sen. David Sibley	$5,000
04/19/2010: Lt. Gov. David Dewhurst	$100
05/10/2010: Sen. David Sibley	$5,000
05/11/2010: Atty. Gen. Greg Abbott	$1,000
05/13/2010: Rep. Charlie Geren	$1,000

05/18/2010: Gov. Rick Perry	$4,800
07/30/2010: Rep. Paula Pierson	$1,000
08/04/2010: Rep. Bill Zedler	$500
09/08/2010: Rep. Mark Shelton	$1,000
09/24/2010: Sen. Craig Estes	$4,000
12/17/2010: Rep. Jim Keffer	$1,000
09/13/2011: Rep. Paula Pierson	$1,000
11/16/2011: Rep. Bill Zedler	$200
01/14/2014: Rep. Jim Keffer	$2,903.97

In an interview with Libby Cluett of the Mineral Wells Index on August 20, 2010, Mike Patterson explained the numbers regarding the laundering process:

> "Everybody for the first year gets to buy their lot for 90 percent of its 2008 assessed value, which in most cases is substantially lower than today's assessed values," said Patterson. "In addition, if they contemporaneously close – I'll probably give them 30 to 45 days – I'll knock another 5 percent off that sales price."

> He said the lowest purchase price for land beneath a lake home is about $3,000; the highest is $350,000. These prices are all based on the land's 2008 assessed value, determined by the Palo Pinto Appraisal District. The PPAD adjusted the 2008 values for lessees – which in many cases reflected a roll back to the 2007 values – because the BRA issued a moratorium on new leases on May 20, 2008, pending divestiture.

> The average BRA lot sales price is about $68,000, according to Patterson, but he added, "That's probably doubled now."[252]

---

[252] Libby Cluett, "Closer to Closure" *Mineral Wells Index*, August 20, 2010, accessed November 28, 2015. http://www.mineralwellsindex.com/news/closer-to-closure/article_f395cb1e-c01e-565a-a89b-ee2c1bd78fd8.html.

Patterson then issued a warning to anyone who was dragging their feet:

"If they don't buy from me the first year," Patterson said,
"They will then have to buy at the current assessed value."

According to the BRA's documentation when the leased shoreline was put up for sale, the most expensive piece of property was actually assessed at $462,000. This lot was located at 1211 Panorama Way.[253]

Perhaps Mike Patterson was referring to the third most expensive lot, which was a three acre piece of raw land located at 1171 Panorama Way. This property was assessed at $343,000 in 2008 and is now assessed at $950,000 as of 2015. It would appear that this leaseholder was smart enough to heed Mike Patterson's warning and purchase the property in 2009. In 2012, a $5 million palatial estate was built on the lot.

Unfortunately for this particular leaseholder, in between this new estate and the water's edge was the FERC buffer zone, which was one-half acre in size. Because of the FERC license, the BRA was required to hold title to the buffer zone and was not able to include it in the sale. Fortunately for this particular leaseholder, the Brazos River Authority surrendered its license to operate a hydroelectric plant at Possum Kingdom Lake and that half acre of lakefront property was gifted free of charge. That portion of the property is now valued at $141,000.[254]

---

[253] Mike Patterson, "Leasehold Roster with Valuations," *Patterson Equity Partners*, May 7, 2009, accessed July 23, 2011. https://web.archive.org/web/20151129120610/http://www.pklandpartnership.com/downloads/PK%20BRA%2010.xls.

[254] Palo Pinto Appraisal District, "Property ID: R000024323," *Southwest Data Solutions*, n.d., accessed November 28, 2015. http://www.isouthwestdata.com/client/webProperty.aspx?db-key=palopintocad&stype=name&sdata=sigel&time=20155161538029&id=R000024323.

Chapter 24

UNANSWERED QUESTIONS

Hopefully it is now abundantly clear that the property at Possum Kingdom Lake was sold for a material fraction of its fair market value. It should also be obvious that this transaction was not the result of a competitive bidding process. And, it should be equally apparent that the Brazos River Authority was adamantly opposed to selling its most valuable asset—except for that short period of time when it wasn't.

Nonetheless, a substantial number of questions remain unanswered. These are best presented politician by politician, and player by player.

Governor Rick Perry and his Staff

The most obvious question to be put to former governor Rick Perry is whether or not any promises were made to any of the temporary board members whom he appointed in exchange for their vote to sell the property. Such promises could include campaign stumping for future candidates or a future appointment to a more prestigious or influential position.

Similarly, the question must be asked as to whether Governor Rick Perry was personally aware and actively involved in the course of events that transpired during 2007, 2008, and 2009. Conversely, we have to ask if this was simply another instance of a governor's staff running amuck as in the case of Governor Chris Christie's "Bridge-gate?"

If the answer to Governor Perry's awareness is affirmative, then you have to question his motives and reasoning for championing such a cause.

If the answer is in the negative, then you have to question his managerial skills. If Ken Anderson, Phil Wilson, and Cody Shorter were acting outside of the governor's direction in 2007 when they were negotiating the first attempt at a forced divestiture, then it seems reasonable to conclude that one byproduct of absolute power was a culture of corruption. If they were acting at the governor's direction, the same conclusion can be drawn.

Likewise, if Governor Perry hand-selected the temporary appointees to the board of the BRA that reversed the position of Presiding Officer Steve Pena and his contemporaries, then you would have to conclude that the governor was driving the process. Conversely, if his staff made those appointments without his knowledge, then, you would have to conclude that the governor's staff was actually running the state of Texas.

Lt. Governor David Dewhurst and his Staff

On September 8, 2008, State Senator Kip Averitt hosted a private meeting for Mike Patterson that included multiple BRA representatives, legislators, and lobbyists. Also in attendance was Ms. Carmen Cernosek, who served as the Natural Resources Director for Lt. Governor David Dewhurst. Why did Ms. Cernosek attend this meeting?

More important, why did Lt. Governor David Dewhurst route House Bill 3031 to the Agriculture and Rural Affairs Committee in 2009, rather than to Senator Averitt's Natural Resources Committee—who had considered the matter in 2007?

Attorney General Greg Abbott and his Staff

On June 5, 2008, Attorney General Greg Abbott issued Opinion No. GA-0634. This opinion addressed how the property at Possum Kingdom Lake should be sold, subject to the laws that were on the books at the time. The key points in this opinion read as follows:

> If the property is offered for sale to the lessees, the Authority would sell the property pursuant to Water Code section 49.226. Section 49.226(a) generally provides that surplus real or personal property owned by a water district may be sold in a private or public sale or be exchanged.

Section 49.226(a) requires that the surplus property be exchanged for "like fair market value."[255]

This opinion was premised on a lot-by-lot sale by the Brazos River Authority directly to each respective leaseholder. By contrast, House Bill 3031 created a vehicle for a bulk sale with a mandatory resale at a formulaic price that was divorced from fair market value.

None of the parties involved submitted a subsequent request for opinion to Attorney General Abbott, asking whether the resulting laundering process violated Article III, Section 52 of the Texas Constitution. This question needs to be put to the former attorney general. Likewise, a formal request for opinion needs to be submitted to the current attorney general, Ken Paxton. And, by the way, if House Bill 3031 is deemed to be unconstitutional, the law should be overturned.

State Senator Craig Estes

While there is an endless series of questions that needs to be put to Senator Craig Estes, the first is whether or not he deceived Senator Mike Jackson when Jackson asked this simple question in regards to HB 3031 in 2009:

And it says "fair market value?"

Similarly, Senator Estes needs to explain why he characterized the sale of property at Possum Kingdom Lake as being a local matter, when the Brazos River Authority was responsible for managing a river basin that stretched for 850 miles across Texas. It would also be enlightening to know if he recognizes, acknowledges, or has any remorse for the financial harm that was done to the state of Texas.

Beyond that, we need to ask Senator Estes to what extent he coerced the board and the staff of the Brazos River Authority to place the property up for sale before House Bill 3031 was even introduced in the legislature.

---

[255] Atty. Gen. Greg Abbott, "Opinion No. GA-0634," *Office of the Attorney General*, June 5, 2008, accessed May 1, 2011.
https://www.texasattorneygeneral.gov/opinions/opinions/50abbott/op/2008/htm/ga-0634.htm.

State Representative James "Jim" Keffer

Representative James Keffer is subject to the same questions as Senator Estes. However, as Representative Keffer was the official author of House Bill 3031, there are particular questions that need to be initially directed toward him.

The first of these regards the original terms of House Bill 3031. The Brazos River Authority put the shoreline of Possum Kingdom Lake on the market on January 8, 2009. This request for bids stipulated that the successful bidder would be required to resell the property for 90% of the 2008 assessed values. In contrast to this, the original version of HB 3031 stipulated that the successful bidder would be required to resell the property for 65% of the 2008 assessed values. HB 3031 was filed on March 11, 2009 which was twenty-eight days before the deadline to submit a bid for the property. The filing of the bill immediately put a cloud of confusion over the BRA's request for bids.

Roughly ten days later, Representative Keffer and Senator Estes met with the leadership of the Possum Kingdom Lake Association to negotiate the mandatory resell price.[256] The primary question to be put to Keffer is this: Why were you tampering with the terms and conditions of the sale of a state asset only days before the sale would be finalized? And, given that these negotiations were being publicized by the ultimate buying parties on the internet, *how was this tampering not tantamount to bid-rigging?*

A secondary and equally obvious series of questions for Representative Keffer concerns his landlord at Southwest Securities Bank in Granbury, Ms. Mary Ward. We should ask Representative Keffer how his landlord and one of Mike Patterson's subordinates wound up on the board of the Brazos River Authority immediately prior to the transaction. While we are at it, we should also ask Representative Keffer if Mary Ward ever hosted a fundraiser for him at her bank during his efforts to become the next Speaker of the Texas House of Representatives.

---

[256] PKLA Staff, "Board of Directors Meeting," *Possum Kingdom Lake Association*, March 28, 2009, accessed July 10, 2011.
https://web.archive.org/web/20151126195624/http://pklakeassn.org/minutes%20 3-28-09.htm.

Former Presiding Officer of the BRA, Steve Pena

The question that needs to be asked of Steve Pena is somewhat awkward given his efforts to prevent this outcome from occurring. Nonetheless, he has to be asked if he was offered a more prestigious appointment to the Texas State Board of Public Accountancy in return for dropping his opposition to the forced divestiture of land at Possum Kingdom Lake.

While it is certainly possible that Steve Pena simply gave up and hoped that the Brazos River Authority would be made whole in the long run, you have to wonder if he knew what was going to happen as soon as he was reappointed elsewhere.

Succeeding Presiding Officer of the BRA, Christopher DeCluitt

The position of the Brazos River Authority changed dramatically when Christopher DeCluitt replaced Steve Pena as the presiding officer. The primary question to be put to DeCluitt is why he reversed the position of the Brazos River Authority in its opposition to the forced divestiture of the shoreline of Possum Kingdom Lake? The secondary question is why he introduced the concept of a residual interest in the FERC property on September 22, 2008? The tertiary questions are innumerable but begin with this:

> Why did you direct the staff of the Brazos River Authority
> to put the property up for sale before House Bill 3031 was
> introduced in the Texas Legislature?

The Board of the BRA, circa 2009

Without a doubt, the most important questions need to be directed toward the temporary board members who were appointed to the Brazos River Authority just long enough to vote to sell the property. The first question is this:

> Were you asked if you would vote to sell the property at
> Possum Kingdom Lake before you were appointed to the
> board of the Brazos River Authority?

Secondly:

> Were you made aware of the letter that was received from Integra Realty advising against the bidding process that was being used to sell the property before you voted to accept the bid? And, if so, why did you vote to accept the bid in 2009?

Obviously, there are many other questions that need to be asked and answered, but for the time being, these will have to do.

Chapter 25

SINE DIE

The Latin term *sine die* translated literally means "without day." When a legislative body adjourns *sine die*, it does so without assigning a day for a further meeting or hearing. The same is true when a politician announces that he will not seek reelection.

On Sunday, June 14, 2015, State Representative Jim Keffer issued the following statement on Twitter:

> Rich fringe have no answers, no vision—want mouthpieces
> for their private follies. Ask questions, seek facts, "sheeple"
> get eaten. #txlege

As I am not advised on the legislative definition of "sheeple," I submitted multiple questions to Representative Keffer in response to this statement. Each of these questions attempted to seek facts in regard to House Bill 3031 which passed unanimously in 2009. None of those questions received a response.

Two days later, the man who was once convinced that he would be the next Speaker of the House in Texas issued the following statement to the *Hood County News*:

> Having now finished my 10th Regular session in the Texas
> Legislature, I intend to complete my current term as State

Representative (District 60) but will not seek reelection in the 2016 Republican primary. It has been the highest honor and greatest privilege to serve you. Since our initial election victory in 1996, Leslie and I strove at all times to put rural Texas families first while working under three Texas Governors (George W. Bush, Rick Perry and Greg Abbott). We now bid an affectionate farewell to the august body of men and women who will carry forward the responsibilities of our state government. At the end of this term (January 2017), we will take our leave of all the employment of public life with no regrets. Having ever-lasting friendships across the district, and with now grown children and young grandchildren, we are ready to share all that is great about being Texans. Thank you! God Bless Texas.[257]

In his farewell address to the taxpayers of Texas, James "Jim" Keffer shamelessly plagiarized none other than George Washington.[258] Given the details of this tale, his final public statement can serve as the final insult to the intelligence of the rest of us.

The term sine die can also be applied to the suspension of a presidential campaign. On Friday, September 11, 2015, former Texas governor Rick Perry announced that he was "suspending" his race for the White House. The timing of this announcement, 9/11, was consistent with his infamous "Oops" moment four years earlier. Three days later, Rick Perry blamed his inability to raise money for his campaign on his criminal indictment.

The indictment by the Travis County district attorney's office, this drunk DA that had used this office, we think,

[257] Ross Ramsey, "Keffer, a Straus Lieutenant, Won't Seek Re-election," *The Texas Tribune*, June 16, 2015, accessed June 16, 2015. http://www.texastribune.org/2015/06/16/keffer-straus-lieutenant-wont-seek-reelection/.

[258] General George Washington, "Address to Congress Resigning his Commission," *Maryland State Archives*, December 23, 1783, accessed July 4, 2015. http://msa.maryland.gov/msa/stagser/s1259/131/html/gwresign.html.

for political purposes… it had a real corrosive effect on
our ability to raise money.

Rick Perry's statement suggested that he and the Public Integrity
Unit in Austin had finally managed to destroy each other. The facts of his
indictment suggest otherwise. Rick Perry's statement also illuminated his
willingness to ignore basic facts and expect the rest of us to do so as well.

The drunken district attorney, to whom Perry referred, Rosemary
Lehmberg, had actually recused herself from the case. In her absence, a
special prosecutor by the name of Michael McCrum was appointed by
the judge of the 379th District Court in Bexar County. This judge's name
was Bert Richardson. Bert Richardson and Michael McCrum were both
Republicans.[259]

The term *sine die* is equally applicable to one of the longest-serving
lieutenant governors in the history of Texas. Roughly one month after
Playing Possum–The Tale of the River Card, Round I was published in 2014,
Lt. Governor David Dewhurst was driven out of office in the Republican
primary runoff election. In this race, David Dewhurst lost to state senator
Dan Patrick in a landslide by a margin of 65 percent to 35 percent.

Similarly, in the race to replace Greg Abbott as the attorney general
of Texas during the same election cycle, State Representative Dan Branch
was defeated by State Senator Ken Paxton in another primary runoff by
the same margin–65 percent to 35 percent. Dan Branch's defeat came in
spite of the fact that his opponent Ken Paxton was facing allegations of
securities fraud at the time. The recently elected Attorney General Ken
Paxton has since been indicted on three felony counts in this matter. As
you may have noticed, David Dewhurst and Dan Branch were both key
figures in the "Texas Miracle."

In contrast, the Gang of 11 has yet to adjourn sine die. Although Jim
Keffer has announced his retirement—enabling him to enjoy the maximum
possible pension from the taxpayers of Texas—Representative Joe Straus
is still the Speaker of the House in Texas. Likewise, the gentleman who
hosted the meeting in his home that ousted Tom Craddick and anointed

---

[259] Abby Livingston, "Perry Blames Indictment, Debates for Failed Campaign,"
The Texas Tribune, September 14, 2015, accessed September 14, 2015. http://www.
texastribune.org/2015/09/14/perry-speaks-first-time-dropping-out/.

Joe Straus, Representative Byron Cook, still represents District 8 in Texas. The same is true for state representative Charlie Geren, who still holds the seat in District 99 that encompasses half of the city of Fort Worth. The rest of the Gang of 11 is now gone.

And, for all practical purposes, the Public Integrity Unit in Texas has also bid sine die. In August 2015, the PIU's prosecutors lost their case against Jerry Cobbs for his role in the CPRIT scandal in what many thought was a slam-dunk case. Roughly one month later, the Public Integrity Unit informed the complainants from Granbury of the following:

> After reviewing the evidence and speaking with a potential
> witness, we found insufficient evidence to move forward
> with a criminal prosecution. Therefore, we are closing this
> matter at this time.

To say the least, the Public Integrity Unit in Texas was castrated by Governor Rick Perry when he vetoed the PIU's funding. In the final scene, they both faded into the history books and irrelevancy.

It is now time to adjourn *The Texas Miracle* sine die as well. In so doing, I submit this matter to the court of public opinion and invite you all to render your own judgment. Was the sale in 2009 *"by the Brazos River Authority of certain residential and commercial leased lots and other real property in the immediate vicinity of Possum Kingdom Lake"* a legitimate transaction?

Or did the taxpayers of Texas get screwed like a bunch of tied up goats?

While I cannot give you a day as to when I will return, I can assure you that I will remain diligent in my casual observations of the Texas legislature. I can also assure you that I remain convinced of the following:

Power tends to corrupt—and absolute power corrupts absolutely.

Printed in the United States
By Bookmasters